MW01623856

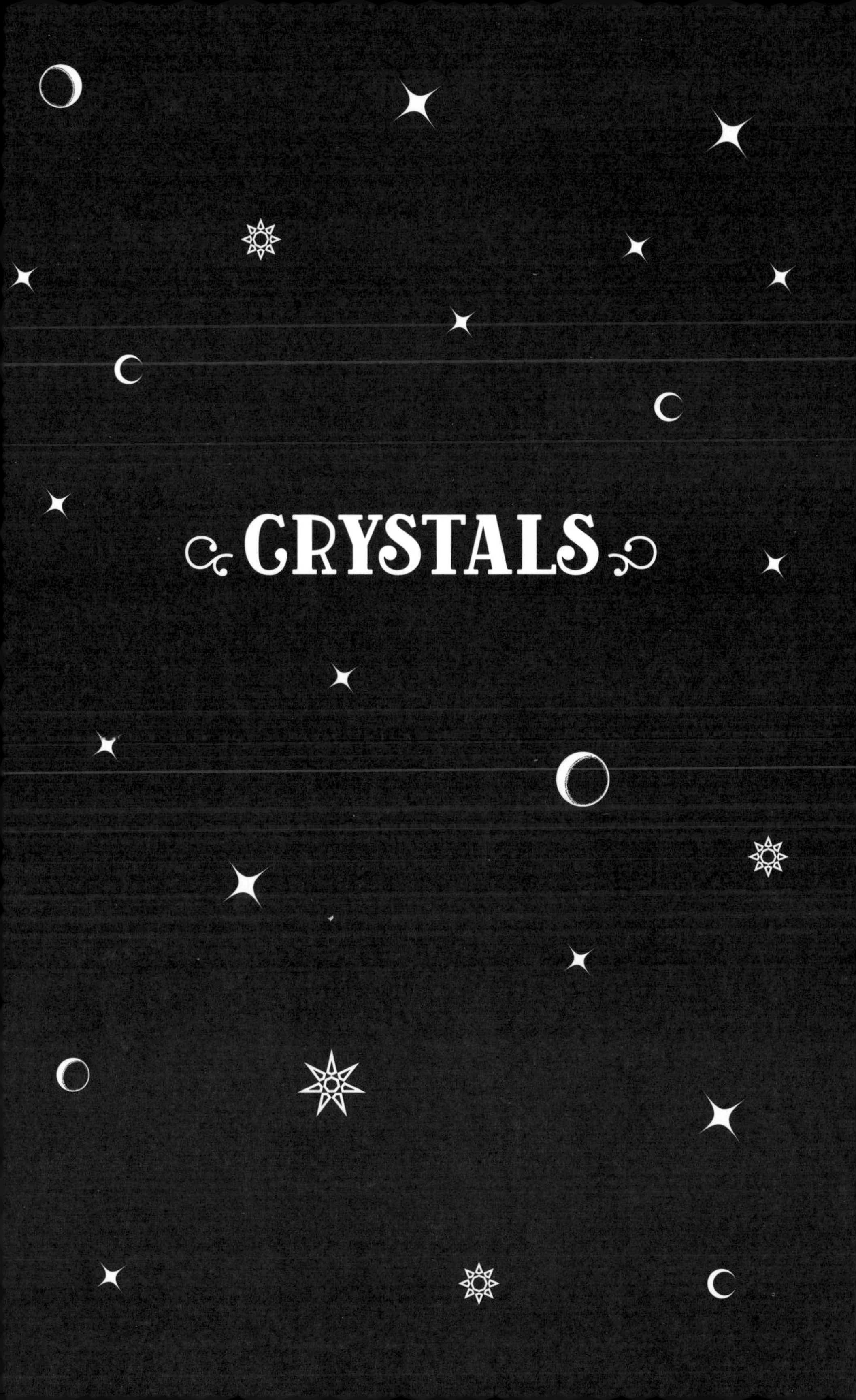

CRYSTALS

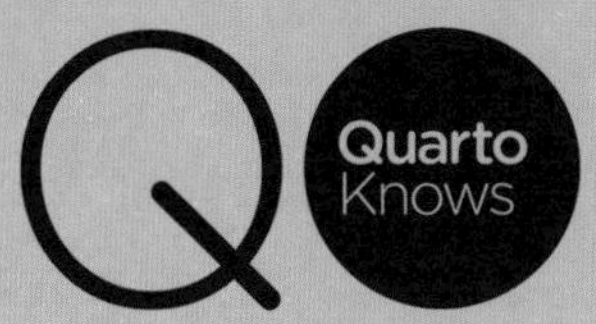

Inspiring | Educating | Creating | Entertaining

Brimming with creative inspiration, how-to projects, and useful information to enrich your everyday life, Quarto Knows is a favorite destination for those pursuing their interests and passions. Visit our site and dig deeper with our books into your area of interest: Quarto Creates, Quarto Cooks, Quarto Homes, Quarto Lives, Quarto Drives, Quarto Explores, Quarto Gifts, or Quarto Kids.

First published in 2018 by Wellfleet Press,
an imprint of The Quarto Group
142 West 36th Street, 4th Floor
New York, NY 10018 USA
T (212) 779-4972 **F** (212) 779-6058
www.QuartoKnows.com

Wellfleet Press titles are also available at discount for retail, wholesale, promotional, and bulk purchase. For details, contact the Special Sales Manager by email at specialsales@quarto.com or by mail at The Quarto Group, Attn: Special Sales Manager, 100 Cummings Center, Suite 265-D, Beverly, MA 01915, USA.

10 9 8 7 6 5

ISBN: 978-1-57715-206-4

Cover and Interior Design: Ashley Prine, Tandem Books

Printed in China

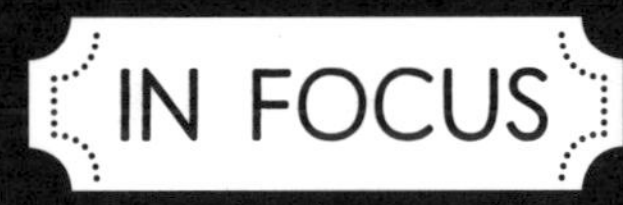

CRYSTALS

Your Personal Guide

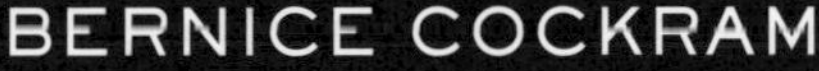

BERNICE COCKRAM

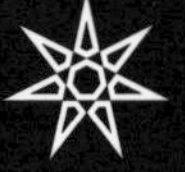

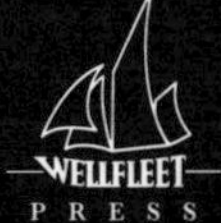

CONTENTS

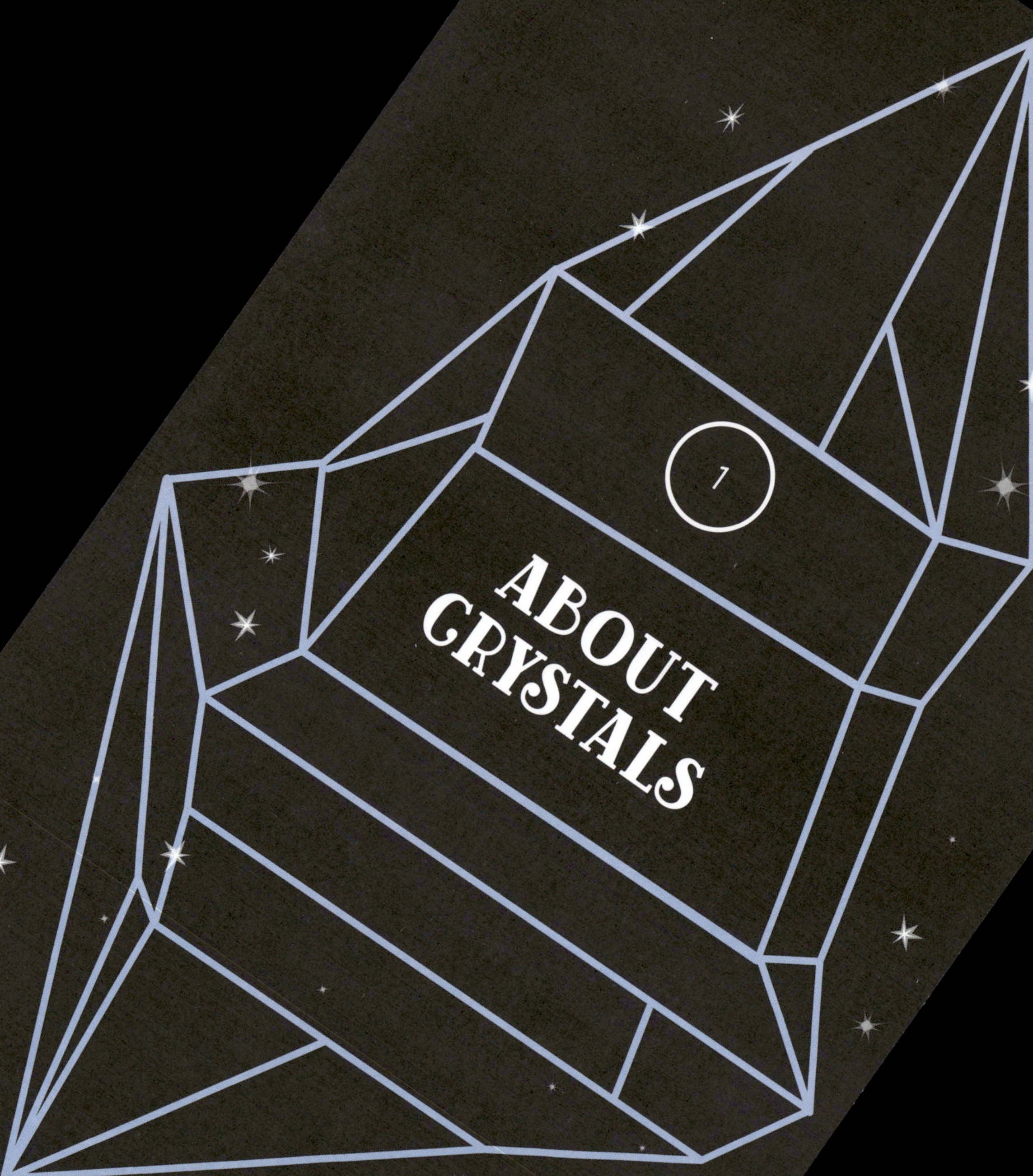
1
ABOUT
CRYSTALS

I discovered crystal therapy and crystal healing by accident. I borrowed a book from the library to identify some tumblestones that my six-year-old son had collected, and the book talked about placing crystals on chakra *points*—locations where energy lines meet or cross within your body. In a slightly different manner, a *crystal point* is a sharp pointed end on a crystal, whether natural or carved. I was very skeptical but decided to give it a go. When I picked up a crystal, I experienced a very strange feeling, which I now know was my energy shifting, and thought that maybe I had done something wrong, so I tried again the next day and got exactly the same result. This fired up my curiosity, and in time, I acquired different crystals to work with and borrowed books from the library, giving me different ways to lay the crystals on and around my body.

Five years later, after attending a workshop and working on other people, I decided to train to become a certified crystal therapist so that I could help other people experience what crystals can do for them.

Crystal Therapy and Crystal Healing

Crystal therapy is a treatment in which crystals are placed on and around the body. Crystals can also be moved over the body—for example, by using a pendulum. Crystal healing occurs when crystal therapy is combined with another holistic treatment, such as massage, Reiki, spiritual healing, and acupuncture.

Working with Crystals

Working with crystals can help us to shift energy and emotions that we have been holding on to, such as issues from the past that are holding us back or affecting our everyday lives. Crystals are also good for clearing away stress or energy that we have picked up from others, and they can enable us to feel calmer and to think more clearly.

On a molecular level, crystals resonate at different frequencies. The frequency depends on factors such as the crystal's structure, which is called the *crystal system* or *crystal habit*, and the color of the crystal. We are aware, subconsciously, of energy around us, and placing crystals on or around the body can help to bring balance by increasing or decreasing the frequency of our own energy. This in turn helps the client we're working on to feel more relaxed and positive, allowing the body to heal itself more effectively.

Crystals will absorb and hold energy, which is why quartz crystals are used in clocks, watches, and circuit boards. The quartz absorbs energy from the power source, and emits it in a regular pulse, making it a useful and reliable technical resource.

The hardness of a crystal affects the way that it works. Hard crystals like quartz work in a direct way, whereas softer crystals such as calcite are gentler and absorb energy more readily. A crystal's hardness is measured on the *Mohs scale*, which was created by mineralogist Friedrich Mohs in 1812. He listed crystals and minerals in order of softest to hardest, which makes talcum number one and diamond number ten. The table opposite shows the scale of hardness as devised by Friedrich Mohs.

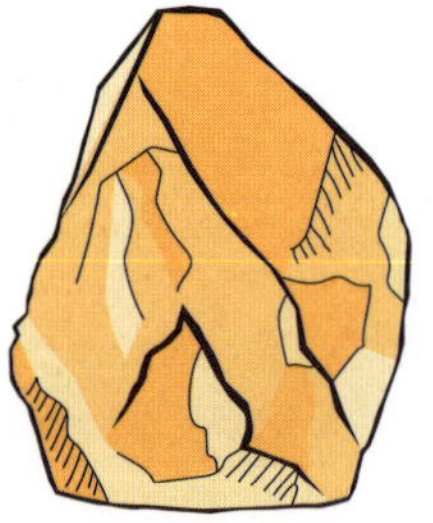

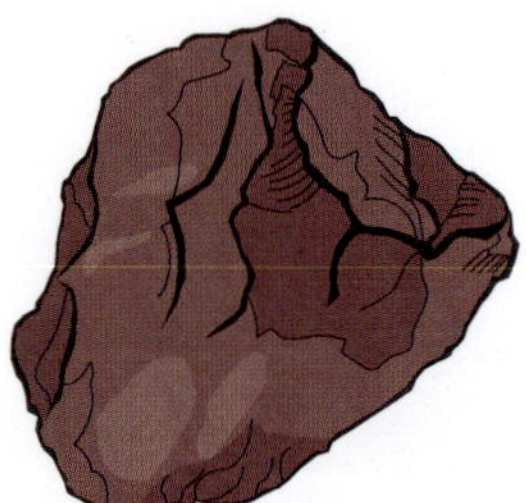

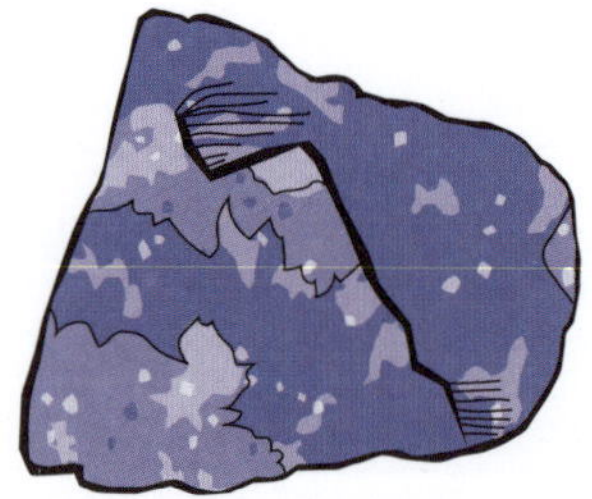

The Mohs Scale		
Number	Crystal	Description
1	Talcum	Scratched by all other minerals and easily marked with fingernails.
2	Gypsum	Can be scratched with a fingernail using greater pressure than needed to scratch a number-one material.
3	Calcite	Can be scratched by a sharp coin.
4	Fluorite	Can be scratched with a penknife blade.
5	Apatite	Can be scratched with difficulty using a steel point.
6	Feldspar	Will easily scratch glass.
7	Quartz	Will scratch most common surfaces.
8	Topaz	Can scratch quartz.
9	Corundum	Easily scratches topaz and quartz.
10	Diamond	The hardest natural substance.

It is useful to know how hard a crystal or mineral is so that it may be stored appropriately. If you keep all your crystals in the same storage box, any hard crystals will damage the softer ones.

Crystal Colors and Properties

Color	Properties
Black, red, brown	Black, red, and brown crystals are generally used when there is a need for grounding and in matters concerning basic needs for survival.
Orange	Orange is enlivening and energizing, and it can encourage creativity.
Yellow	Yellow boosts confidence and cheers people up, so it is good to use when there is fear or sadness.
Green	Green helps with issues concerning love, although pink helps when there is a need for self-love.
Light blue	Light blue governs expression and communication.
Dark blue	Dark blue and any purple can encourage "knowing"—that is, intuition and seeing the whole situation.
Purple	Purples connect us to the energy around us, such as gods and goddesses, universal energy, our higher selves, and so on.
Clear	Clear stones bring in white light, so they are very good for clearing and bringing clarity.
White	White stones are similar in energy to clear crystals, but the energy is less direct, so they are a bit gentler and more diffracted.

The energy of multi-colored crystals varies, because there is often more than one mineral involved. For example, quartz will enhance the energy of any mineral inclusion, such as tourmalinated quartz that is bonded with black tourmaline, whereas ruby in zoisite is more green than red. On the other hand, labradorite is a greenish-gray stone with flashes of yellows, blues, and purples and works more in a dark-blue and purple way.

Crystal Systems and Crystal Habit

The structured form in which a crystal grows is called a *system* or *habit.* It may sound technical, but a crystal's system can tell you a bit about the type of energy a crystal emits. Some crystal books explain the crystal systems in detail, and you can find in-depth information about the systems on the Internet. Unfortunately, length restrictions prevent this book from going into a great amount of detail, but you will find more about this in chapter ten on crystal grids.

When you see a crystal listed as helping with a certain issue or condition, it is often based on the *habit* of the crystal as well as its color. So, for example, amethyst is often suggested for headaches and migraines. This makes sense, as purple resonates with the crown chakra, but amethyst is also a *trigonal* crystal, which helps to calm excess energy.

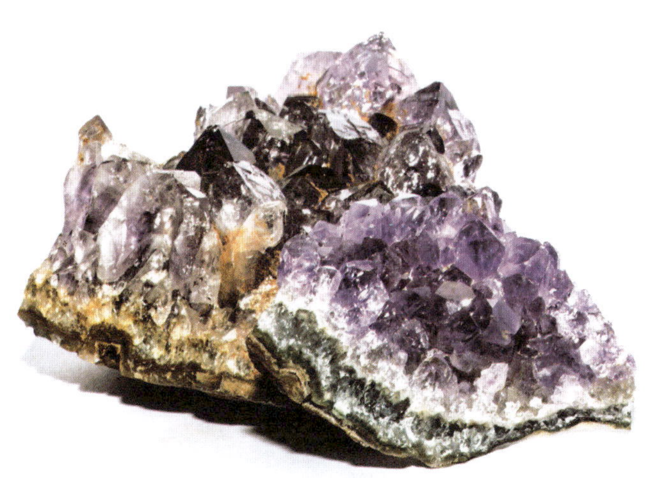

❋ ❋ ❋

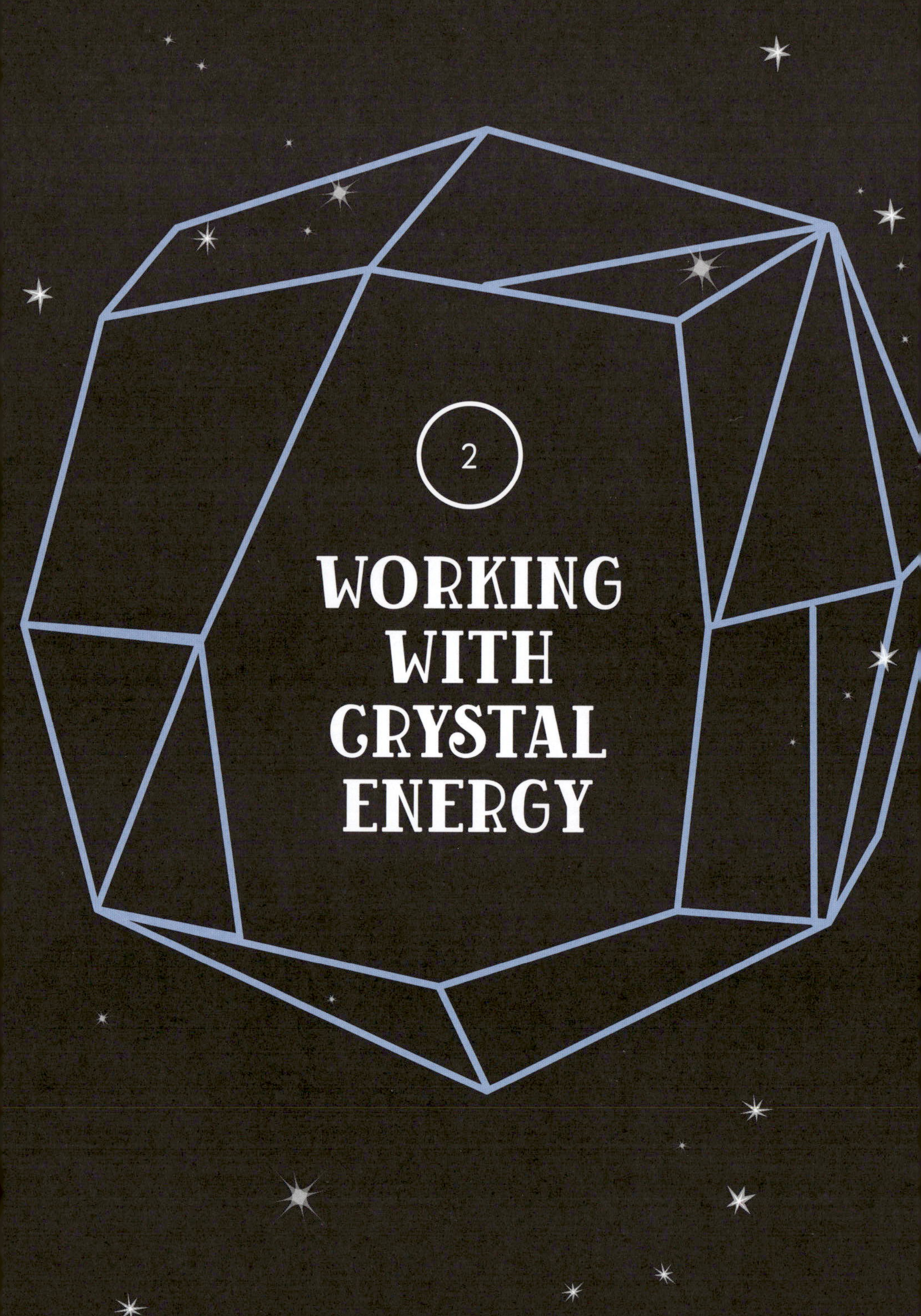

2

WORKING WITH CRYSTAL ENERGY

We can experience crystal energy in a few different ways, as you will see in this chapter.

Wearing Crystals as Jewelry

Jewelry is a lovely way of attuning yourself to a crystal's energy. As well as the precious and semi-precious stones themselves, you may hold within them the energy of gold, silver, or platinum, depending on the type of jewelry. I purchase spiral cage pendants so that I can pop in a tumblestone of my choice and wear it on a necklace. Jewelry should be cleansed often, as the stones may pick up other types of energy while you are out and about, in addition to your own unwanted energy. You will see how to do this in chapter three on cleansing, dedicating, programming, and charging your crystals.

Crystals on Display

Crystals on display in a room will energize the space around them, and, obviously, the type of energy will depend on the size of the crystal, because a larger crystal will energize a larger area than a smaller crystal. If you are just starting to work with crystals, or you are particularly sensitive to energy, you may want to limit the amount of display crystals you have in your bedroom or beside your bed so that your sleep is not disturbed.

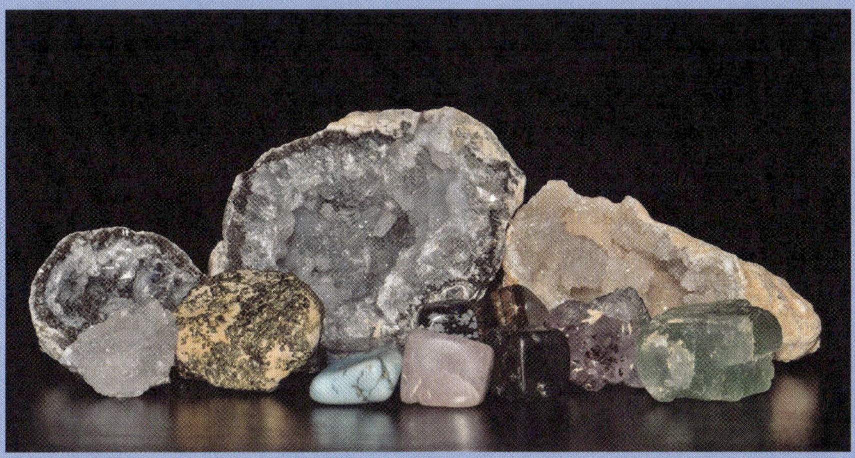

Nets

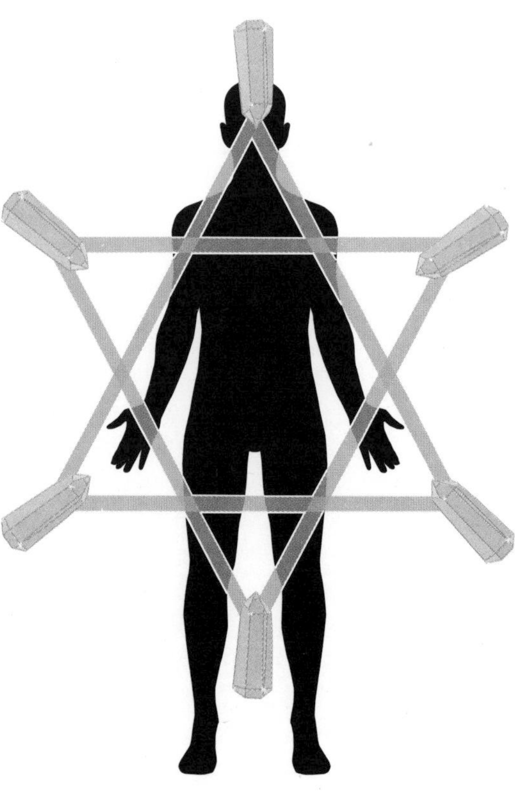

Nets refer to the placement of crystals in a symmetrical pattern around the body using a single type of crystal to form an energy field. You may use tumblestones, raw crystals, or terminated points. Nets around your body are created with an even number of stones to make the net symmetrical. You may also like to place some crystals on your body as you lie within the net—these don't need to be symmetrical.

When working with single terminated points, such as quartz, you should consider in which direction you would like the energy to travel: for example, the Seal of Solomon layout in chapter seven on using a pendulum first releases unwanted energy by facing the points outward, then brings in energy by directing the points inward. You can also create a symbol to lie beneath or inside, for example, a zodiac or planetary sigil. Make sure that all the points are facing in the same direction to ensure the energy runs smoothly. With a net like this, it isn't necessary to have an even number of crystals.

Large Crystal Grids

A large crystal grid is similar to a net, but the crystals are placed around a property or area or, alternatively, set up on your altar or other sacred space. Setting a grid around your house or just in the four corners of your room

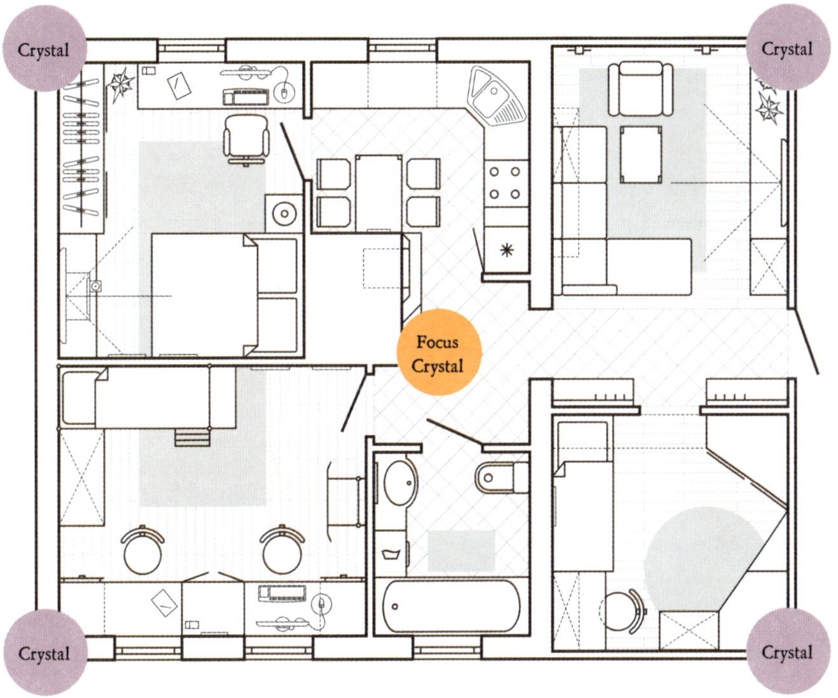

brings a protective energy to that space. The frequency you will need in order to cleanse these crystals will depend on whether the crystals are hard or soft (see the Mohs scale in chapter one) and the type of energy in that room. For example, a room used for meditation is different from a study containing lots of electronic equipment.

Mandala Grids

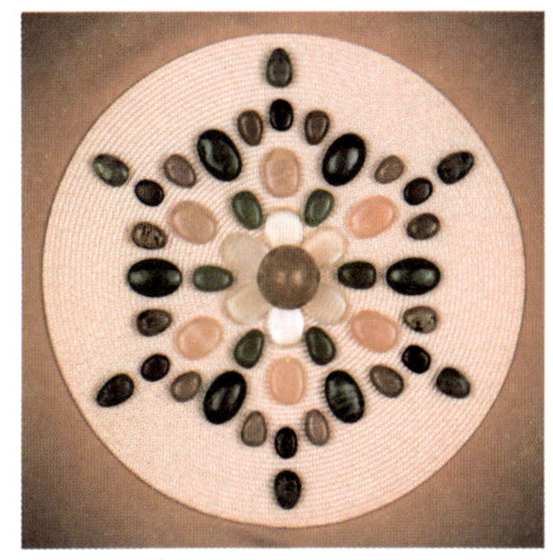

A *mandala* is a grid in a circular repeated pattern that is based on sacred geometry. You can create a mandala on your altar or sacred space for a particular purpose, such as healing a place or person, or perhaps for helping you to cope with the energies that are around you at a specific moment. Often a mandala will be symmetrical, but this is not crucial if you are just drawn to creating a pattern. A mandala does not have to be made with crystal alone, so you may like to include flowers or feathers as well. Having the mandala in your line of sight is a good idea, because every time you notice it, you will link in with its energies.

Placing Crystals on the Body

Crystals can be placed on someone who is lying down, and they can be placed on the chakra points, or you may place one on a specific point of pain. For example, if you have a headache you could put a crystal on your forehead or on your stomach to help with stomachache.

Carrying Tumblestones

Crystals can be carried around in your bag or in a pocket. I like to tuck mine in a pocket or even in my bra! Even if you don't actually feel the energy of the crystal, your energy will still be interacting with the stone. Tumblestones can be carried around for as long as you need them. Just be aware of how you feel if it is a new crystal you are attuning yourself to. For instance, if you start to feel ungrounded, remove the crystals and try again later. I recommend cleansing the crystals at the end of the day.

Elixirs and Essences

An *elixir* or *essence* is water that is attuned to the energy of a crystal. An easy method is to place one or more crystals in a glass or jug of water—ideally, distilled or spring water—and leave them there for a few hours.

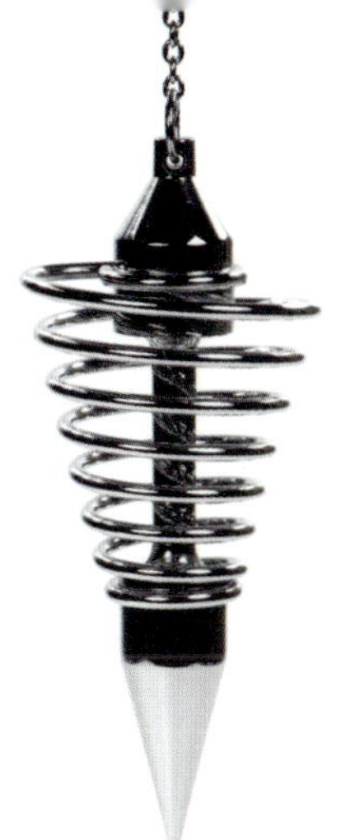

Using a Pendulum

You can swing a pendulum over an area of pain, or you can use it to clear negative energy away from someone. It is usual for a pendulum to swing in a circle when it is clearing energy away and either to stop swinging or to swing forward and backward when that area has been cleared.

Working on Yourself

Some people may feel energy from a crystal straight away while others do not. All it takes to feel energy from a crystal is a bit of practice and experimentation with different crystals. The layouts I have included in this book are safe to

Making Safe Essences

To make an essence using a water-soluble or toxic crystal, place the crystal in a glass, and then place the glass in a bowl of water for a couple of hours so that the water doesn't come into contact with the crystal. The water will absorb some of the crystal's energies as a result of having been close to it for a while; after this, the energized water can be safely consumed or used on the skin.

You can also make what is called a *mother essence* by storing the gem water with an equal amount of alcohol, such as vodka or brandy, in a brown or blue jar. These colors have been found to preserve the liquid, as the dark color helps to block the corresponding light frequency that causes the liquid to degenerate. This is why most beers are kept in brown bottles—the brown keeps the hops fresh. Beers with minimal or no hops content can be kept in green or colorless bottles. This mother essence contains the vibration of the crystal or crystals, and a few drops can be used in drinking water or placed on the skin.

use as often as you like. The more often you experience the layouts, the more sensitive you will become to crystal energies.

In my experience, I have come across crystals that affect my moods. For example, I was training to become a therapist when I first worked with fossilized or petrified wood, and it actually brought me to tears. Other crystals can affect my focus; for instance, if I hold big pieces of moldavite, I soon begin to feel ungrounded. Then there are crystals that shift energy in such a way that I can feel it—for instance, as a pain in my chest while it clears a blockage, or a large energy buildup in my abdomen as energy feeds into an underactive chakra.

Chakras are the seven psychic centers that line up along the body from the base of the spine to the crown of the head. You will discover more about these mysterious centers later in this book.

While working on a child, I asked her if she had any problems with her ankles or feet, as my pendulum had spent a long time clearing in this area. She said she didn't have any pain or issues there, and I was left wondering why the pendulum had spent so long at that part of her body until at the end of the session she admitted she had felt the pendulum moving and had used her own energy to "play" with the pendulum!

Some people I have worked on do not experience any feelings during a session, but they still benefit from the clearing properties that crystals exhibit.

Spells

Spells are used to help manifest your desires, or as a form of protection. Crystals can enhance the energy of such spells. Intention is the most important part of casting a spell, and a crystal that is programmed with your wish (see chapter three on programming crystals) can assist you. *Intention*—in the context of mind, body, and spirit activities—means deciding what you hope to achieve before setting out to do something. The "intention" is always to bring about a positive outcome from your work.

Other "ingredients" for spells include herbs, candles, and hair or nail clippings (often used in love and relationship spells). I suggest you use a pendulum to select which crystal to use in your spell. Candle color plays a part as well, such as pink for love, yellow for banishment of fear, and black for protection. Herbs also have different meanings: rosemary is protective, lavender is used to encourage love, thyme can be used for healing. Your intention for the spell should be positive, so remove any negative words such as *don't*, *not*, and *never*.

There are many ways of casting the spell, ranging from simple to elaborate. I keep it simple: I write my wish on a piece of paper (making sure I add the phrase "with harm to no one") and then light a candle. While holding my crystal, I meditate on my desire and then burn the piece of paper to send my spell out to the universe. I keep the programmed crystal where I can see it every day for as long as I feel I need to.

Keep in mind that spells should always be for the highest good of all involved, or they may come back on you.

Sleeping with Crystals

Tumblestones can be kept under your pillow or on a bedside table while you sleep. This would be a way of connecting with a crystal subconsciously and benefiting from the crystal's energy while you sleep. Make sure that the crystal is not too stimulating, though, as it could interfere with your sleeping pattern. It may be a good idea to use calming stones, such as sodalite or amethyst, to start with, until you get used to having different energies around you.

Crystals in the Bath

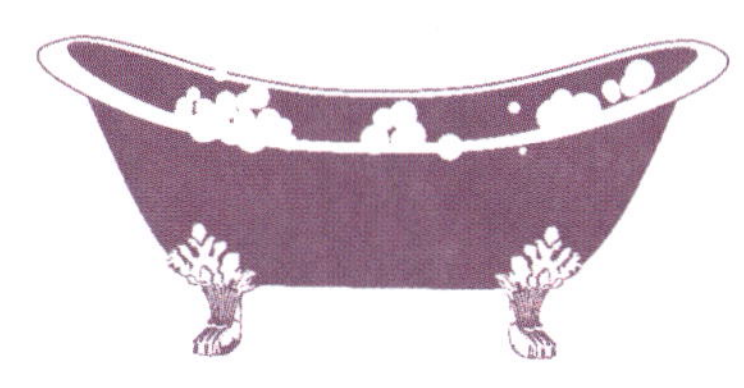

You can take crystals into your bath to energize the water. Make sure that the crystals are not water soluble or toxic. Harder crystals would be more suitable, as softer crystals may be damaged by the hot water.

❋ ❋ ❋

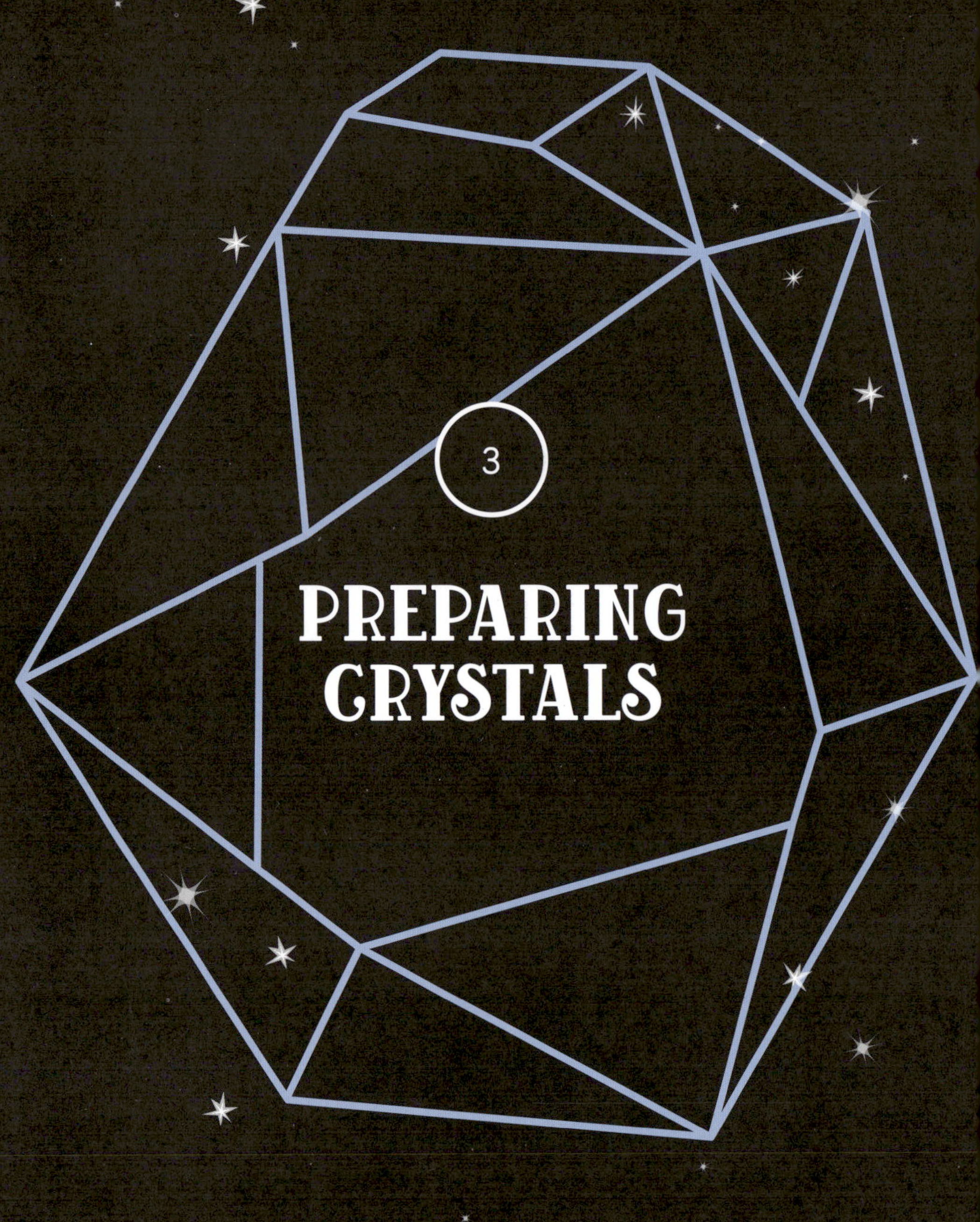

3

PREPARING CRYSTALS

Cleansing

Crystals absorb energy, so we must cleanse crystals to clear away any unwanted energy. This will also clear any programming that you have previously put into the crystal. It is important to cleanse crystals that you have bought or that have been given to you, because the crystals will have picked up energy from being handled by many people or even from the room they have been stored in, and such energy may not be beneficial.

Ideally, any crystal jewelry that you own should be cleansed before you wear it—this is especially important if the jewelry has had a previous owner. Crystals can hold only so much energy before that energy is radiated out again—as per quartz in a watch—and you may end up processing someone else's unwanted energy! The same is true for any tumblestones or other specimens with which you wish to meditate, to carry with you, or to use for healing layouts. I have heard stories of some people's crystals randomly cracking or splitting, and while this could be due to softer crystals being kept in a humid environment, it could also be due to the crystal containing too much energy and being in need of a good cleanse.

When you cleanse your crystals, hold the intention in your mind that you want to clear the crystal of any energy that does not belong to the crystal.

There are several different ways of cleansing; they are all equally effective, so it is a matter of preference for which method you choose.

Rice

Place the crystal or crystals in a bowl of brown rice overnight, as the rice will absorb the energy from the crystal. Throw the rice away the next morning.

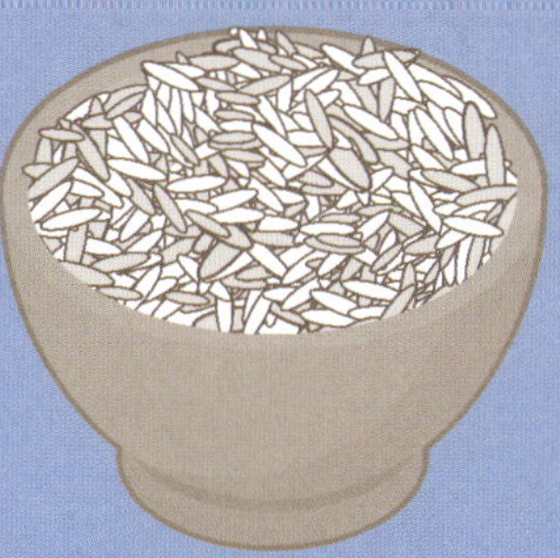

Salt

Place the crystal or crystals in a bowl of salt overnight. Some care is needed with this method so that the salt does not scratch soft crystals or get trapped in cracks or pits in the crystal's surface. Dispose of the salt the next morning.

Water

Take care, because some crystals are water soluble, so check before using this method.

Note: Take care when placing hard and soft crystals together to prevent damage.

- Crystals may be held under cold running water for a minute or two. Make sure the plug is in the sink if you are holding a small crystal or you could lose it down the drain. Don't use hot water, as this may cause the crystal to crack.
- Crystals may be placed in a pillowcase and held in a running stream.
- Crystals can also be cleansed in the sea, but some crystals may be damaged by the saltwater.
- Although running water is the best, some people leave a bowl outside when it rains so that they can collect some rainwater for cleansing their crystals.

Earth

You can bury your crystals in the garden overnight to let mother earth cleanse and reenergize the crystals. If you are going to use this method, it's a good idea to put the crystal in a flowerpot, then bury the pot in the earth and place a marker of some kind so that you can find your crystal again when you want to dig it up.

Note: This method may not be suitable if you live in an area where the soil is acidic or rocky. In addition, some crystals are water soluble, so check the type of soil that exists in your area before using this method.

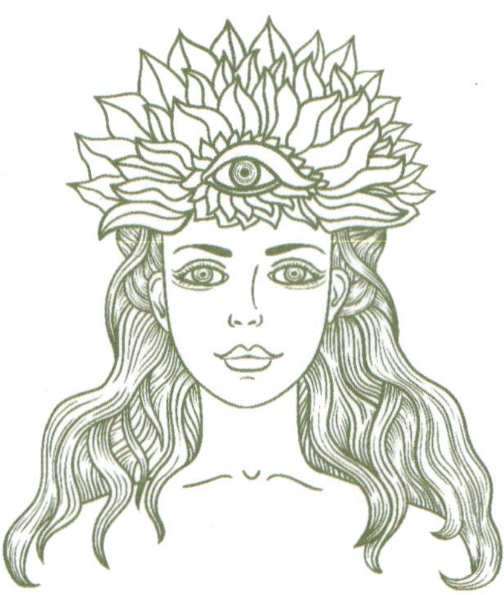

Light

Your third eye is located between—and slightly above—your eyes. Visualize bright white light coming from your third eye and penetrating the crystal, clearing away all energy that does not belong to the crystal. Use your intuition to tell you how long to do this.

Breath

Blow gently on the crystal, with the intention of clearing away all energy that does not belong to the crystal. Use your intuition to tell you how long to do this.

Sound

The vibration of sound can be used to clear a crystal of all energy that is not part of the crystal. These are some useful methods:

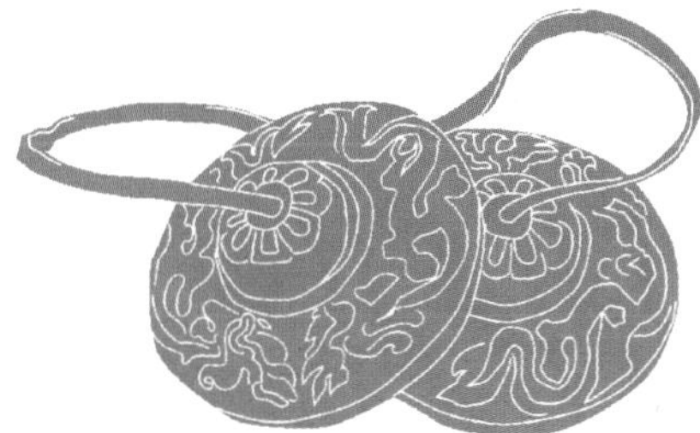

- Tingsha bells, which are also called Tibetan cymbals, can be rung above or beside the crystals.
- Crystals can be placed inside a singing bowl, then you tap or rub the rim of the bowl with a beater to create sound. If a crystal is too large to fit in your bowl, the bowl can be rubbed beside or above the crystal for cleansing.
- You can strike a tuning fork above or beside the crystal.

Smudging

Pass the crystal through smoke from burning sage or incense with the intention that the smoke will carry away all energy that is not part of the crystal. Sage leaves can be dried and tied into bundles; when lit, the leaves smolder with a cleansing, fragrant smoke. You will usually find pre-bundled sage in your local metaphysical store. Sage can also be used for cleansing the energy in rooms.

Selenite

This crystal is very good at moving energy, both in other crystals and within people. A small selenite crystal (either raw or tumbled) can be placed next to a crystal that needs cleansing and left there for a few hours. Care should be taken with selenite as it breaks easily, and it will dissolve if it gets wet.

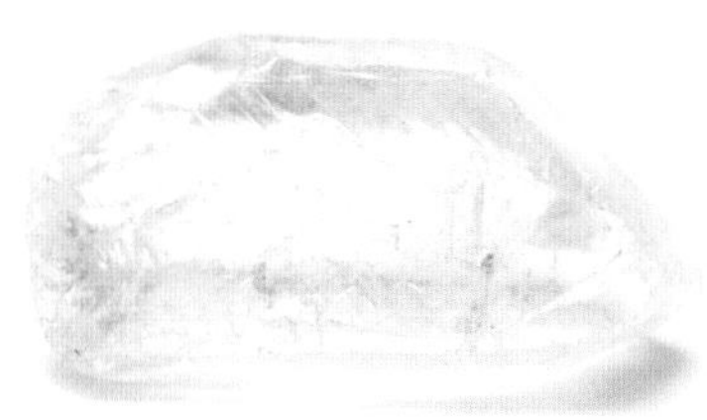

A Crystal Bed or Cluster

Crystals can be placed on a large crystal cluster or a *geode* (a hollow, roughly oval mineral object) overnight. The larger crystal will clear energy from the smaller crystal. The same applies to the geode method.

Some crystals, such as selenite and large crystal beds, do *not* need cleansing, as you will see below. In the case of selenite, this situation comes about owing to the way that it is formed, which is in long, straight striations. The energy in this crystal is constantly moving, so the crystal does not absorb energy. In large crystal beds, such as amethyst, quartz, and citrine, there are so many individual crystals that any energy that is absorbed is gradually dissipated, although I use my singing bowl or some sage every so often on these types of crystals to help clear them.

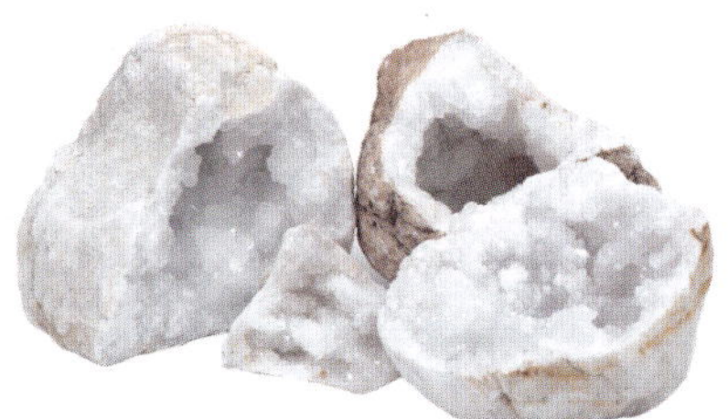

Dedicating

Once a crystal is cleansed, you may hold it in your hands and dedicate it to a form of energy, or you may dedicate it to a particular purpose. This will focus your mind on the use to which you want to put the crystal.

- You may like to dedicate your crystal to God, a pagan god or goddess, or universal energy.
- You may like to dedicate your crystal to healing or to being part of a grid that clears or energizes a space.

Programming

Programming directs your crystal to work in a specific way. Either this can enhance the way a crystal already works, such as to help with a health condition or an emotional issue, or it can alter the vibrational energy of a crystal. For example, if you only have a clear quartz available, and you want to work with something else, you could program the clear quartz crystal to match the frequency of the crystal that you would use if you could.

I programmed a crystal before giving it as a gift someone who was being bullied—I chose a crystal that already had protective energies and further programmed it to protect the bearer from any negative energy directed at her.

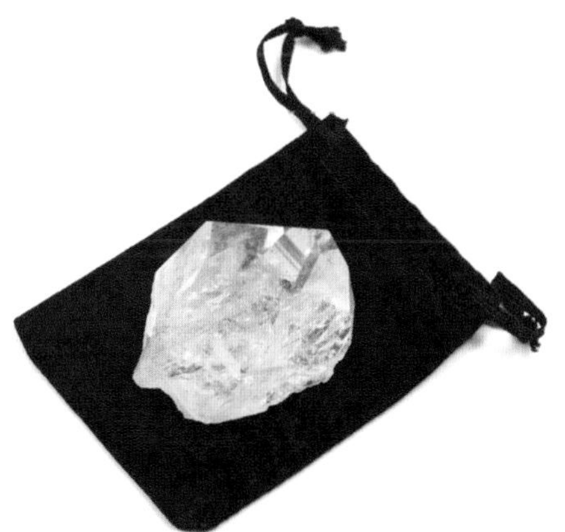

Ask the crystal's permission before programming, or carry out a short meditation to attune yourself to the crystal's energy. If you sense the crystal has no objection to being programmed, then there are a couple of different ways to begin the programming.

For Phrases and Ideas

Hold the crystal up to your third eye, which is on your brow, and visualize your programming flowing from you into the crystal. Keep going until you feel that the crystal has accepted the program. If you aren't sure whether the crystal has accepted your programming, try asking your pendulum to give you confirmation (see chapter seven on using a pendulum for how to do this).

For Colors

Place the crystal on a piece of paper or piece of cloth that is the color you want the crystal to take into itself, or perhaps write the name of the color on a piece of paper. Check with our pendulum to see how long the crystal should remain in place.

Essences

Put a couple of drops of vibrational essence or a flower essence onto the crystal. This type of programming will take longer, so use your pendulum to see how long the crystal has to remain in place before the program will be accepted. The program will remain in the crystal until the next time you cleanse it.

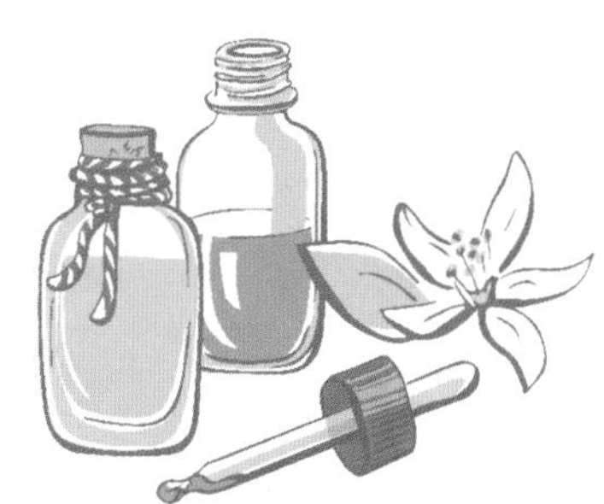

Charging a Crystal

Charging a crystal means filling it with a type of energy, but it can also be a good way of enhancing the crystal's own energy. Here are some methods of charging.

Sunlight

Crystals may be left on a windowsill or another safe place to absorb the rays of the sun. Keep in mind that some crystals may fade in bright sunlight, while others could magnify the light and start a fire.

Moonlight

Crystals may be left on a windowsill or another safe place while the moon is full to absorb the energy of the moonlight. This is a gentler form of energy than sunlight.

Take Care

When you program a crystal, the program needs to be for the *highest good*. Do not try to program a crystal to cause harm or discomfort to people, as this may come back on you. This is also true when it comes to programming crystals to heal other people because there can be times when, for whatever reason, people do not wish to accept healing, either consciously or subconsciously. Any such programming needs to be along the lines of "to bring healing energy to X, for his or her highest good."

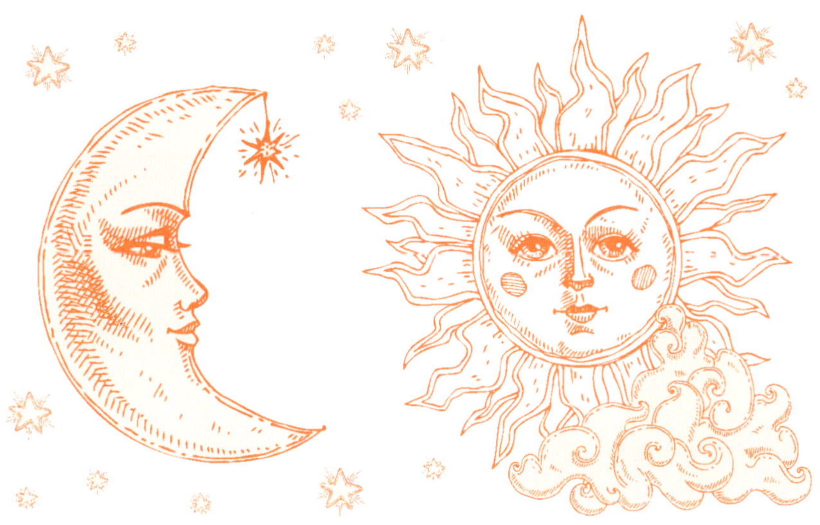

Reiki

If you are Reiki attuned, you may like to channel Reiki energy into your crystal.

Spiritual Healing

As with Reiki, you may like to channel the particular healing energy that you work with into your crystal.

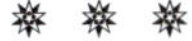

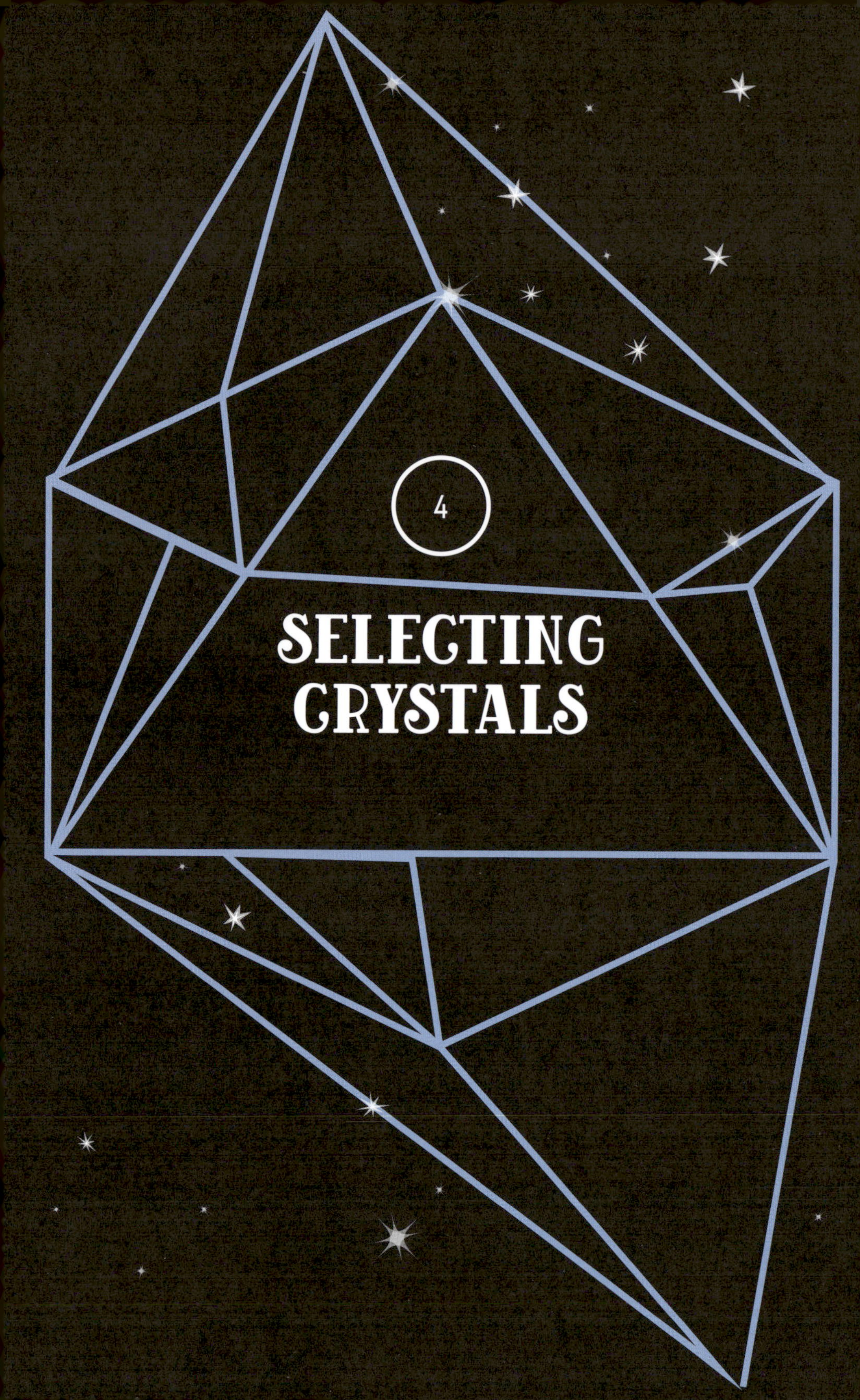

4

SELECTING CRYSTALS

When I first started working with crystals, my set contained only seven different colors, one for each chakra, and I gradually built up my collection by one or two stones at a time. I found that by collecting crystals this way, I remembered the names more easily and didn't need to cope with a variety of different energies all at once.

Deciding Which Crystals Are Right for You

If you are buying crystals, I suggest you consider which stones you are drawn to, as they will generally be the crystals you need to work with at that point in time. You may use a pendulum to select exactly which crystal is best for you (see chapter seven on dowsing), or you may just know intuitively, as soon as you look at the crystal, which one is right for you.

Pay no attention to anyone who tells you that if your hands aren't tingling, then it isn't the crystal for you (as someone once told me!). You may feel an instant connection with a crystal when you hold it, and you may experience tingling hands, a rush of energy, or just a feeling of belonging—or you may feel nothing. These responses are perfectly normal. I have purchased a crystal and felt nothing at the time, only for the stone to become the one I work with and carry around with me most often.

If you have a specific ailment or issue that you would like to work with, you might like to make a list of the things that are bothering you and then use your intuition or a pendulum to select the right crystal. Everyone is different, so while the store or online shop may label a certain crystal as helping with a particular condition, that may not be the one you need.

If there is a crystal you really do not like the look of or if you feel uncomfortable with its energy, this could indicate that it will bring up issues that you are not ready to deal with at this time.

Crystal Shapes

Crystals come in different forms and shapes, and it is a good idea to think about the purpose of your crystal before purchasing it. For example, if you are intending to carry the crystal in a pocket or bra, you may want to choose the tumbled version so that there are no sharp bits to poke into you. A raw crystal could be used for nets or placed on the body in a chakra layout. I have found that the energy from raw crystals is more "earthy" than of tumblestones, which have a smoother, more uniform energy. One is not better than the other; they are just different.

Tumblestones, or Tumblies

These are raw crystals that have been placed in a large drum with some grit and lubricant and rotated so that the crystals are gradually eroded, which makes them smooth. Tumblestones, or "tumblies" as they are sometimes called, are good for carrying around in a pocket or bra, or they can be put in

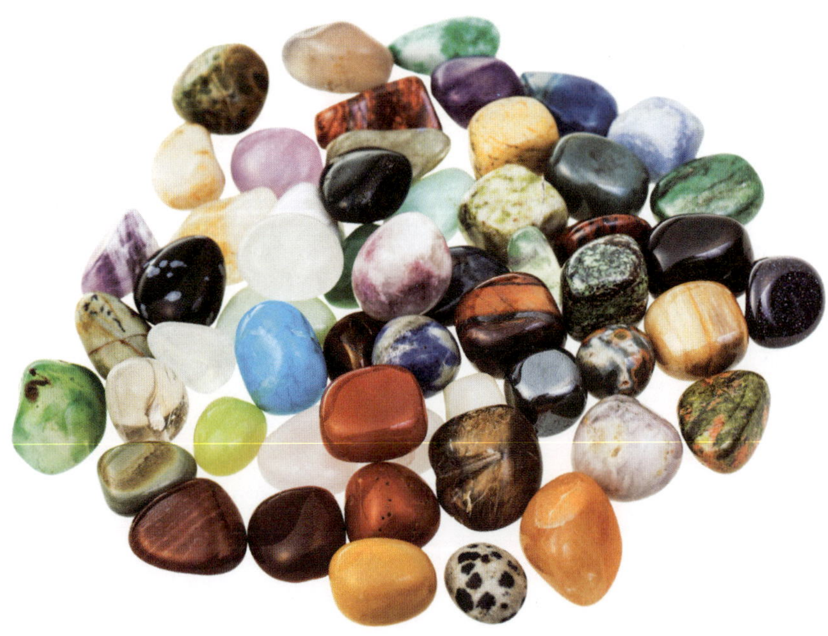

a spiral cage and hung from a necklace. Spiral cages can be purchased from most metaphysical stores in a variety of sizes to suit most tumblestones. Tumblestones are also useful when placing on or around the body, although if they are too spherical they will roll off, so these crystals may need taping in place with microporous tape.

Wands and Points

These can be cut to shape, but some minerals naturally form in a wand shape, like quartz. Wands and points are good for directional energy, so they can be used to bring energy into a specific point on the body, or to draw energy away from an area. Some wands have rounded bases, so by gently rubbing an area of pain, these can help to bring relief by drawing the unwanted energy away from the body. This activity also has a slight massage effect, which can be beneficial.

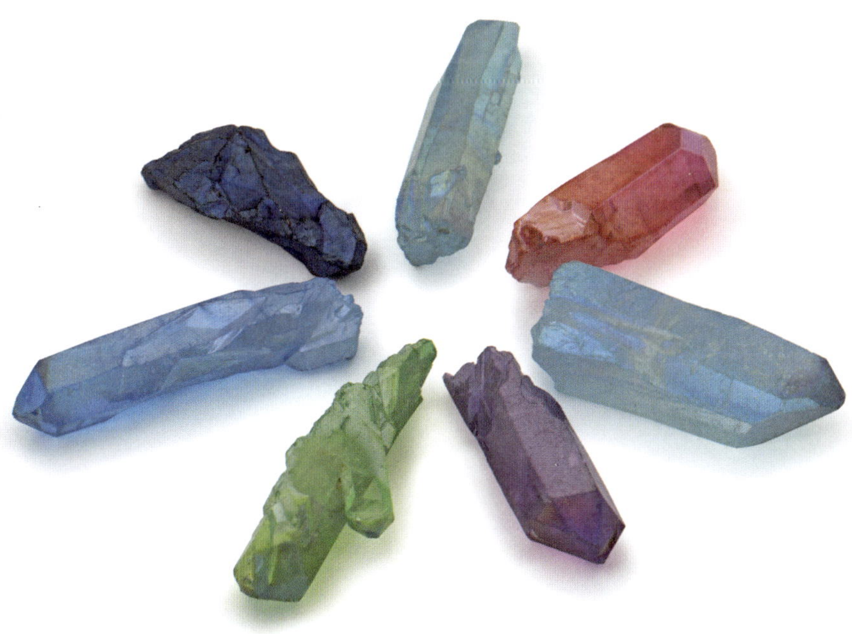

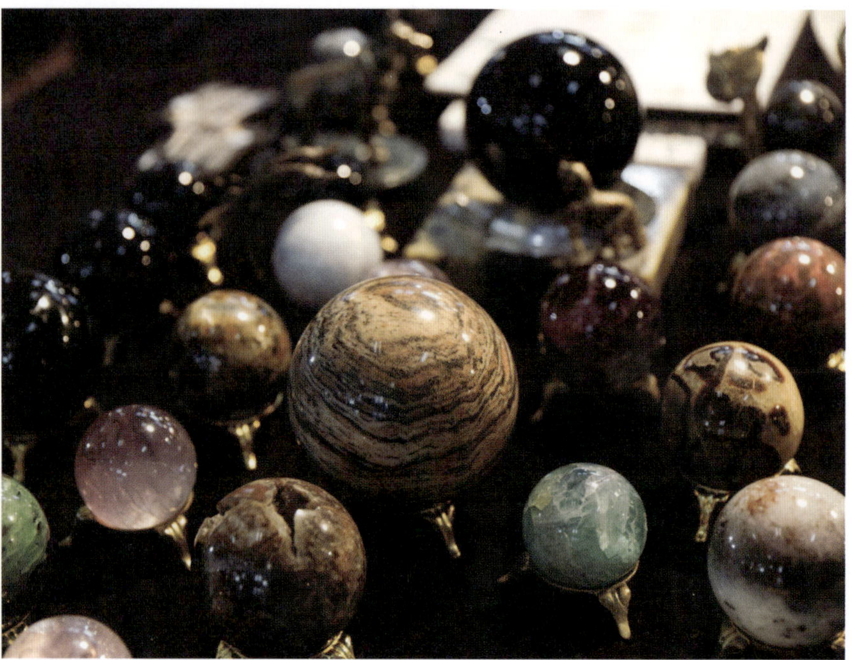

Crystal Balls and Eggs

Some crystals are shaped into spheres and egg shapes. As with tumblestones, the energy of these shapes will not be directional. These crystals can be difficult to use for crystal therapy, as they roll away when you try to place them on or around the body, but they bring positive energy into an area or room and can be used for meditation.

Pyramids

Crystal pyramids usually have four sides, and this shape allows for channeling energy, which is then directed from the upward point. There are many written accounts that claim that placing food and water underneath a pyramid shape keeps the consumables fresh for longer.

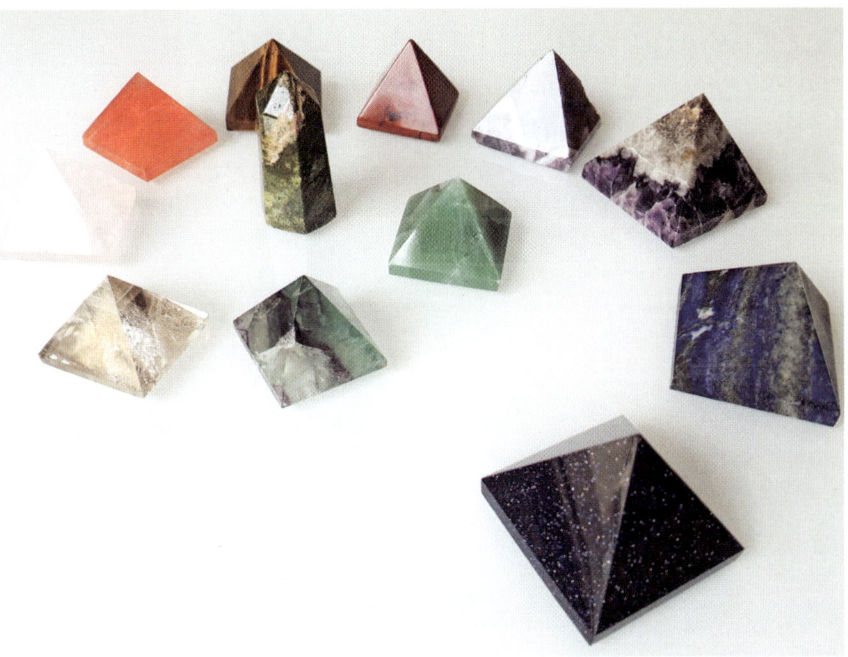

Skulls and Animals

Crystals are often carved into animal and skull shapes. These will not appeal to everyone, but they make lovely display pieces, and, although they are not practical for therapy use, the crystals can still be used for meditation or to energize a room or an area.

Merkaba

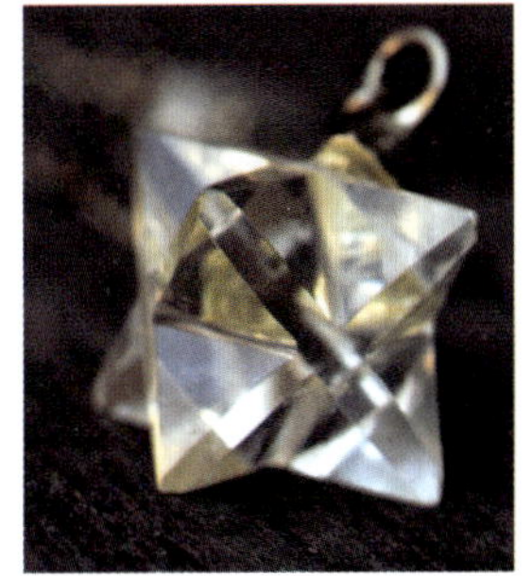

A *merkaba* is a 3D shape consisting of two four-sided pyramids (tetrahedrons). One has a point that faces upward, which represents male energy, and the other point facing downward, representing female energy. This sacred geometric shape is used to connect with higher realms of consciousness, so it is a good tool with which to meditate.

Geodes and Crystal Beds

A *geode* occurs where there was a pocket of gas inside rock or lava as it cooled. This means that crystals, which are usually agate or quartz and its variations, are formed inside the gas pocket. Quartz-variety geodes (amethyst and citrine being the most popular) are usually cut in half to create a beautiful cave-like display. They can be found in various sizes, from palm sized to huge structures that are taller than an average person. Agate geodes are frequently cut into thin, translucent slices that look beautiful with a light behind them, or cut into segments to form bookends.

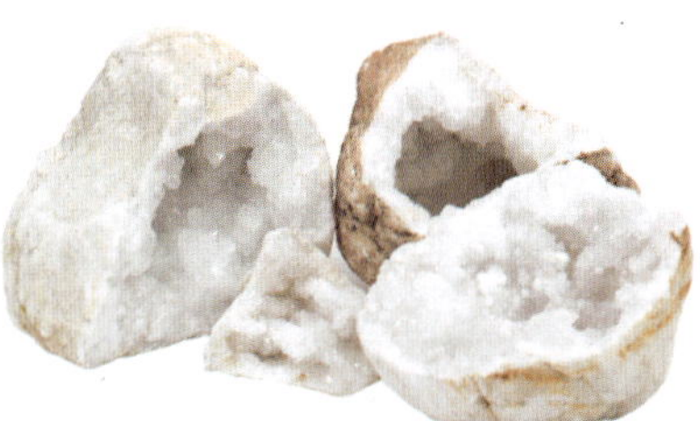

A *crystal bed* is a large chunk that has many small crystal points; amethyst and citrine are the most common.

Take Care When Purchasing a Crystal

Care needs to be taken when purchasing crystals to ensure that the stone you have selected is safe to carry around and work with. If you are buying crystals from specialist dealers, they often provide information on this, but some smaller shops or bargain stores may not. Some crystals can contain elements that are faintly dangerous, which means you will need to wash your hands after using them. For instance, malachite contains copper, which can be toxic. In its tumbled form it is safe, but care should be taken with raw malachite. Stibnite contains antimony sulphide, which is toxic. Other crystals are very soft, such as desert rose (gypsum), which will break easily if carried around.

If you are intending to go crystal shopping, you could take an identification book with you and look up any special requirements before you buy. If you have purchased a crystal impulsively, do check it out before you start working with it.

Broken Crystals

Unfortunately, sometimes crystals can break. This can be due to being dropped, or sometimes a crystal can absorb so much energy (especially the softer crystals) that it cracks or splits. The damage will manifest according to the way the crystal grew in the first place; for example, some crystals will cleave perfectly, and you will end up with two crystals, each of which will have a flat side, like calcite. A quartz point I have that I dropped on the floor ended up with a conchoidal chip. The word *conchoid* comes from the Greek word for "mussel," because the chip resembles the rippled curved shell.

Although it is extremely disappointing when one of your favorite crystals gets damaged, it will still work, and you may wish to meditate with your broken crystal to get a feel for the way the energy has changed. A crystal wand that I use for therapy broke in half during transit, so I glued it back together and cleansed, dedicated, and charged it by leaving in on my windowsill in the sunshine for a day. Then I meditated with the wand and discovered that the energy traveled normally from the bottom, but once it got to the super-glued bit, the energy seemed to slow down somewhat as it traveled toward the point. However, the wand still worked because on a molecular level, the energy vibration of the crystal was still the same.

Some people say that working with broken crystals helps us to work on self-healing. You may also read that some people believe it is better to bury broken crystals in the ground for a while to be healed by mother earth. I suggest that you go with your intuition and do what you feel is best.

Man-Made Crystals

Some crystals that occur in nature are enhanced by creating them in a lab, for example, bismuth. Lab-grown specimens create beautiful rainbow-colored square spirals, whereas in nature, bismuth is an inclusion that is often mixed with other minerals and just looks like a piece of rock. Recently there have been many lab-grown specimens of green chlorite quartz coming onto the market as well. Although chlorite

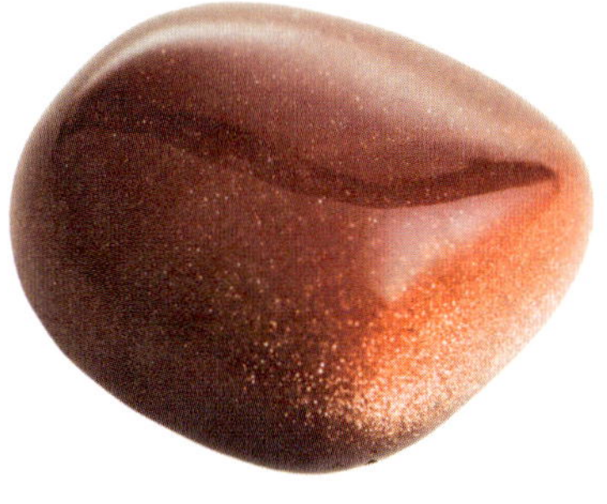

quartz does occur in nature, the green of the chlorite is usually contained within the clear quartz; the man-made crystals are recognizable by the appearance of a coating of green or a covering of tiny points called *druzy*.

A large majority of citrine available is actually amethyst that has been super-heated to replicate the process that happens naturally to turn amethyst into citrine. Natural citrine is usually very pale and can look similar to smoky quartz. Heated citrine can be quite dark, with some pieces being nearly orange in color. There is nothing wrong with heat-treated citrine, and it can still be used for healing, but some people prefer to work with naturally occurring specimens rather than crystals that have had changes forced on them. The same goes for smoky quartz, as the smoky effect only occurs in nature when quartz is irradiated. If you see smoky quartz for sale that is a very dark brown—almost black—these are pieces that have been subjected to radiation in a laboratory.

Opalite, which is sometimes called opal moonstone, is glass, as is goldstone. Goldstone has inclusions of copper, which are a brown color, or manganese or cobalt, which are a blue color. There is some debate over whether opalite and goldstone crystals actually work, but if you are attracted to owning one of these crystals, then you could work with the stones by using them for color therapy. Colors have different frequencies, as you will see in chapter eight on chakras.

In recent years, there have been claims that andara crystal (sometimes called andara glass) has been formed from slag glass picking up high-vibration energy from a sacred site. I'm unable to comment on the energy of the glass, as I haven't encountered any examples. Some people say that because glass is a man-made product created from melting sand, it doesn't have an energy that can help with healing; on the other hand, obsidian is volcanic glass formed by nature and has a very strong energy. You may have to hold a piece of andara glass and see if it resonates with you before purchasing. Even if it doesn't have an energetic vibration, the glass comes in beautiful colors and may be useful for color therapy.

Attuning Yourself to Crystals

Attuning yourself to a crystal is simply a way of getting used to its energy. This can be done by meditating with a crystal or carrying it around with you, but make sure you have no other crystals with you so that you focus on only one type of energy. You could even put the crystal under your pillow while you sleep.

Crystal identification books often give a list of physical, emotional, and spiritual uses for a crystal, but actually attuning yourself to your own crystal

Trademarked Crystals

Sometimes crystals are given created names in order to persuade people that there is a new crystal on the market. These names may also be trademarked and include a certificate of authenticity. Some examples include Cinnazez™, which is cinnabar in quartz, or Rosophia™, which is feldspar and quartz. Larimar is sometimes sold as dolphin stone, and kambaba jasper also has an alternative name of nebula stone. It may be worth doing some research before purchasing a crystal, as you may find that there is a difference in price for the newly named stones.

will help you to learn how its energy *feels*. Once you know how the crystal's energy feels, even if it's only on a subconscious level, your intuition will draw you to that stone whenever you need it.

Storing Crystals

I use a plastic compartmental box of the type that you can buy from a hobby or craft store. I like to line each compartment with a bit of cloth to minimize any damage from rattling around during transportation. Ideally, soft crystals are best stored separately from hard crystals in order to minimize damage. I also put a note with the crystal's name in the compartment in case I forget it! This is especially helpful when the crystal that you own looks different from the pictures in the identification books.

It is lovely to have crystals out on display, but be aware that some crystals will fade if left in sunlight for long periods, such as on a windowsill. In addition, if you are planning to have crystals in the kitchen or bathroom, check whether the crystals are able to withstand a humid atmosphere; for example, gypsum and selenite will slowly deteriorate if kept in damp conditions.

❋ ❋ ❋

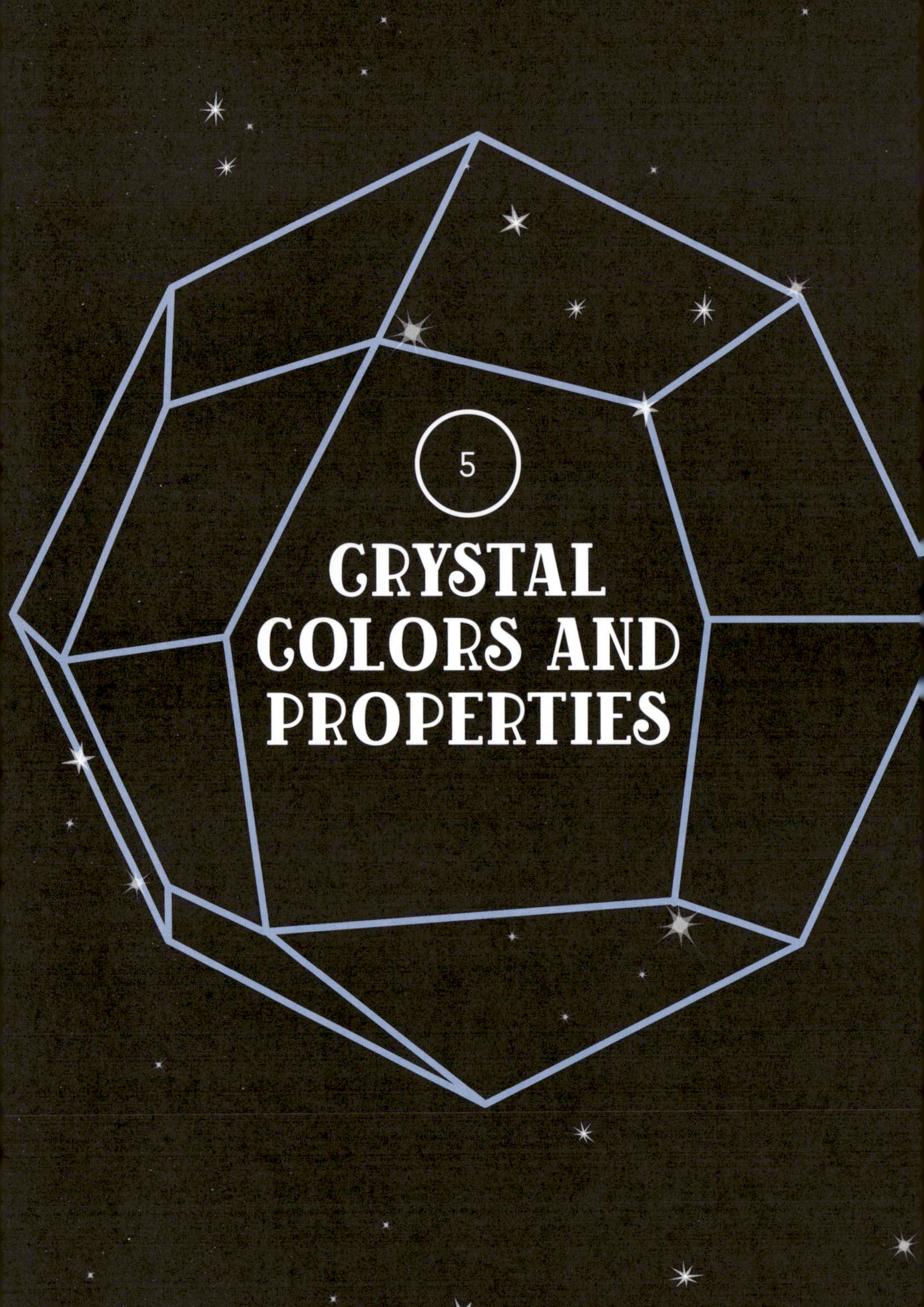

5

CRYSTAL COLORS AND PROPERTIES

Crystals come in different colors and many shades. Often you will have a choice of color for one particular mineral; for example, fluorite comes in purple, green, blue, yellow, pink, and clear; tourmalines are found in black, green, blue, and pink; and moonstone is commonly a creamy white, but is also available in shades of brown and orange.

Crystals of the same color share certain attributes, which I have listed below, but as mentioned in chapter one, the way in which a crystal works also depends on its hardness and structure, so I have added a summary for each crystal.

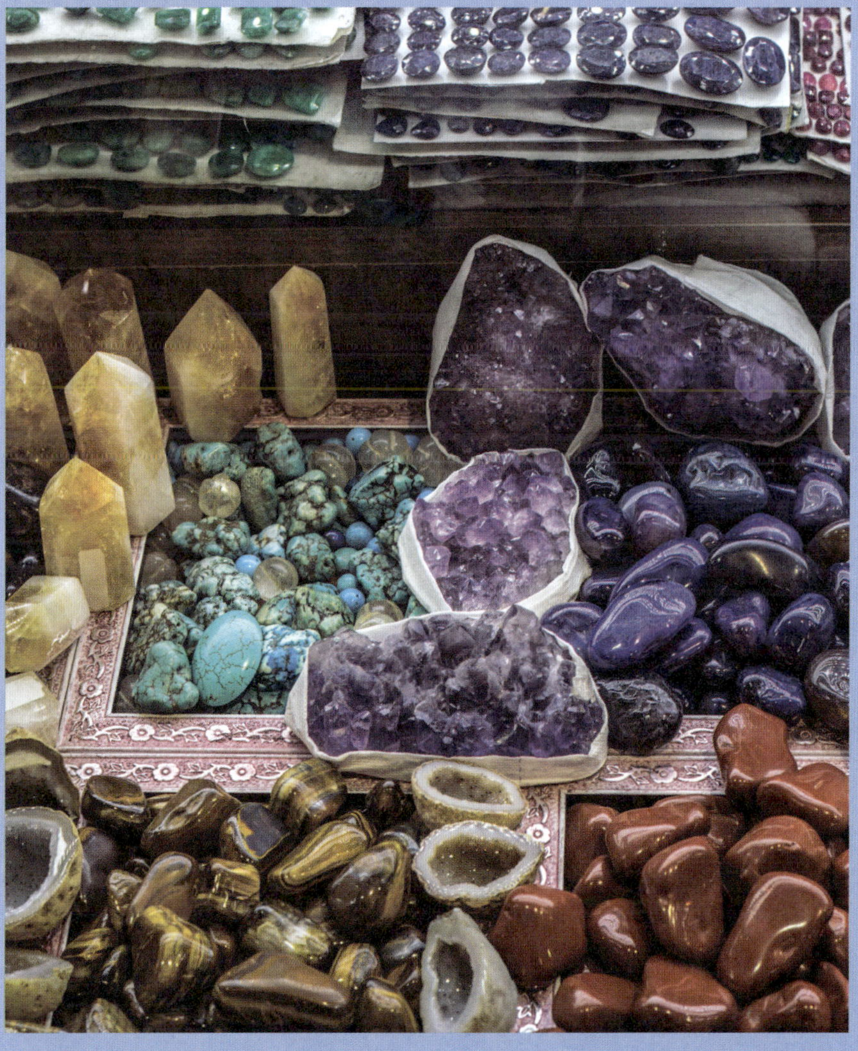

Black

Crystals of this color are very grounding and are also used for protecting one's aura from other energies. The aura is a subtle energy field that surrounds every living thing, and in the case of those who work on a psychic or healing level, the aura can easily pick up energies from others that can leave one feeling weak, spaced out, or uncomfortable. Black is often used for grief as well, aiding a person in grounding and transmuting energy.

Black Tourmaline

A good grounding stone, this crystal is often used for protection. It reflects negative energy back to the person who is directing it at you and is gentle enough to carry around for long periods of time.

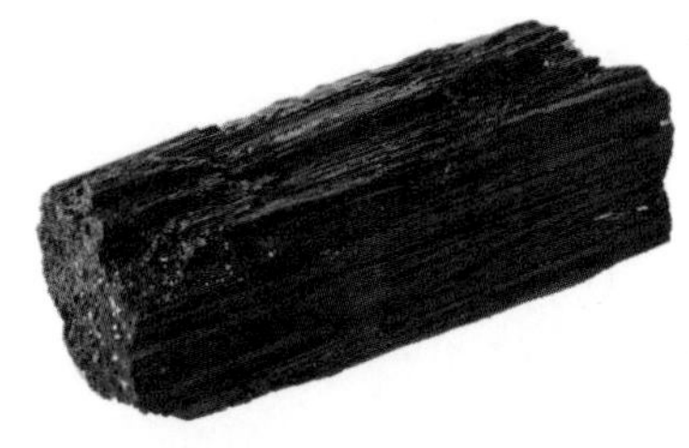

Obsidian

This can be a powerful stone to work with, as it is amorphous and works in a very direct way; it will bring to the surface any issues that you need to deal with in order to make progress.

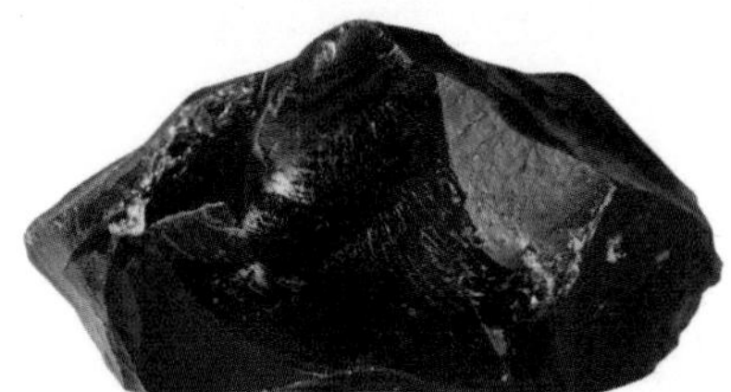

Hematite

A stabilizing crystal that helps to calm. Hematite contains iron and can be useful in situations that require strength of patience or will.

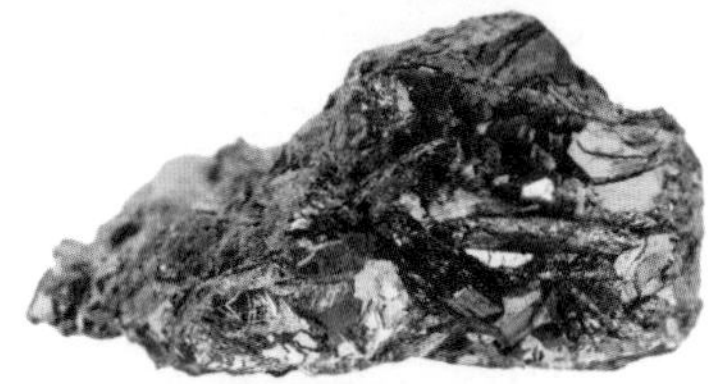

Black Kyanite

This crystal is good for getting energy moving on different levels and helps bring everything into focus.

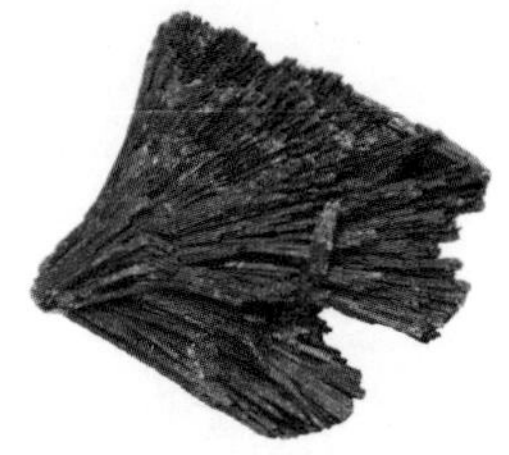

Brown

This color is very earthy and grounding, so it strengthens one's connection to the earth.

Smoky Quartz

Formed when quartz is subjected to radiation in the earth, smoky quartz is a gentle grounding crystal, also helping to remove earth energy that is no longer needed, in order to move on.

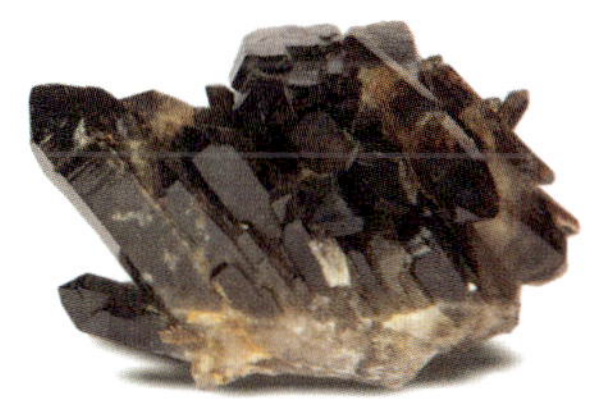

Chiastolite

As well as calming fears by gradually grounding, chiastolite renews determination to get a job done.

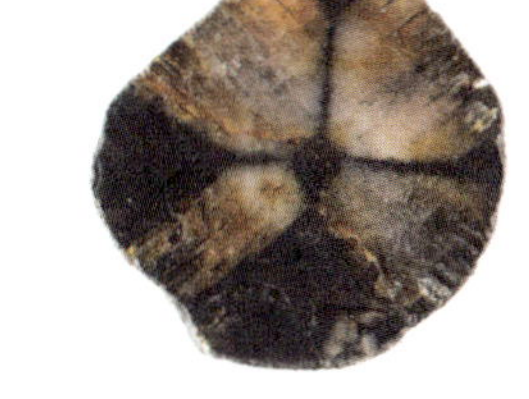

Brown Agate

This stone can help with digestion, both physically and mentally. It also assists a person in assimilating information.

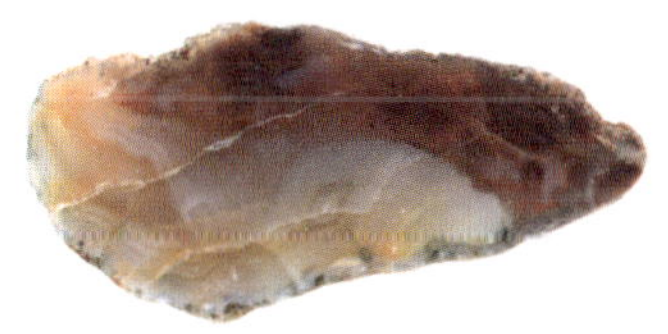

Aragonite

This crystal is slowly grounding and assists in calming excitable or nervous behavior.

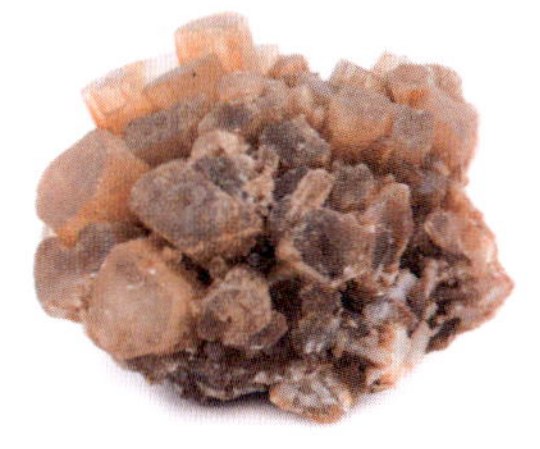

Red

These crystals work with survival instincts or issues, often connected to feelings of security and stability. Red is stimulating, so you should limit the length of time you continuously work with crystals of this color. Although associated with survival, red is also the color of passion.

Red Jasper

Red jasper is a gently grounding stone and is sometimes found mixed in with hematite, which creates brecciated jasper. Red jasper is an energizing stone and a good one to work with if you are feeling physically worn out.

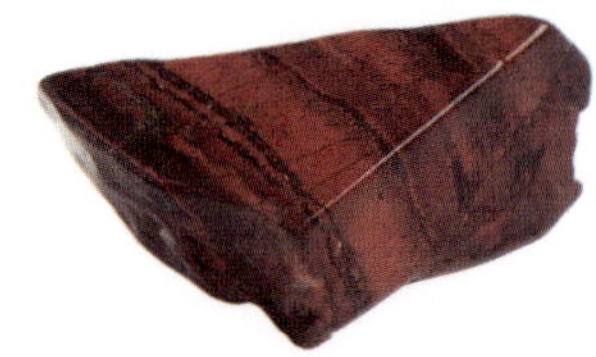

Ruby

This is an energetic stone that can increase energy and passion for a project.

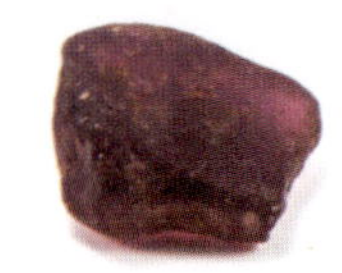

Red Muscovite

Sometimes called red mica, this beautiful sparkly crystal helps to release a buildup of stress and exhaustion.

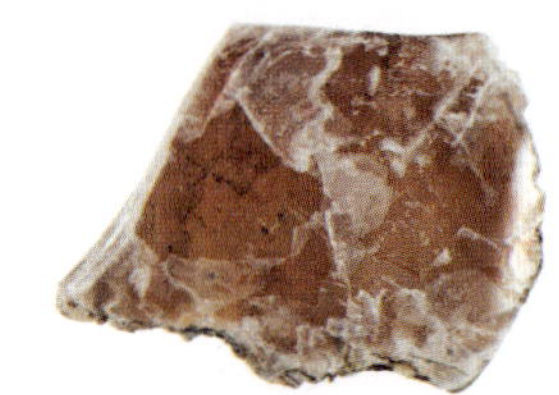

Garnet

This crystal can help with emotional wounds and release of tension concerning basic needs.

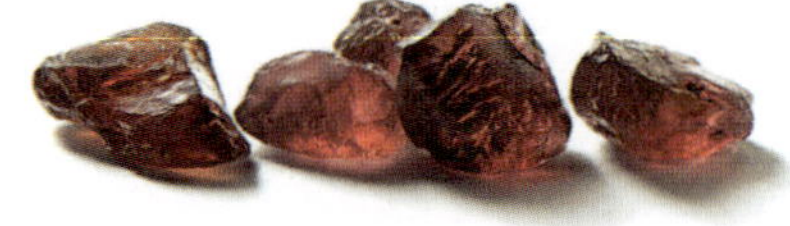

Orange

Enlivening and energizing, crystals of this color can encourage creativity and raise energy levels.

Carnelian

This crystal is very good at exciting energy and can be a good pick-me-up if you are feeling worn down.

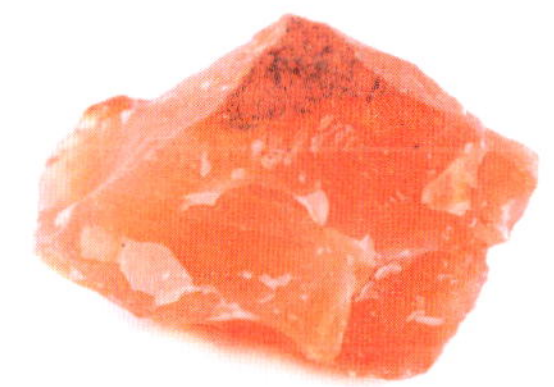

Orange Calcite

This is a good crystal to keep with you if your creativity has been stifled by others. It also helps with releasing the emotional effects of abuse.

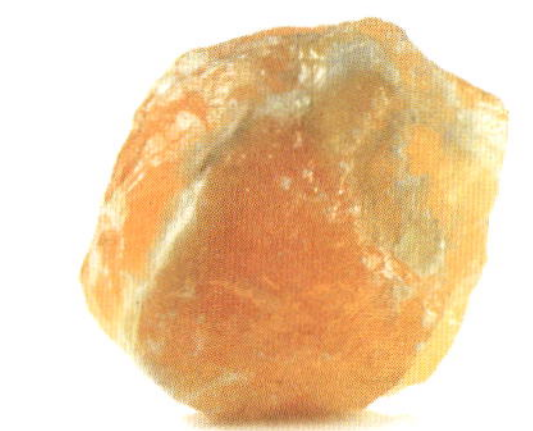

Sunstone

The energy of this crystal is cheering, and it aids with transforming negative thoughts into a positive attitude.

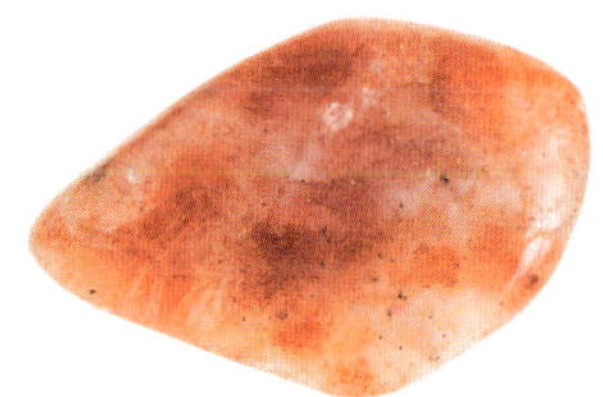

Tangerine Quartz

This is quartz that is coated with hematite or iron, which means its energy can aid in making decisions, so it helps when you need to get something done.

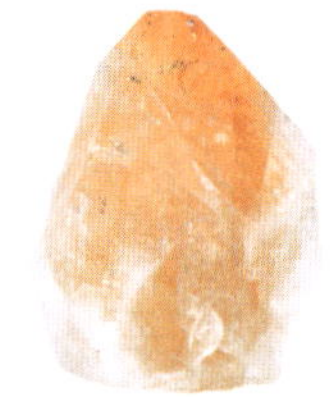

Yellow

This is a warm color that boosts confidence and brings cheer, so it is good to use with fear or sadness. Yellow can also be used in times of mental stress to stimulate positivity. This color can bring prosperity, joy, and wisdom.

Amber

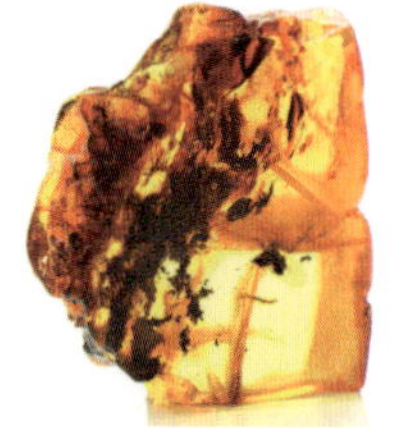

Amber is fossilized tree resin and has an amorphous structure. It can become statically charged. Working with amber assists courage.

Yellow Jasper

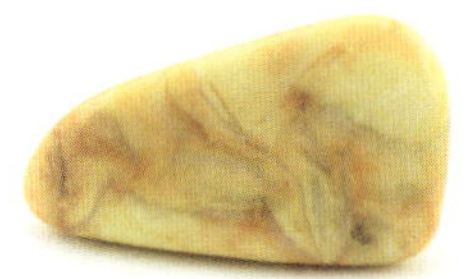

This crystal works slowly, so it is good for carrying around with you for long periods of time. It helps to gradually increase confidence in yourself and protects against stress from external sources.

Citrine

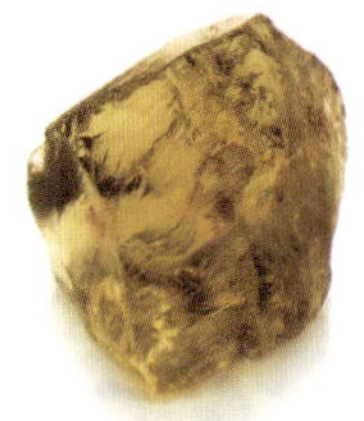

Citrine that is actually heat-treated amethyst will be either a very bright yellow or a dark, almost brown, yellow. Real citrine more closely resembles smoky quartz with a yellow tinge. Both versions are good at promoting optimism and helping to banish fears.

Tiger's Eye

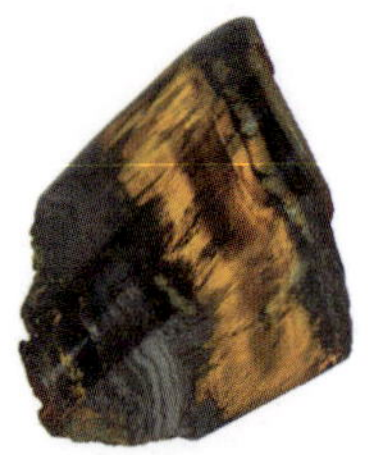

This is a great crystal to carry around at times when you need a boost of confidence and belief in yourself, such as when you're taking an exam or going for an interview.

Green

Green crystals are good to work with if there are issues concerning emotions and how much of yourself you give to others. This color is great for those who need a fresh start in life and love.

Green Aventurine

This crystal helps us to reach out to opportunities with confidence and also imparts hope and gratitude.

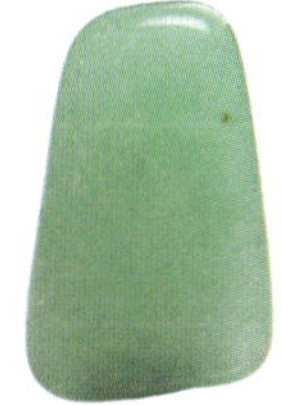

Emerald

Emerald enhances and renews love, encouraging passion and playfulness in relationships.

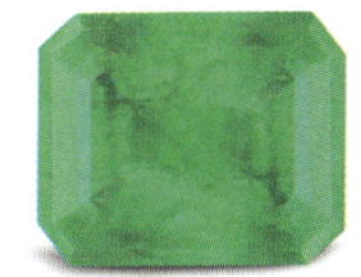

Peridot

This stone aids facing one's fears of being unlovable. It also encourages love toward a situation that is causing emotional upset.

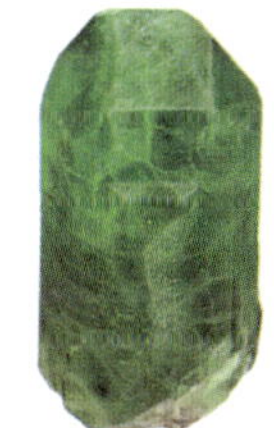

Malachite

This crystal helps us to look at the reasons we give to other people and to assess whether certain people in our lives are good to be around. Malachite can be a strong vibration, so you may want to use it for only short periods at a time.

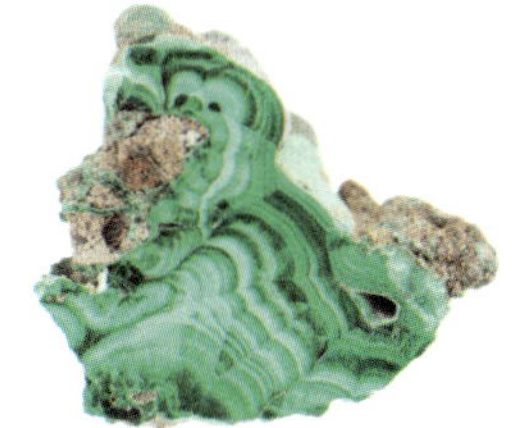

Light Blue and Turquoise

These colors represent expression and communication—speaking your truth. Turquoise has a touch of green, so it can help you express what is in your heart. Light blue is a mix of dark blue and white, feeling calming and clearing at the same time.

Turquoise

Turquoise encourages us to speak out, rather than keeping everything bottled up, but in a way that is diplomatic. It is also a very good crystal for immunity and protection. Be aware that some crystals labeled turquoise are sometimes just dyed howlite.

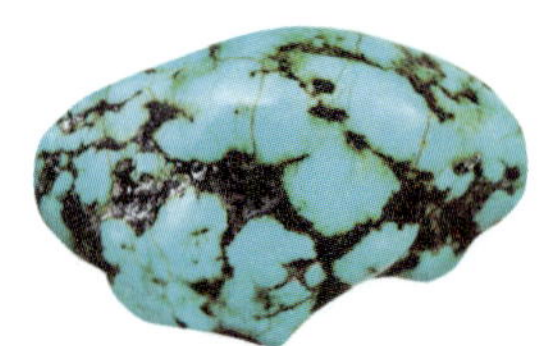

Celestite

This gentle stone enables us to listen as well as calmly discuss. It is a good crystal to aid speaking in public or if you are shy and struggle to talk to people.

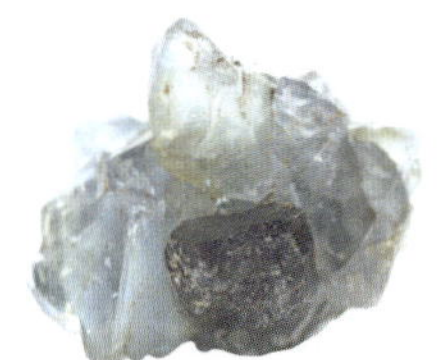

Kyanite

This crystal moves stagnant energy and can be used wherever you feel a blockage of energy. It is also good at deflecting any negative energy directed at you back to the person who sent it, but in a more gentle way than black tourmaline.

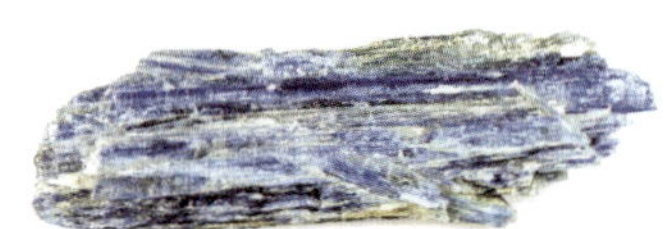

Blue Lace Agate

A beautiful crystal with a peaceful cooling energy, blue lace agate is an ideal stone to use in inflamed situations where you want to speak your mind but feel you have to hold back.

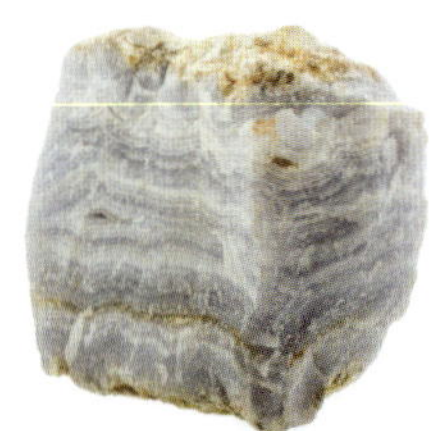

Dark Blue

This color aids intuition and seeing the whole situation. It reminds me of watching the night sky; working with dark-blue crystals brings enlightenment, like seeing stars gradually appearing. Stones of this spectrum also have a calming feel to them, making this a good color to work with to soothe feelings of anger. A stone of this color is good for those who want to increase their level of intuition.

Sodalite

Sodalite has an energy that helps us to be realistic. It also calms the mind and aids the evaluation of daydreams to see whether they are achievable.

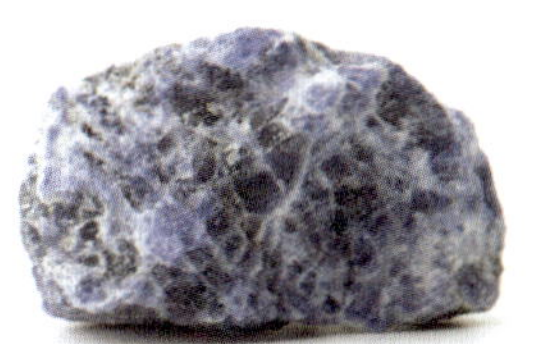

Dumortierite

A calming crystal, easing stress and assisting us with seeing all points of view. It is a good crystal to carry if there is a situation that makes you angry.

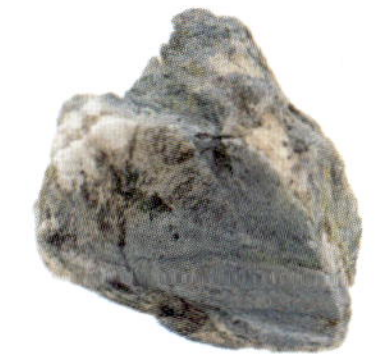

Lapis Lazuli

An ideal stone to boost confidence, inspiring us to push forward with ideas. If you are concentrating on self-development, lapis lazuli aids spiritual studies.

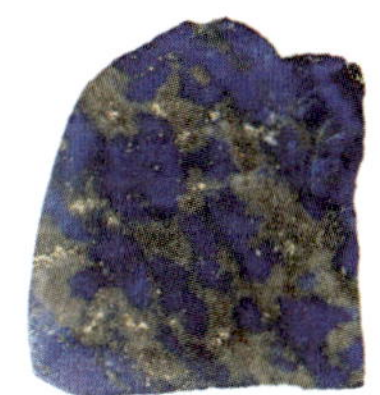

Iolite

Iolite aids intuition and clear vision by calming a chaotic mind, enabling us to discern which course of action we wish to take.

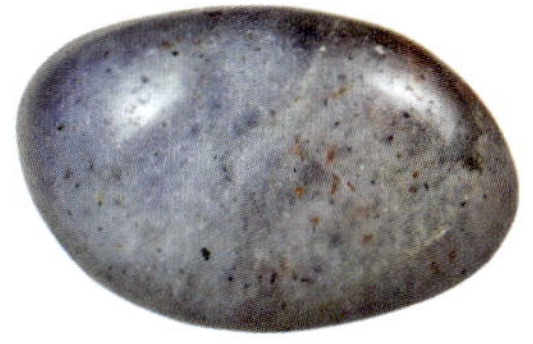

Purple

Purple helps us work toward enlightenment and also connects us to the energy around us, such as gods, goddesses, universal energy, and the higher self.

Amethyst

A crystal that is often recommended to use with headaches and migraines, amethyst gently calms and encourages positivity; simply place it on the brow when you feel a headache coming on.

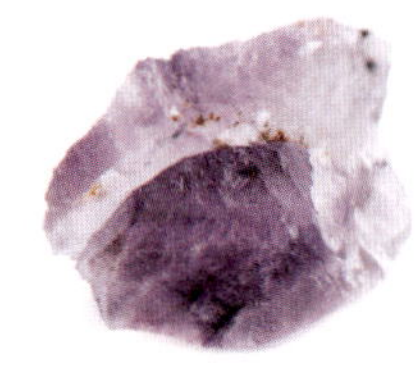

Tanzanite

This crystal aids the expansion of spiritual awareness, and it calms and opens the mind to new possibilities. It is a helpful crystal for deep meditation.

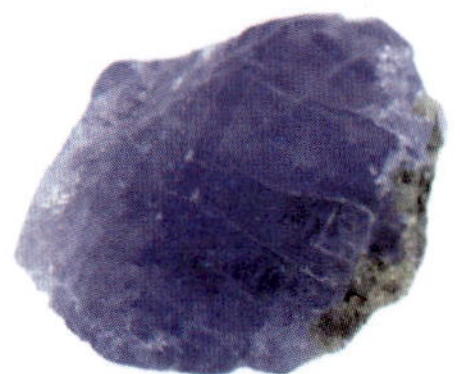

Charoite

Charoite is a beautiful stone that is often used in jewelry. This crystal aids going with the flow, releasing the old and welcoming the new.

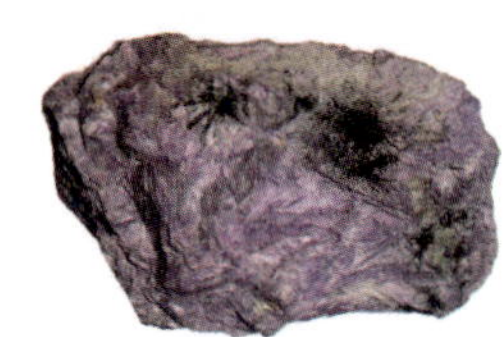

Lepidolite

Lepidolite has an optimistic energy and aids relaxation, gently lifting one's mood.

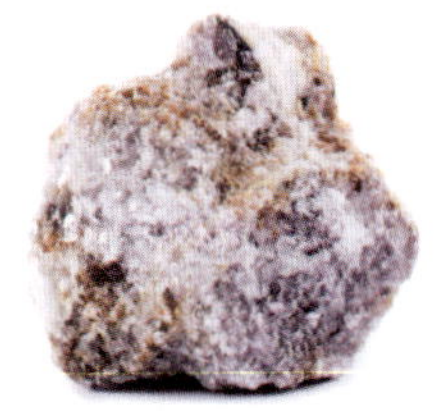

Pink

A mixture of red and white, pink can bring stability by encouraging self-love and self-acceptance. It is a good color to work with if you are feeling rejected or unloved.

Rose Quartz

Rose quartz is commonly available and often recommended for emotional problems, but for people who have very low self-esteem or dislike the way they look, this may be a difficult stone to work with due to the fact that, being a hard crystal, it works in a direct way.

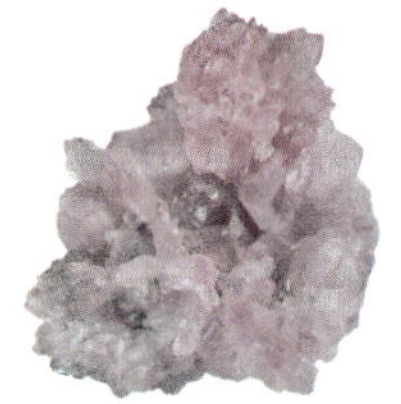

Morganite

This crystal gently assists us in setting aside feelings that we don't need to hold on to. Morganite also encourages patience and compassion, with others and the self.

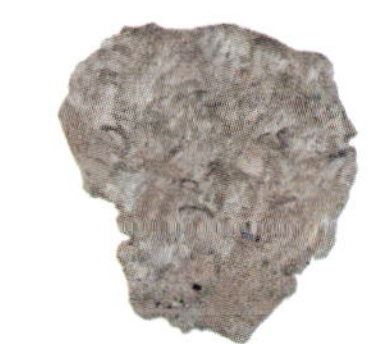

Mangano Calcite

This is a very gentle pink stone and an ideal crystal to work with if you find it hard to love yourself, as it's not as direct and hard as rose quartz.

Rhodochrosite

A beautiful crystal for working with old emotional issues, bringing loving energy in to heal the situation. Rhodochrosite also helps us to send love to the small part of us that believes we're not good enough.

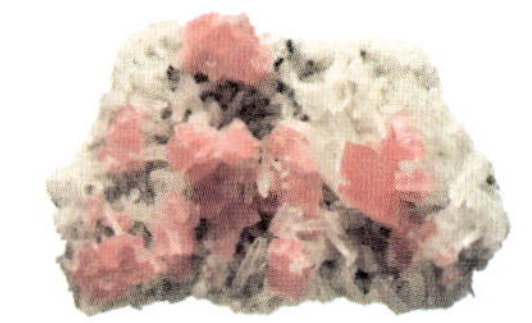

Clear

Clear stones bring in the whole spectrum of light, so they are very good for clearing and bringing clarity.

Quartz

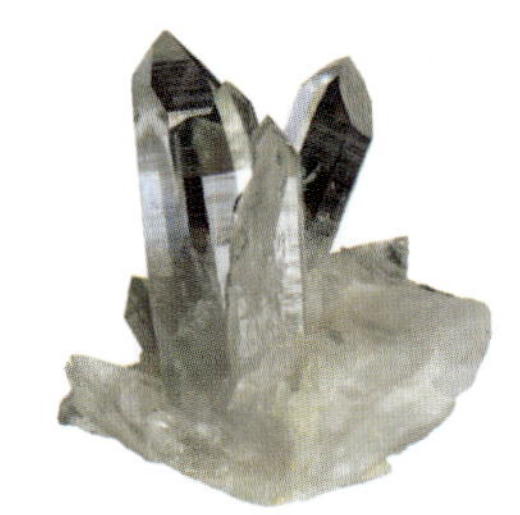

A good crystal to use for general healing situations, it has a hardness of seven on the Mohs scale and works in a very direct way. Quartz is also often found with other minerals, such as when it forms with black tourmaline to create tourmalinated quartz. When this happens, quartz will amplify the energy of any mineral inclusion.

Danburite

This crystal has a lovely bright energy that, like quartz, clears blockages and unwanted energy, but, being a soft stone, it works in a gentler way than quartz.

Apophyllite

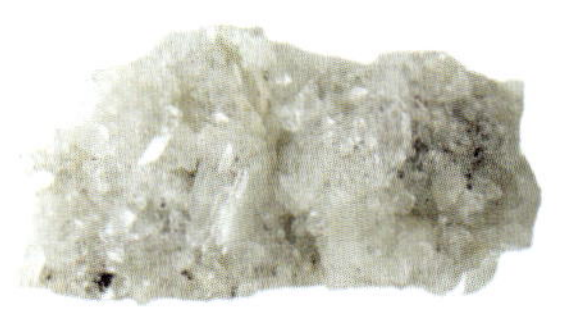

Another crystal with a bright energy, apophyllite facilitates joy by helping to clear away outdated beliefs and negative patterns of thinking.

Clear Topaz

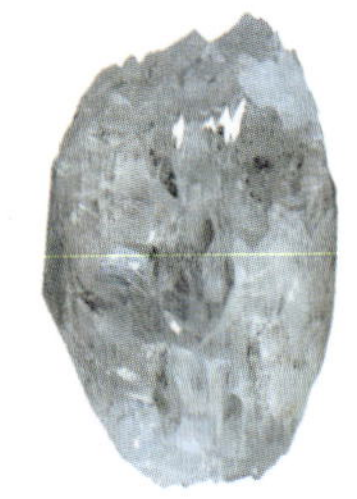

This crystal enhances spiritual development by aiding understanding and enlightenment. Clear topaz can also help with trusting our own psychic abilities.

White

Crystals that are white are similar in energy to clear crystals, but the energy is less direct—a bit gentler and more diffracted. The color white is representative of purity and innocence.

Howlite

This is a calming crystal that brings peace and eases stress or anger. Howlite can also help to clear the mind and is a useful aid to meditation or sleep.

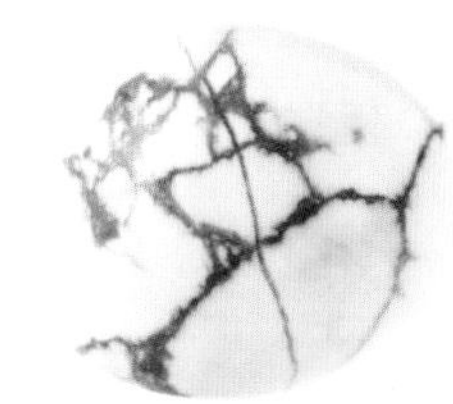

White Jade

Jade is a very serene and accepting stone. White jade helps us to slow down when we need to focus or concentrate on a task.

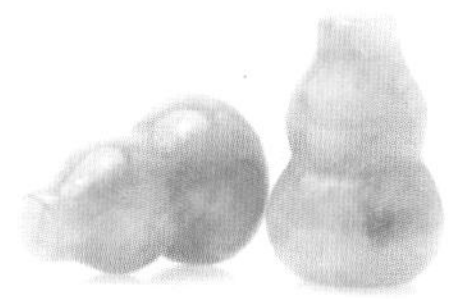

Snow/Milky Quartz

This crystal is clear quartz with microscopic bubbles inside, giving it a white, opaque appearance. As with clear quartz, this stone is good for clearing, but it does so in a slower way. It is good for all healing situations.

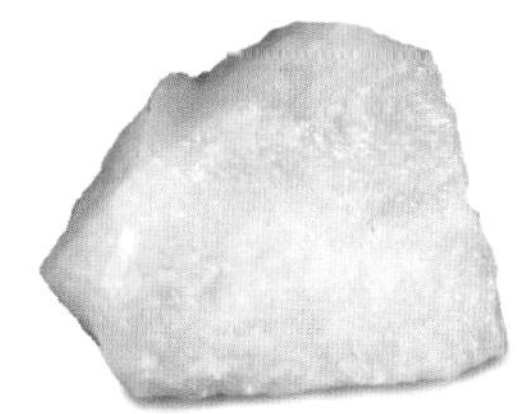

Selenite

Selenite's energy moves quickly and can shift energy blockages easily.

Multi-Colored

Some crystals are made of one mineral but are more than one color. They can encompass either the traits of all the colors in their makeup or the traits of the color that is predominant.

Single Mineral

Fluorite

Fluorite can be found as singular color crystals, but sometimes there will be a mixture: I have a chunk of clear fluorite with pink, blue, and green stripes running through it. This stone assists with coordination and integration, bringing peace and calm.

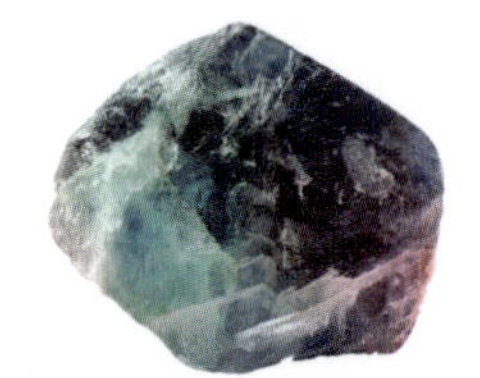

Peacock Ore

Showing colors including purple, green, and blue, peacock ore is the name given to bornite or chalcopyrite that has oxidized. This stone can help with joy and confidence to take action.

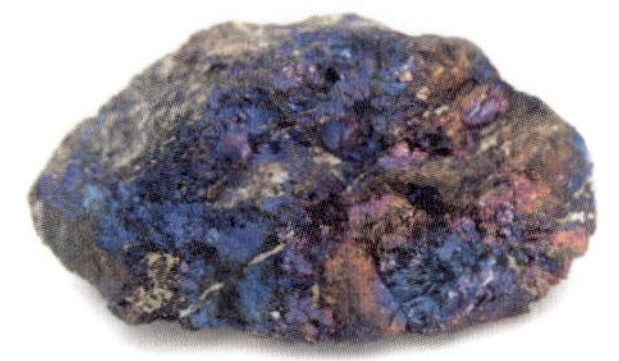

Tourmaline

Watermelon tourmaline is a form of tourmaline that consists of a pink center surrounded by green. There are also beautiful examples of multi-colored tourmaline. This crystal brings balance and harmony by shifting unwanted energy.

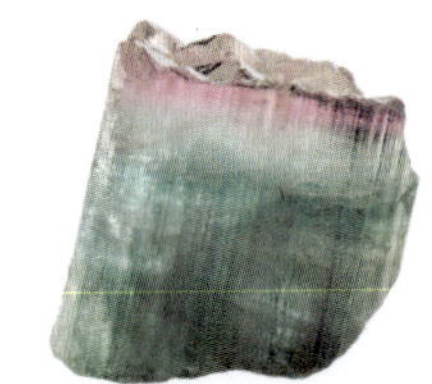

Ametrine

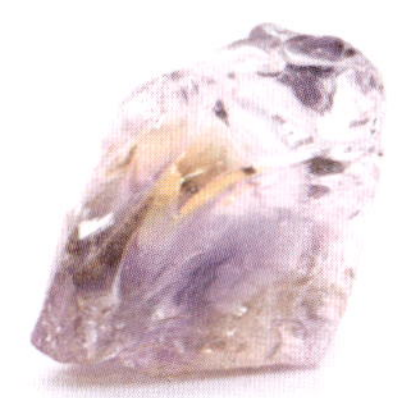

This crystal is a mixture of the calming healing of amethyst and the joyful energy of citrine.

More Than One Mineral

Tiger Iron

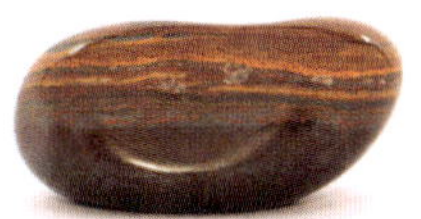

Contains jasper and tiger's eye with hematite. It is a good crystal for stamina and staving off exhaustion.

Ruby in Zoisite

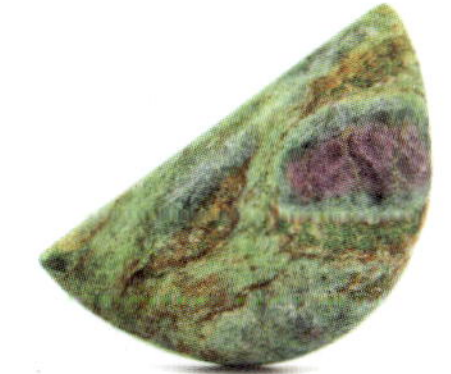

Balances energies, including the balance of male and female energies within a person. It also calms passions of the heart.

Super 7

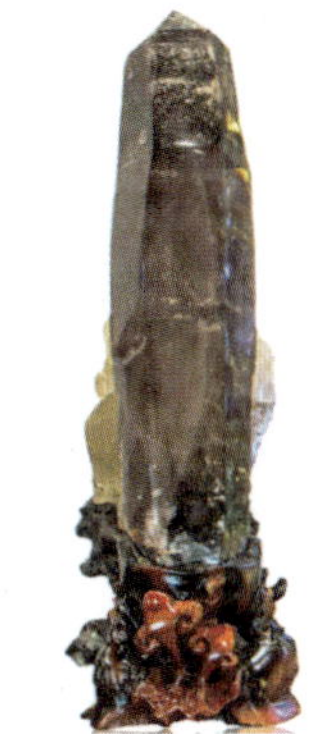

Contains amethyst, quartz, rutile, smoky quartz, goethite, cacoxenite, and lepidocrocite. It is said that this crystal never needs cleansing. Super 7 has a high vibration and can help us to develop spirituality by assisting self-development.

✵ ✵ ✵

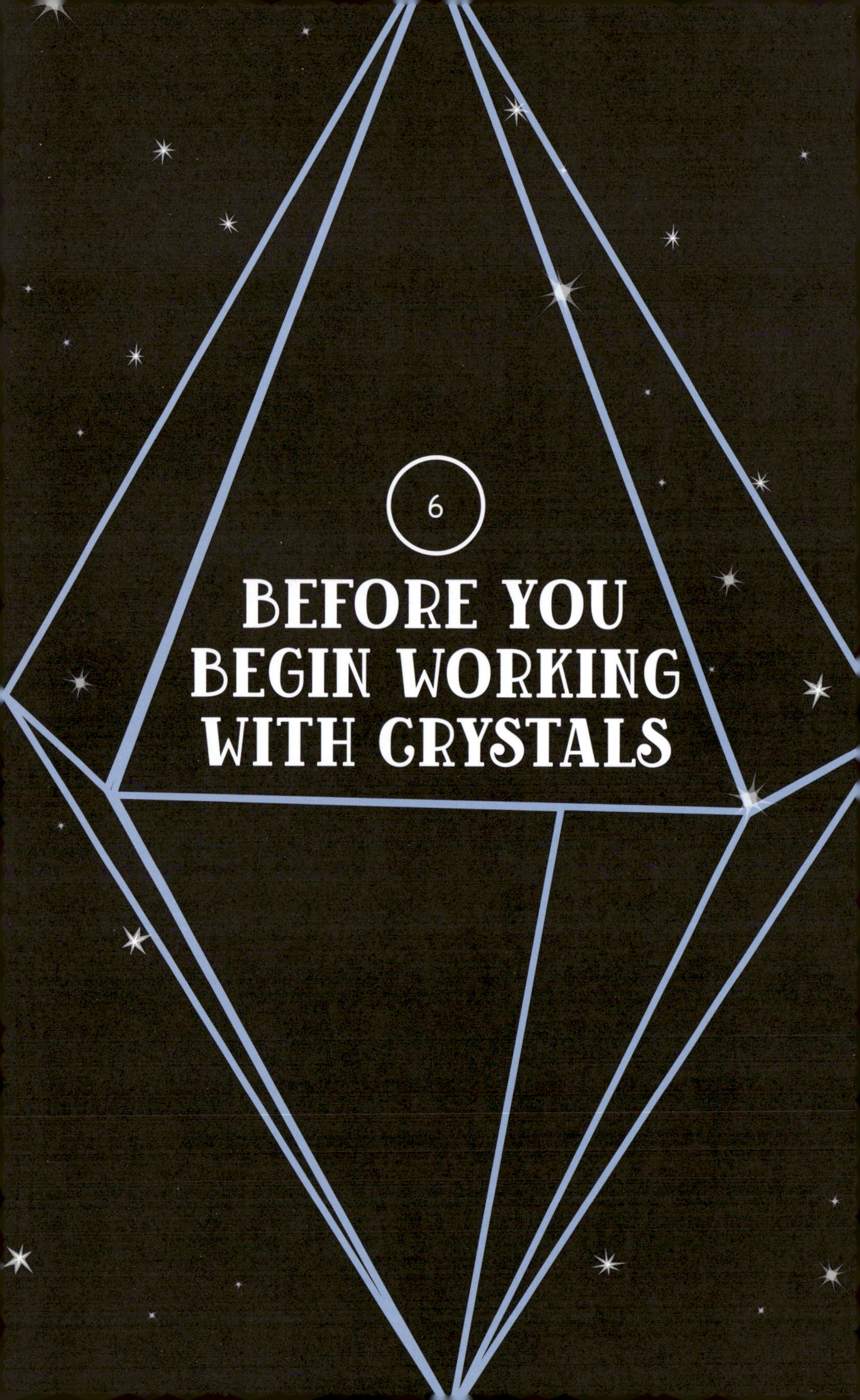

6

BEFORE YOU BEGIN WORKING WITH CRYSTALS

Before you begin working with crystals, it is a good idea to set up a routine of grounding and centering yourself, and eventually this will become second nature. Each time you start your grounding and centering routine, you will automatically start to relax and open up to the energy of the crystals.

Grounding and Centering

Being grounded will make you feel fully in your body, while you are also alert and aware. You could be ungrounded if you find it hard to concentrate, if you feel light-headed or fuzzy-headed, or if you feel as though you are not in your body. Other symptoms of being ungrounded include feelings of anxiety or even of panic.

To center yourself, you need to focus your energy either on your solar plexus, which is around your diaphragm, or on your heart. Being centered helps you to feel balanced, enabling you to make decisions and cope with daily life.

Methods of Grounding and Centering

TAPPING IN

Tapping in is a quick and easy method of grounding and centering. The sternum, or breastbone, is halfway between your throat and your belly button, so now, using three fingers, tap your sternum between ten and twenty times, then tap your sternum again in a counterclockwise circle for the same number of times that you tapped the first time. This method has the benefit that it can be carried out unobtrusively. For example, if you are out in public and feeling overwhelmed due to all the different energies around, you can discreetly "tap yourself in" to bring your energy back into yourself.

COOK'S HOOKUP

For this exercise, you will need to be seated. Place your left foot across the right foot. Then hold your arms out horizontally in front of you and place your left hand across the right hand. Turn both hands inward so that the palms face each other. Interlace the fingers of both hands and slowly bring your hands in toward your chest, then up toward your neck. Hold this position for a couple of minutes while breathing in and out, deeply and slowly.

If you find it more comfortable, you can cross your feet and arms the other way, starting with the right foot and right hand.

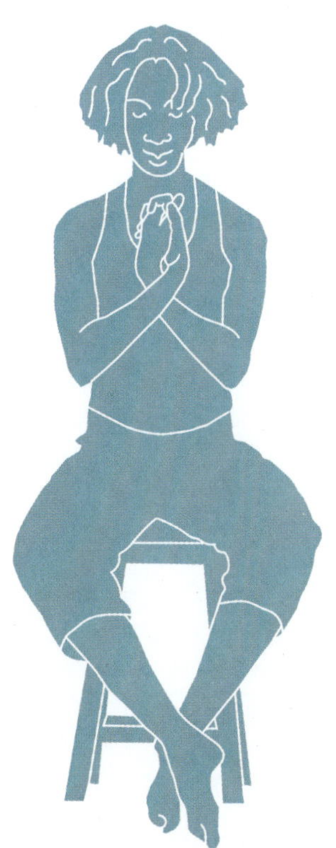

Color

Black, brown, and red crystals are known to be very good for grounding, but I have found the best ones for me are black tourmaline, smoky quartz, and brecciated jasper. You'll have to experiment to find the best crystal for you. Placing crystals by your feet gently draws your energy downward and slowly grounds you, but holding the crystals in your hands and concentrating on the way they feel will work as well.

An easy grounding and centering layout to do at the end of a crystal healing session, for yourself or someone else, is to lie down and place a single terminated smoky quartz point on your chest pointing toward your feet and another one between your feet pointing away from them. This gently directs your energy downward and away from your body.

FIGURE OF EIGHT, OR ELEPHANT'S TRUNK

Put one shoulder up to your face as if you are pretending that your arm is an elephant's trunk, and wave your arm around in a figure of eight for a minute or so. Although you may feel silly doing this, moving around and concentrating on your body is an easy way of grounding and centering. You can alternate this exercise by using the other shoulder.

VISUALIZATION

Visualize bringing your energy down from your head to your feet and growing roots into the earth. Continue the visualization and focus your attention on your heart or solar plexus chakra until you feel focused and clear-headed. A visualization has one great benefit, which is that no one can see what you are doing; however, this method is good only if you are not concentrating on something else—for instance, please do not try to do visualizations while driving!

PREPARING A NET

Different practitioners use different names for the same technique, so while I tend to call the following method a "net," others call it a "layout." No matter what you call it, it means placing crystals in a symmetrical pattern around the body using a single type of crystal to form an energy field (see more on page 14 in chapter two).

When preparing to do a net on myself, I lay some crystals at my feet and lower legs, then place other crystals beside me so that I can reach them when I'm lying down. I also make sure either that I'm wearing a watch or that I can see a clock so that I can keep an eye on the length of time I stay in the layout. After every five minutes spent in a net the energy will go a little deeper, so it is a good idea to dowse (see chapter seven) beforehand to see how long you actually *need* to spend with the crystals. Spending longer in the net will not hurt you, but it may clear away more energy than you were expecting, leading to a feeling of emotional imbalance or to being ungrounded.

If you are planning to use nets or to place crystals on your body, always make sure you have enough black, brown, or red crystals left over so that you can use them to ground yourself afterward. Until you get used to working with crystals, you may feel "floaty" and spaced out at the end of a session. It is important not to panic—just work through a couple of grounding exercises, such as placing dark crystals at your feet and doing visualization. Also, eating and drinking after a session can help you to ground.

Always drink plenty of water for the next three days after working on yourself, as this will help to keep your energy flowing and will also help your body to detoxify if it needs to.

SEAL OF SOLOMON

A good net to do on yourself if you are feeling stressed or overwhelmed is the Seal of Solomon, which is also known as the Star of David. This layout uses six single terminated (pointed at one end) quartz points, which will face outward to start with so they can release unwanted energy; then they will be turned to face inward to bring in fresh energy.

- You will need six quartz points.
- You may like to dowse to see how long the points should face in each direction—usually about three to four minutes each way. Either set an alarm or check your watch or clock to see when to turn the points inward. Alternatively, you can just use your intuition to tell you when to turn the points.
- One point goes below and between the feet, one on either side of the calves, one at each shoulder, and one above the head.

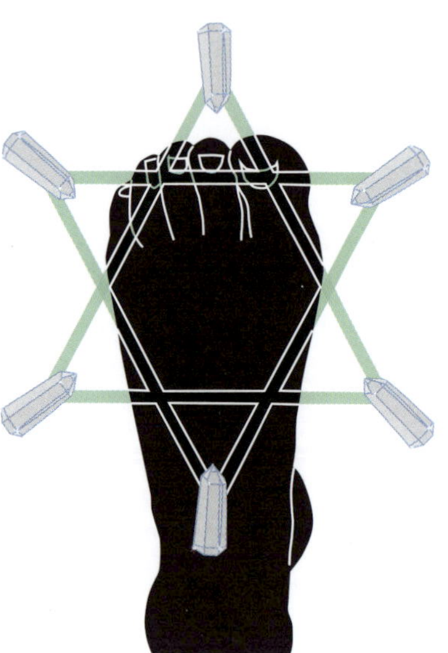

This layout can also be used around a specific body part to release unwanted energy and then bring in healing energy. A pendulum (see chapter seven) can help you to narrow down the area to cover, and it can tell you how long the points should face inward and outward.

This layout is gentle enough to be used every day. Don't worry if you spend longer in this net than the amount of time you dowsed for, because there will be no ill effects. If I'm feeling a bit tired or run-down, I sometimes put a Seal of Solomon around my bed before I go to sleep, with the points facing inward to bring in healing energy during the night.

❋ ❋ ❋

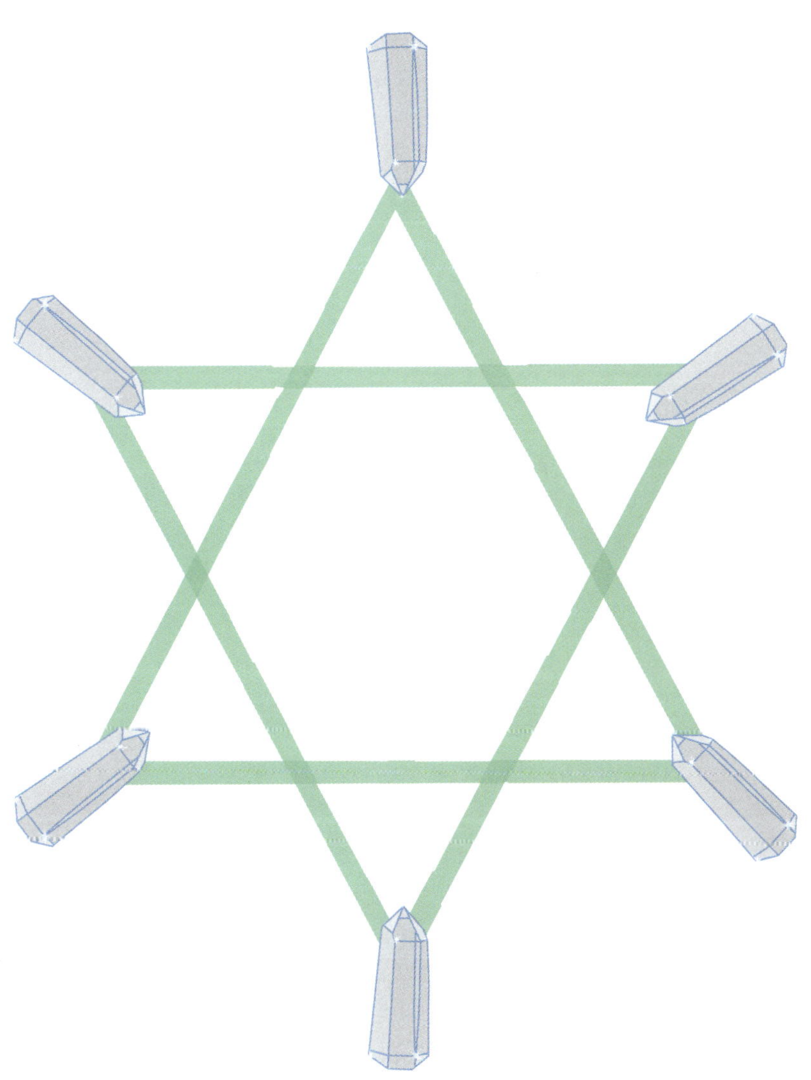

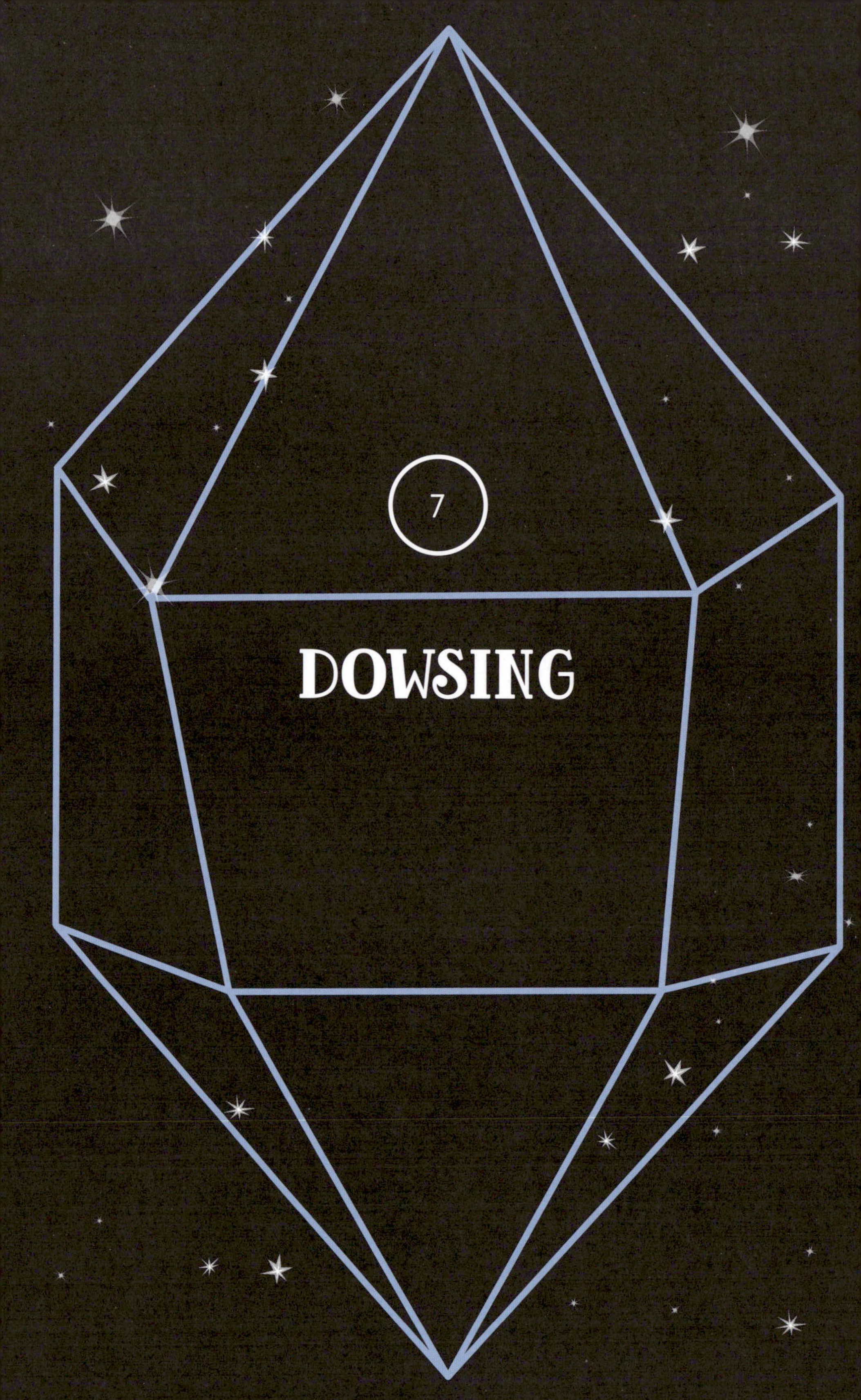

7

DOWSING

Dowsing is also called divining, as in water divining, which is where someone uses pieces of copper wire or a piece of wood to find water that is hidden belowground. When working with crystals or for any other subtle purpose, dowsing enables us to find answers to questions by watching the movement of a pendulum or a pair of dowsing rods. Logic says it shouldn't work, but it does, and it is a surprisingly easy and successful technique for an absolute beginner to use.

Using a Pendulum

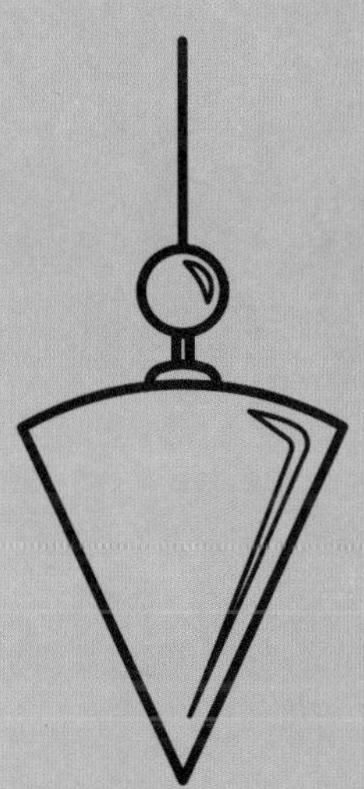

A pendulum is a weighted object on the end of a string or chain. I work with crystal pendulums, but there are also metal, wood, and seed pendulums, to name a few. You could easily make a cheap pendulum by tying a fishing weight on the end of some fishing wire or, if you have a necklace with a heavy pendant, this works just as well.

A pendulum's movement is caused by minute muscle movements in your arm in response to a question. You will get the best results if you are relaxed and open-minded.

Asking Questions

- Tap yourself in (see chapter six).
- You may like to start your pendulum swinging forward and backward in what is called a neutral swing so that you can experience a change in direction quite quickly. This is not essential, because some people prefer to keep their pendulum still until it gives an answer to a question.
- Ask the pendulum to show you "yes"––it should now start swinging in a regular pattern, maybe side to side, or maybe in a circle.
- Ask the pendulum to return to neutral swing (forward and backward), or gently still the pendulum by pulling it upward or by using your other hand.

- Now ask the pendulum to show you "no"— it should move in a different way to your "yes."
- If you want to check your answers, ask a simple question, such as "Am I awake?" or "Am I asleep?" The pendulum should respond appropriately.
- Once you are sure of how the pendulum moves for your "yes" or "no," ask the pendulum if it is happy to work with you. If you receive a "no" answer, cleanse the pendulum, or tap yourself in and try again, or select a different pendulum and ask if that one is happy to work with you.

Not all pendulums work in the same way, and you may find that different pendulums move in different directions for "yes" and "no." It is always a good idea to check out a new pendulum to see how it will respond to your questions. Once you have ascertained the direction of swing, your pendulum should give the same response each time you use it. Also, you may find that a pendulum swings differently for someone else than it does for you.

You may prefer to hold the pendulum halfway down the chain, tucking the rest of the chain inside a closed fist, rather than holding the bead or ring at the end. I find that I get a quicker response with a shorter chain.

Using an Arc

An arc is useful if you have more than one answer, for instance, "Which layout do I need to use on this person today?"

- You can easily create an arc by using a compass to draw a fat semi-circle on a piece of paper and then joining the ends with a straight line so that

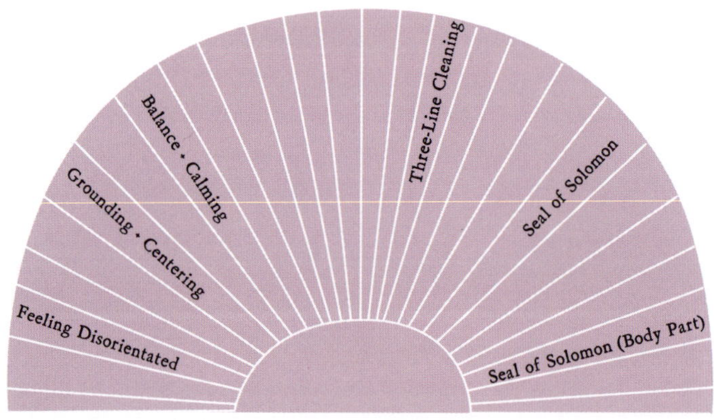

Solving Pendulum Problems

A woman who attended a workshop I was running could not get her pendulum to respond to her questions, but it transpired that she always used this pendulum for healing, so when she chose a different pendulum to use for dowsing, she had no problems.

Some people recommend that you use a particular crystal for only one purpose and keep it for that purpose only. This is because you will get used to working with that crystal's energy in a particular way, and it can be difficult to retrain your subconscious mind to interact with the crystal in a different way.

it resembles a half-moon. From the center of the straight line, draw regularly spaced lines to the rim of the semi-circle. You will end up with something that looks like a fan.

- Now write one "answer" in each section. For example, if you were to have an arc for the layouts in this book, you may have a Seal of Solomon in one section, a rainbow chakra layout in the next, then grounding and centering, followed by balancing and calming, an earth net in the next section, and lastly a three-line clearing.
- Hold the pendulum over the arc.
- You may like to start the pendulum stationary, or swinging in a neutral direction.
- Ask the appropriate question and see which answer your pendulum swings toward.
- If your pendulum jiggles about rather than swings, or moves in a direction other than "yes" or "no," this could be for a couple of reasons.
  - Your question may be a bit vague, so try making your question more specific. If you get the same result again, try tapping yourself in, or leave it for the time being and ask the question again later.
  - You may be too emotionally invested in the answer—for instance, you want the pendulum to answer in a specific way rather than in the way it wants to go. Tap yourself in and try to relax before asking the question again.

Using a Pendulum to Ease Pain

Pendulums may be used over a site of pain. The pendulum will swing in a circle as it draws the painful energy out, before returning to a neutral swing when finished.

Pendulums are also used to ascertain the length of time that someone should remain in a layout. For every five minutes spent in a layout, the person will go a little deeper, so when you are just starting to work with crystals, don't do too much too soon on either yourself or the people you are working on.

Ask your pendulum if it is safe and appropriate for you to use that particular layout. If you get a "yes" answer, then ask how long you should remain in the layout. Ask "One minute?" and wait to see if your pendulum confirms the answer. If not, then ask "Two minutes?" or "Three minutes?" and so on until your pendulum confirms the correct answer.

Dowsing with Rods

Some people find it hard to dowse with a pendulum, but almost anybody can dowse with rods, even if they have never considered doing anything remotely metaphysical before. The downside of rod dowsing is that there are no crystals involved. For instance, you can dangle a crystal on the end of a string as a pendulum, but where rods are concerned there are no crystals in the picture.

Obtaining Dowsing Rods

You can buy dowsing rods on the Internet or you can find them in any metaphysical shop, most crystal shops, or even in "witchy" shops. They are usually made of metal, with handles that allow the rods to move freely.

Alternatively, you can make your own. To do this you will need two metal coat hangers, two inexpensive ballpoint pens, and two bits of tape.

- Cut the hangers into an L shape.
- Pull the middles out of the pens so that you have only the plastic shells left.
- Fit the short ends of the rods into the pen "holders." They should be able to swing about easily.
- Wrap a bit of sticky tape on the ends of the rods to make them safer to use.

Energizing Your Dowsing Rods

The first thing you need to do is to establish your "yes" and "no." Stand up and hold your rods in front of you so that they are about eight inches apart. Make sure they are far enough away from you to be able to swing about, but not so far that your arms become uncomfortable.

Now mentally ask the rods to give you their "yes." They may cross or swing apart. Now ask your rods to give you their "no." The "no" result should be different from the "yes."

The usual scenario is for the rods to cross over each other for "yes" and open away from each other for "no," but anything can happen. For instance, one rod can move inward or outward while the other stays still. Whatever happens, try the system again on a subsequent day to make sure you and your rods are working well together.

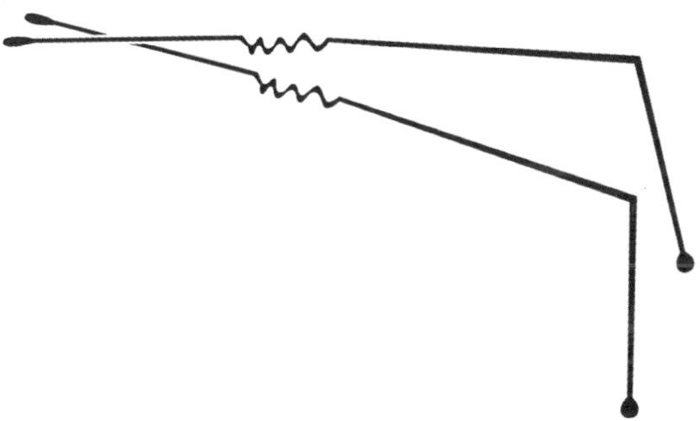

Using Your Rods

Now that you know you can get a "yes" or "no" answer, you can ask the rods to tell you how long you should stay in a net or you can dowse over a crystal to discover the best use you can make of it. For instance, you can ask a new crystal if it will act as an energizer or as a calming agent, or if it will work on an emotional vibration or a health one, or if it might help with decision making and clarity, and so on. If you work with a computer, you may wish to discover whether a particular crystal should be placed on your desk to help keep you safe from the electrical and other energies that you are absorbing during the course of your working day.

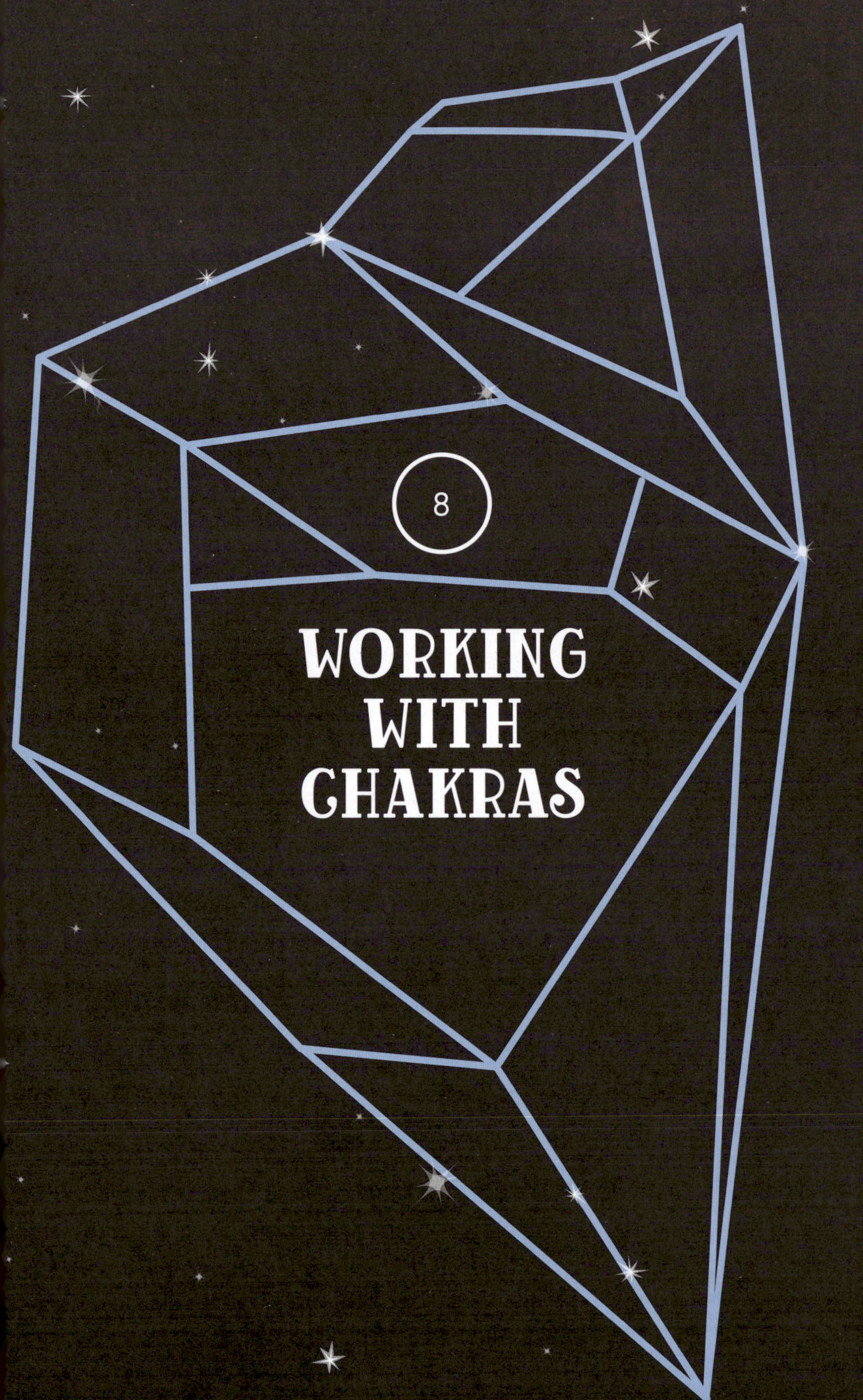

8

WORKING WITH CHAKRAS

Chakras are an Eastern concept that has made its way to the West. We work with the seven main chakras that run from the base of the spine to the top of the head. When the concept of the chakras came to the Western world, the color system was changed to represent the colors of the rainbow—red, orange, yellow, green, blue, indigo, and violet—but it was different in the Eastern tradition.

In the original Sanskrit, the word *chakra* means "wheel." Some traditions see the chakras as spinning funnels. In each chakra, one funnel lies at the front of the body, meeting its opposite funnel that lies at the back of the body. There is some debate about the direction of the spin, but this doesn't affect us in this book.

Chakras are often depicted as lotus flowers, but according to those who can see energies and colors, the chakras look more like spinning funnels.

The chakras settle in areas where there is a large concentration of energy, and psychically they are linked to the endocrine system. The endocrine system is the collection of glands that produce hormones. In terms of frequency, the base chakra has the lowest frequency, and each chakra's frequency increases so that the crown chakra has the highest frequency.

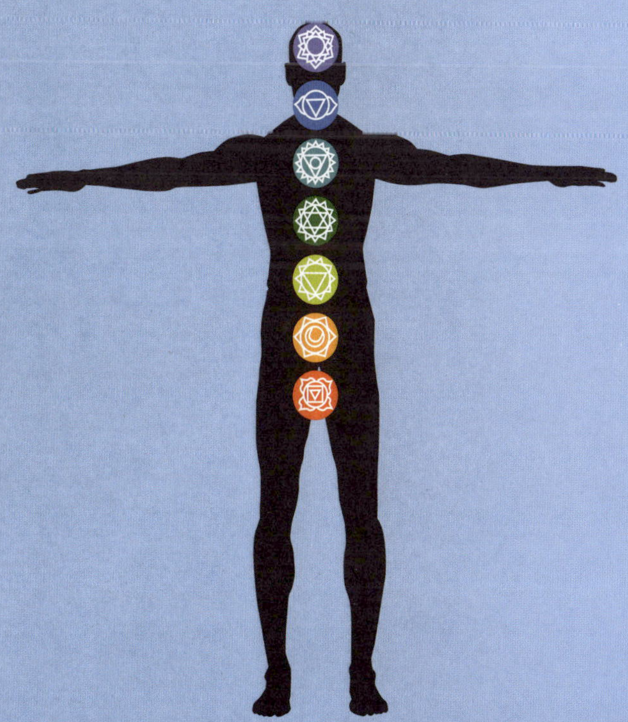

The Base Chakra

Sanskrit Name: Muladhara

Color: Red

- The base chakra is located at the perineum (between the legs), although crystals may also be placed anywhere from the knees to the pubic bone. If you have two crystals of the same type, these may be placed where the legs join the body.
- Physically this chakra is linked with the adrenals, male gonads, and genitals.
- A person with an overactive base chakra could be undisciplined, have a lot of tension or anger, be hyperactive, or even be too fond of exercise. This person may be a hoarder or have a tendency to be self-centered.
- An underactive chakra may mean a person lacks energy, has no motivation, has problems with movement, or suffers from low self-esteem.
- Working on this chakra aids you in staying grounded, clearing confusion, and maintaining healthy boundaries.

Crystal Suggestions

As well as using red crystals on this chakra, you can work with brown or black crystals. The list below gives useful suggestions.

- Red jasper
- Mahogany jasper
- Ruby
- Garnet
- Red aventurine
- Black tourmaline
- Obsidian
- Mookaite

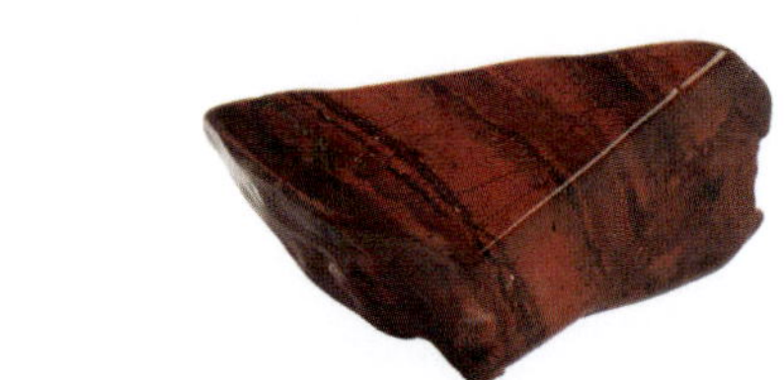

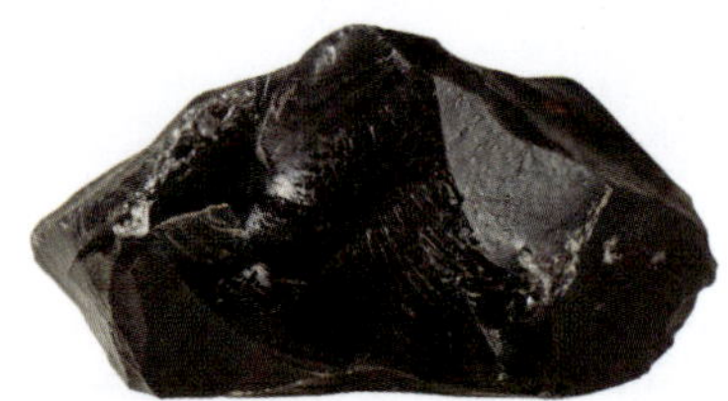

The Sacral Chakra

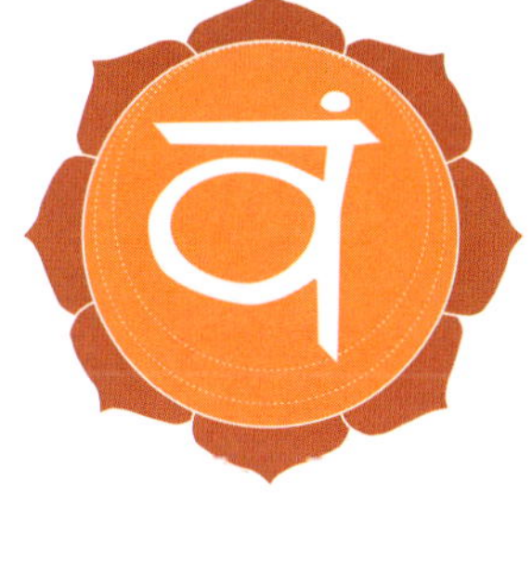

Sanskrit Name: Svadisthana

Color: Orange

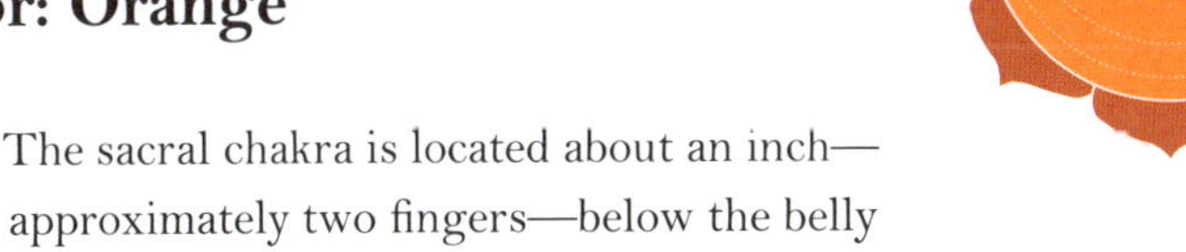

- The sacral chakra is located about an inch—approximately two fingers—below the belly button.
- Physically this chakra is linked with the female gonads, large intestine, bladder, spleen, lower back, lymphatic system, and hips.
- Someone who has an overactive sacral chakra may feel frustration or suffer from addictions. Such a person may also be unstable or possibly manipulative.
- A person with an underactive sacral chakra can exhibit traits such as emotional dependency, hoarding, frigidity, impotence, or oversensitivity. An underactive sacral chakra could also manifest as constipation.
- Working on this chakra enhances creativity and helps the person to be secure in their sexuality as it balances male and female energies and enhances the enjoyment gained from lovemaking.

Crystal Suggestions

The orange color associated with this chakra points to the following crystals:

- Carnelian
- Peach selenite
- Orange calcite
- Sunstone

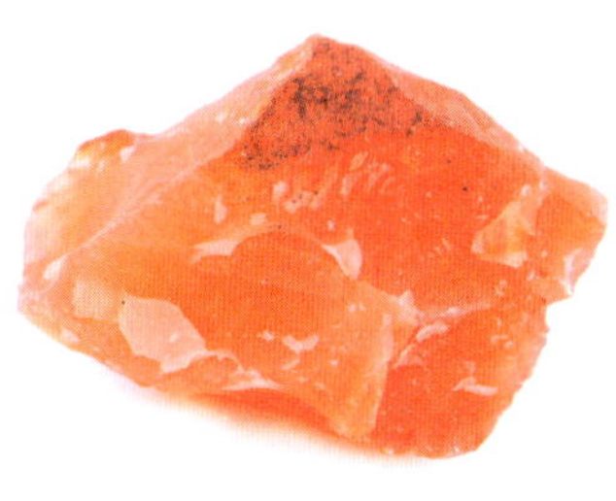

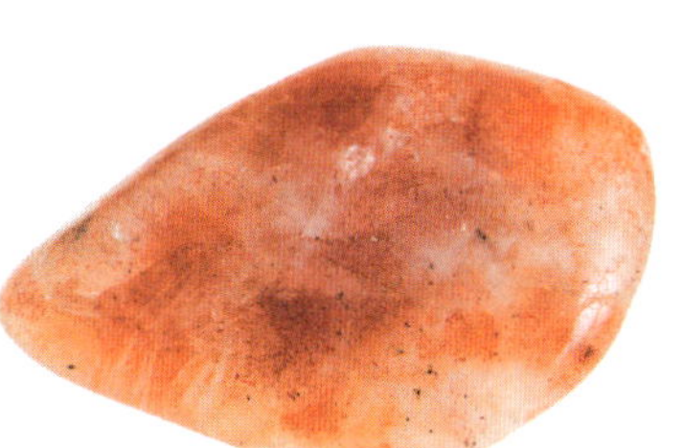

The Solar Plexus Chakra

Sanskrit Name: Manipura

Color: Yellow

- The solar plexus chakra is located at the stomach, about three finger widths below the base of the rib cage.
- Physically this chakra is linked with the pancreas, digestion, nervous system, immune system, spleen, gallbladder, liver, small intestine, and stomach.
- Someone with an overactive solar plexus chakra may show traits such as arrogance and irritability. The person may also be judgmental or suffer from digestive problems.
- If the solar plexus is underactive, it could make a person feel powerless and insecure. The person may suffer from low self-esteem or a lack of enthusiasm, or may procrastinate or even be continuously apologetic.
- Working on this chakra improves confidence, decisiveness, and self-esteem. It can bring a feeling of joy into a person's life.

Crystal Suggestions

These are all yellow or orange-yellow colored crystals that work well with the solar plexus chakra:

- Citrine
- Amber
- Yellow fluorite
- Yellow jasper
- Honey calcite

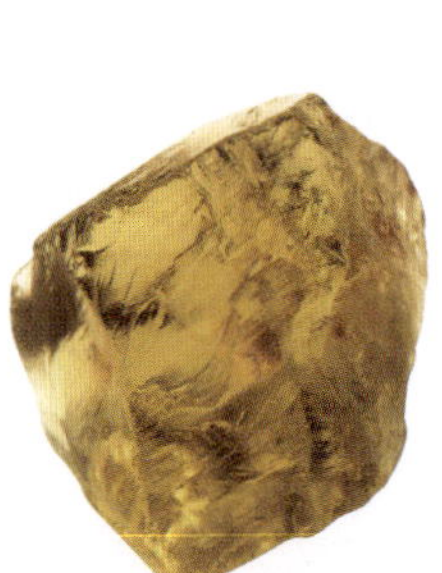

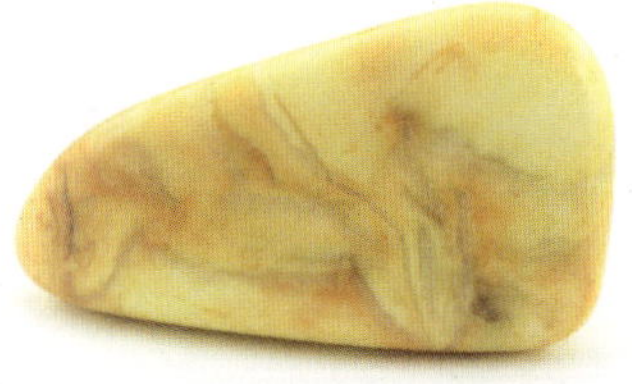

The Heart Chakra

Sanskrit Name: Anahata

Color: Green or Pink

- The area of this chakra is in the center of the chest.
- Physically this chakra is linked with the chest, thymus, respiration, heart, circulatory system, arms, and hands.
- Overactivity in this chakra can make a person manipulative, or it can mean that they have a lack of boundaries and give too much of themselves to others.
- Underactivity can cause a person to be emotionally dependent, repressed or inhibited, lonely, detached, or selfish.
- Working on this chakra enhances all forms of love, and it can help us to give of ourselves freely, with no expectation of reciprocation. For those people who give too much of themselves, pink is a good color to work with as it can aid self-love.

Crystal Suggestions

The crystal colors needed for this are green or pink.

- Green aventurine
- Ruby in zoisite
- Green fluorite
- Jade
- Emerald
- Mangano calcite
- Rhodonite
- Rhodochrosite
- Rose quartz

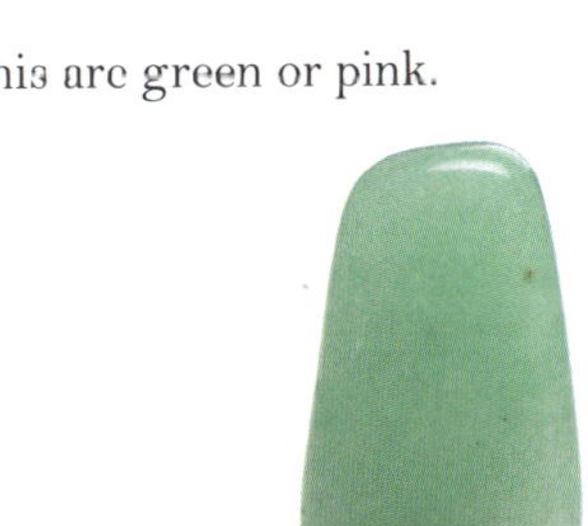

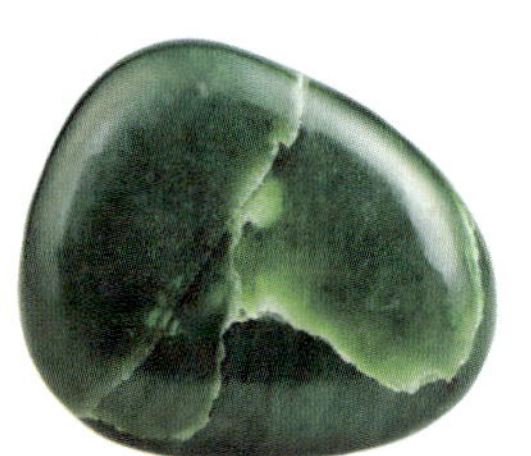

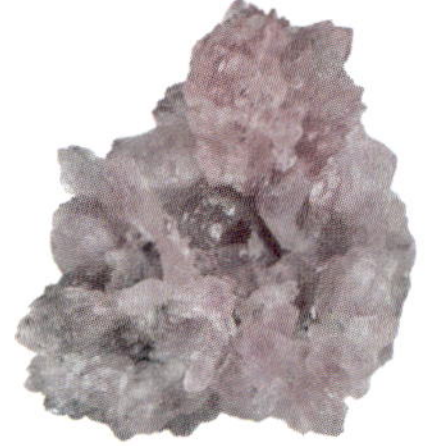

The Throat Chakra

Sanskrit Name: Vishuddha

Color: Light Blue or Turquoise

- The throat chakra is located in the dip at the bottom of your neck, between the two notches. If you feel uncomfortable placing crystals here, you can place them just below the dip.
- Physically this chakra is linked with the throat, neck, thyroid and parathyroid, voice, ears, mouth, teeth, jaw, and hearing.
- An overactive throat chakra may cause someone to dominate conversations or gossip.
- A person could have an underactive chakra if they are shy or afraid to express views. They may also stutter or suffer from frequent sore throats.
- Working on this chakra aids expression and communication, and it can also help those feeling overwhelmed with responsibilities.

Crystal Suggestions

Pale blue and turquoise-colored crystals are used here.

- Blue lace agate
- Turquoise
- Amazonite
- Chrysoprase
- Chrysocolla
- Blue tourmaline
- Angelite

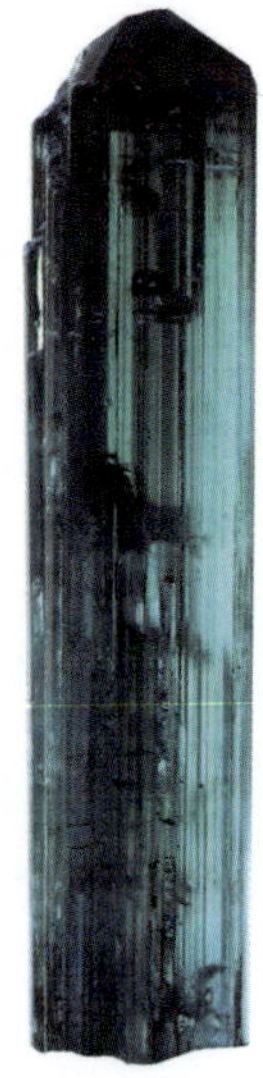

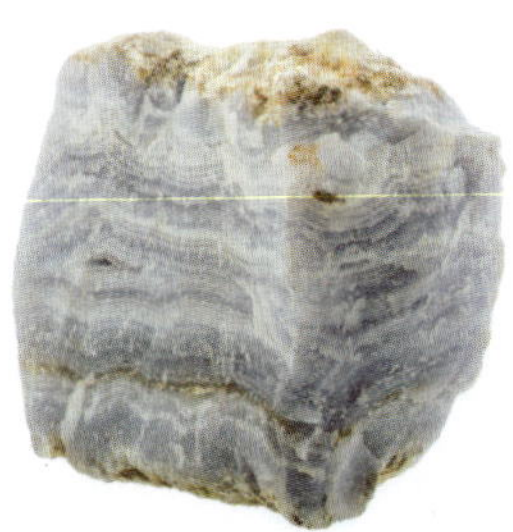

The Brow Chakra

Sanskrit Name: Ajna

Color: Dark Blue or Purple

- The brow chakra is located between and just above the eyebrows.
- Physically it is linked with the forehead, ears, eyes, neurological system, and brain.
- Someone who has an overactive brow chakra may exhibit such traits as selfishness, arrogance, and inflexible thinking. Some people may suffer from hallucinations and delusional nightmares.
- An underactive brow chakra could cause a person to be distracted or undisciplined, with scattered thoughts, and, in extreme cases, to experience schizophrenia.
- Working with this chakra can help to increase perception, insight, and intuition.

Crystal Suggestions

Dark blue and purple shades of crystal are needed for this chakra.

- Sodalite
- Lapis lazuli
- Dumortierite
- Amethyst
- Tanzanite

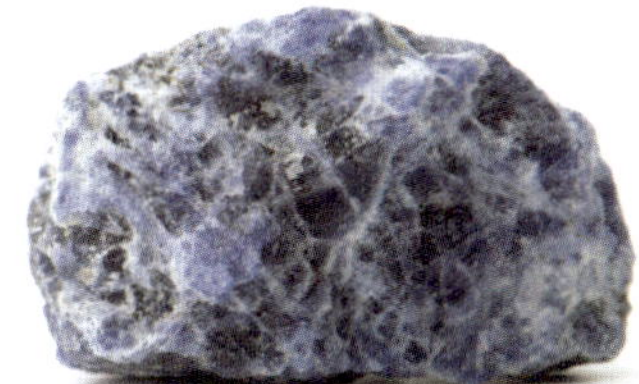

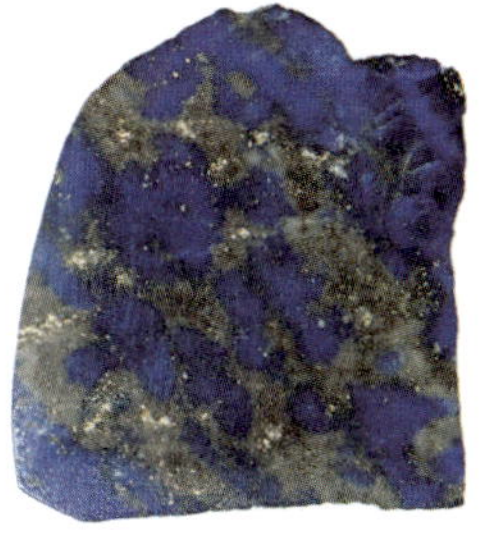

The Crown Chakra

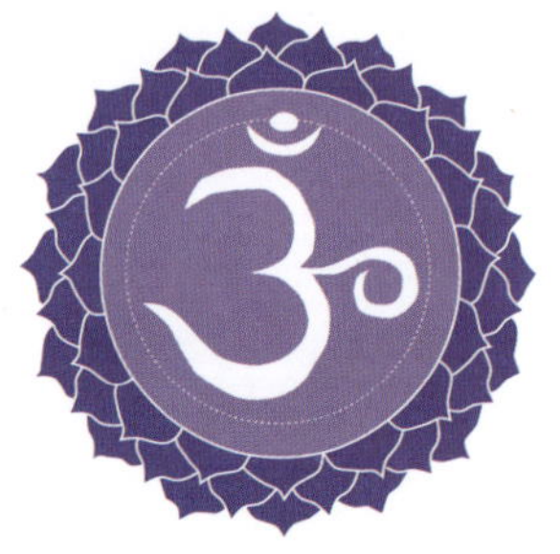

Sanskrit Name: Sahasrara

Color: Light Purple, White, or Clear

- This chakra sits above the head.
- Physically it is linked with the pineal gland, brain, and cerebral and pituitary glands.
- An overactive crown chakra could cause someone to feel ungrounded and delusional, possibly resorting to escapism in their own fantasy world.
- If the crown chakra is underactive, a person may feel empty and indecisive and have a lack of coordination and faith. The person may feel disconnected or detached from others.
- Working on this chakra can help you to realize a connection with whatever deity you revere, so this could be God, a pagan god or goddess, mother earth, or universal energy.

Crystal Suggestions

Purple, white, and clear crystals are ideal for work with this chakra.

- Howlite
- Clear quartz
- Herkimer diamond
- Danburite
- White jade

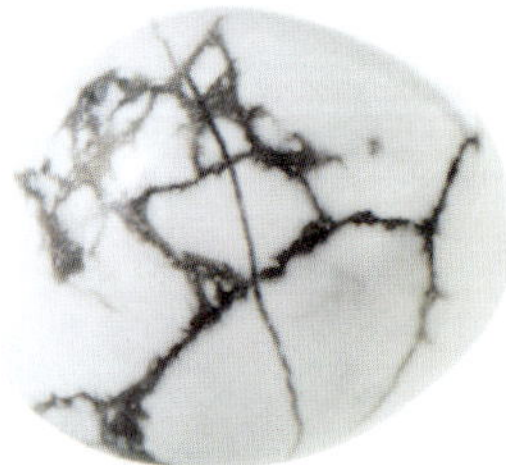

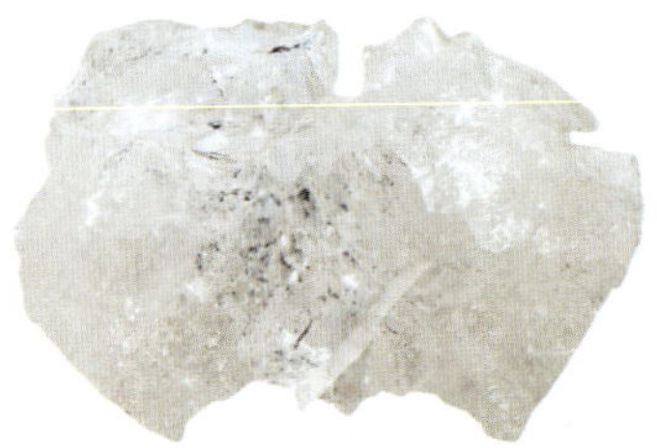

Complementary Chakras

Each chakra also has a *complementary* chakra (except for the heart chakra):

Base = heart
Sacral = throat
Solar plexus = brow

The complementary chakra can also be good to work with to help bring balance to an overactive or underactive chakra. This can be done by placing an intuitively picked crystal on each complementary chakra. For example, if you wanted to work on your throat chakra, you could place a blue crystal at your throat and an orange crystal at your sacral chakra for a couple of minutes. Or you could place an orange crystal at your throat. Or you may wish to simply visualize orange light coming down through your head and balancing your throat chakra.

Minor Chakras

There are many minor chakras around the body. A few are worth noting:

- The palms of the hands.
- The soles of the feet.
- The elbows.
- The knees.
- The higher heart chakra, which is three finger widths above the heart chakra. This is sometimes called the thymus.
- The soul star chakra, which is about six inches above the crown.
- The earth chakra, which is between and just underneath the feet.

Rainbow Chakra Layout

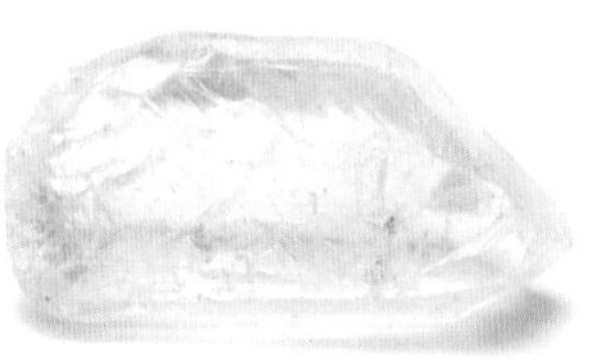

This layout is good for times when you need to bring your energy back into balance. As explained earlier, each color resonates at a different frequency, and choosing a crystal of the same color as the chakra can help to bring that chakra back into balance if it is over- or underactive. This technique can be used daily, or as often as you feel the need.

You will need seven different-colored crystals: red, orange, yellow, green, blue, indigo, and violet. If you don't have one or more of these crystal colors, you can always program a clear quartz crystal to a particular color frequency and use it in place of the missing crystal. (You can find out how to program a crystal in chapter three on preparing crystals.)

The stones are placed in the position of each chakra, with the color of crystal matching the color of each chakra; so you will have red at the base chakra, orange at the sacral, yellow at the solar plexus, green at your heart, blue on the throat, indigo at your brow, and violet above your head at your crown, in the positions noted under each heading. You do not have to remove any clothing, as the energy of your aura will interact with the vibration of the crystal, rather than your physical body doing so.

If you have several crystals of each color to choose from, you may want to use a pendulum to select the ones you will use, or you can pick them intuitively by asking your higher consciousness to help you pick the crystals that you need or that are best for you at this time.

Dowse before placing the crystals to see how long you need to remain in the layout. It doesn't matter if you leave the crystals in place for longer than you intend to. I have sometimes fallen asleep in this layout and find that I wake up automatically when I've spent enough time with the crystals.

Notes on Other Crystal Colors

Black and Brown Crystals

Crystals of these colors can be placed either at the base chakra or just below your feet—often referred to as the *earth* chakra. Placing crystals at the earth chakra helps to bring an extra level of grounding energy to the healing session.

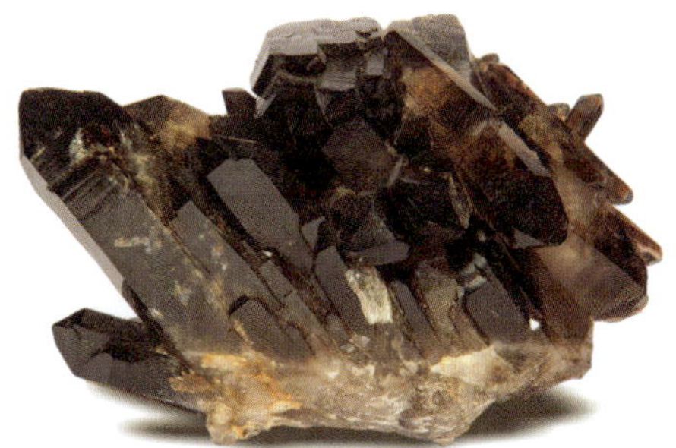

Clear Crystals

Although I have listed clear crystals as working with the crown chakra, crystals that are clear can work with any chakra, as they contain the full spectrum of light.

Mixed or Combination Crystals

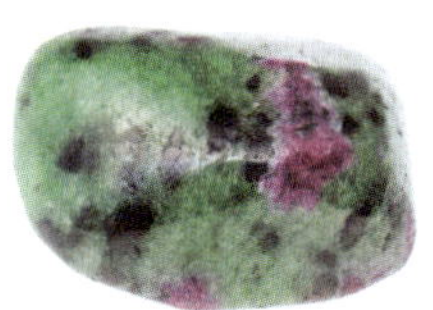

The placement for these crystals can vary. Sometimes the chakra associated with the crystal will depend on the color that most of the crystal contains. For instance, the ruby in zoisite is mostly green and, therefore, associated with the heart chakra.

Sometimes the way you use a crystal will depend on the vibration of the stone; for example, labradorite has a high vibration and is placed at the brow or the crown.

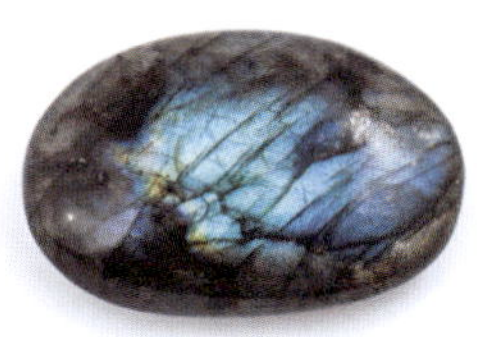

✵ ✵ ✵

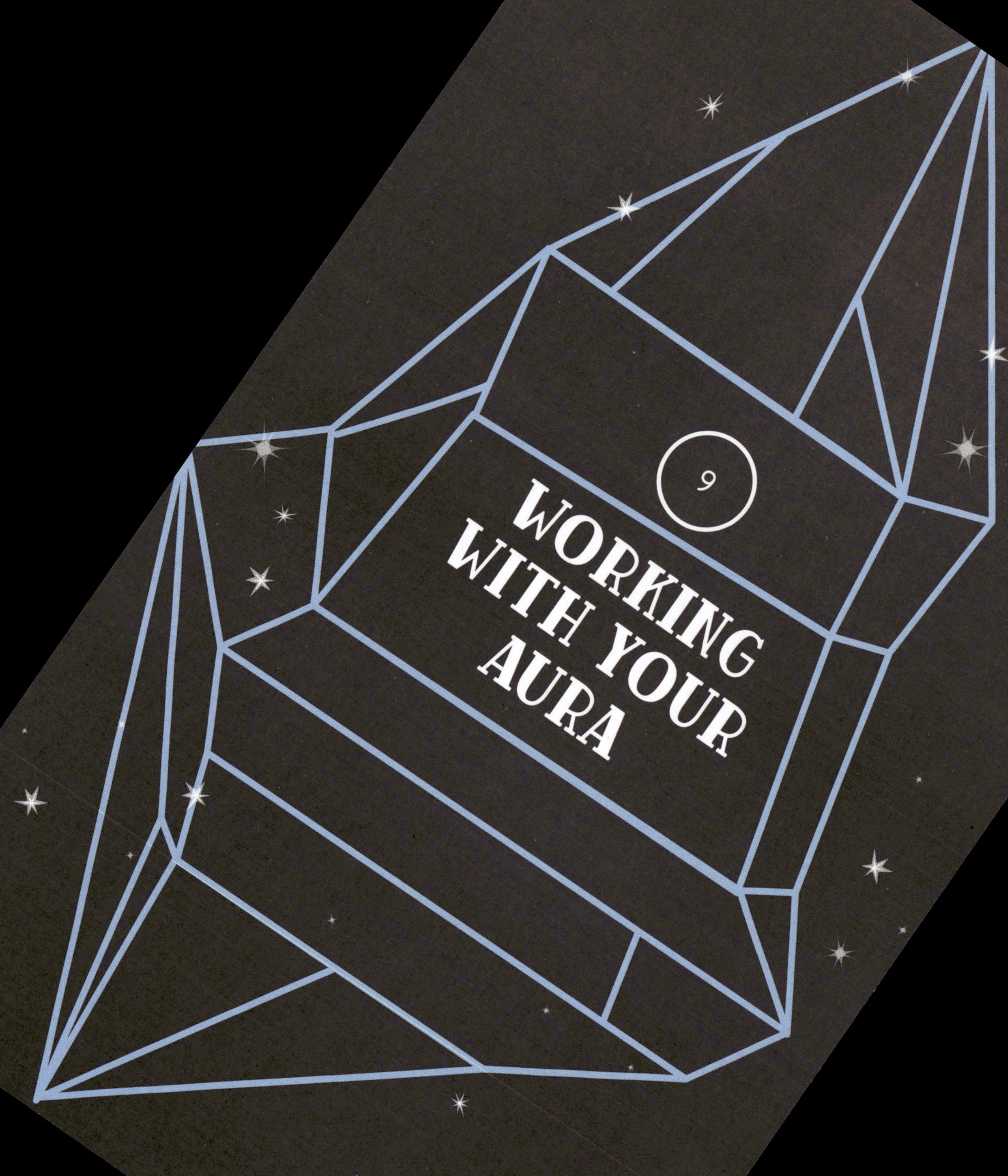
9
WORKING
WITH YOUR
AURA

An *aura* is the term used to describe a person's energy field surrounding his body. This energy gives us information about a person on a subconscious level, and it even explains why we sometimes feel uncomfortable around someone we've only just met; it means that on some level, we do not share the same beliefs with the other person. This subconscious connection is also why we sometimes instinctively know that someone we are close to is unhappy, even when the person hasn't mentioned anything.

There are seven levels called *subtle bodies* that make up the aura, each layer blending into the next, and each subtle body is connected with a chakra:

- The *etheric body* is the aura immediately surrounding the physical body and is energetically linked with all the physical components of the body. The etheric body is often referred to as a "blueprint" of the physical body and is linked to the base chakra.
- The *emotional body* contains information on our emotional state and fluctuates in accordance with our changing emotions. This subtle body is linked to the sacral chakra.
- The *mental body* processes ideas, thoughts, and beliefs and is linked to the solar plexus chakra.
- The *astral body* is the connection between the lower subtle bodies that make up the personality and the spiritual aspects of a person and is linked to the heart chakra. It also influences the way we form relationships with others.
- The *causal* (sometimes called *etheric template*), *soul* (or *celestial*), and *spiritual* (sometimes called *ketheric*) *bodies* all deal with higher levels of our being and our connection to higher levels of consciousness. The *causal body* is linked to the throat chakra, the *soul body* to the brow chakra, and the *spiritual body* to the crown chakra.

Although we are subconsciously aware of someone's aura, it is possible to train yourself to be consciously aware of someone's energy field. Ask a willing partner to stand at one end of a room and focus on sending their energy out as far as they can. Starting at the other end of the room, walk toward the other person with your palms facing them and stop when you feel a change in energy. Then ask your partner to pull their aura in so that it is as close to them as possible. This time when you walk toward them, you should get a lot closer before you feel the change in energy.

It is also possible to learn how to see auras. The etheric layer is the easiest to see. Ask someone to sit with a plain-colored background behind them. Look at the person's head and then soften the focus of your eyes. Keep staring at the same spot for around thirty to sixty seconds. Eventually you will see a light gray-blue layer surrounding the person. If you don't have anyone to practice on, try looking at your hand. If you hold your hand with your fingers apart in front of a plain-colored background and stare at the top of your middle finger for thirty to sixty seconds, you should be able to see your etheric body surrounding each finger.

If there is a disturbance in any of the subtle bodies, this may eventually lead to "dis-ease" (when a person does not feel at ease) and possibly physical illness if they are not brought back into balance. This disturbance can be caused by external energies and experiences, but negative patterns of thought and behavior can also affect the subtle bodies.

The subtle bodies can be brought back into balance with crystals, either by placing them in a net around you or by dowsing for a particular crystal and specific placement. If you don't have several crystals of the same type, you can use a pendulum to select one crystal to balance a particular subtle body and to find the exact right place for it. Depending on the placement, you may be able to tape the stone in place with microporous tape and carry on with your day, whereas a net would require you to lie down for a period of time.

A layout that can be particularly useful is the earth net:

- You will need eight black tourmaline crystals.
- Place one above your head, one below your feet, and one on each side of your body, about level with your solar plexus, creating a rectangle.
- Then imagine the rectangle rotated slightly to the right as you look down at the net, and place the four remaining crystals in the same positions, but at an angle.

This net is useful when you want to work with the physical body; I often use it when I have an aching back. It can be used for grounding, and I also lie in this net to help me integrate and assimilate any energy work that I've done on myself or when I've received healing from someone else.

A technique to help protect your aura from external energies is to visualize a protective boundary, such as a bubble, around your aura in the morning, with

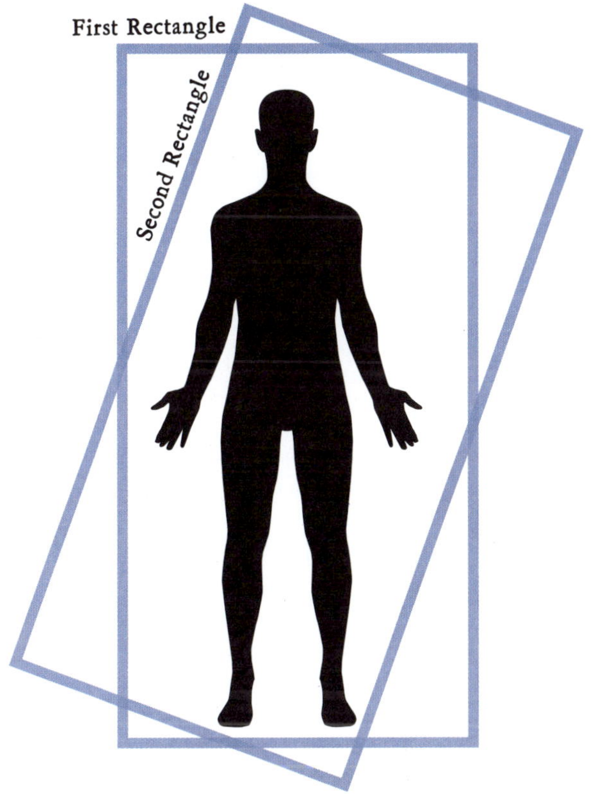

the intention that it will allow only positive energy through and will block any negative energy from entering your aura. The only potential problem with visualization is that it's only effective while you are actively visualizing. To overcome this issue and keep a protective boundary in place throughout the day, you can ask your higher consciousness to maintain the bubble while you're awake. Connecting to your higher self is based on trust, and the more you trust your intuition and intention, the more effortless it will be to become aware of answers and insights in the future.

Another way of protecting your aura is to spray some gem essence through your aura. See chapter two on working with crystals to learn how to make a gem essence. This can be decanted into a clean, empty spray bottle. A couple of drops of essential oils can also be added if desired, as not only does this add the energetically protective qualities of the oils, it also smells lovely!

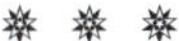

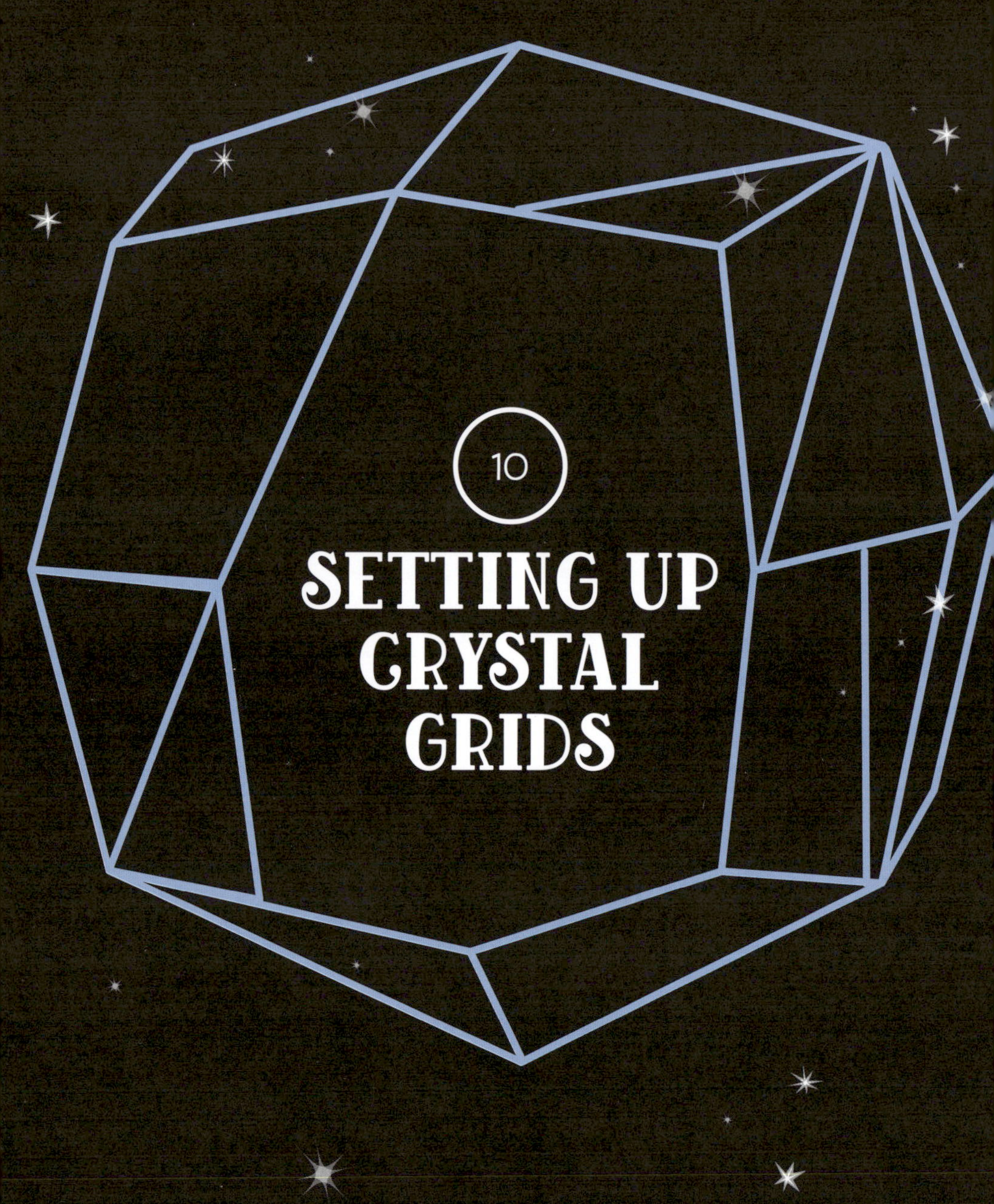

10 SETTING UP CRYSTAL GRIDS

Creating a grid means setting up crystals to make a field or area of energy. Lately there has been an interest in creating mandalas for the purpose of helping to manifest goals or desires (sometimes called "cosmic ordering"), and these are now also referred to as grids; so, for the purpose of this book, when I use the word *grid*, it can also mean *net* or *mandala*.

Grids can be created with crystals of the same type or with different and complementing stones. I frequently use single terminated clear quartz in my grids, as not only does the point direct the energy, but quartz energy amplifies the energy of other minerals as well.

You can choose your crystals intuitively or dowse for the appropriate stones. Or you may like to research which crystal's metaphysical properties match the purpose of your grid. For example, if you wanted to increase abundance, then you might look up which crystals can assist. A quick search of the Internet suggests golden crystals such as tiger's eye, topaz, and citrine.

Before setting up, make sure your crystals are cleansed and dedicated to the purpose of creating a grid.

"Grid" vs. "Net"

The terms "grid" and "net" are used to describe encircling an area with crystals to create a field of energy in the middle.

A net is when crystals are placed around the body as described on page 57.

A grid is the practice of setting up crystals around a room, house, altar, mandala, etc.

Gridding a Room or Building

When gridding a room, there are a couple of different ways you can choose. You can put a crystal in each corner. If the corner doesn't have any furniture to hide the stone behind, or a shelf or windowsill to put it on, then it might be a good idea to hang the crystal, perhaps in a little organza bag with string ties that you can loop over a small tack in the wall. Putting crystals of the same type in all the corners will create a uniform energy in the room, but this is not essential—you can use different crystals to equal effect. Otherwise, you could place a crystal at each of the four compass points, starting with east, then south, then west, and finally north. Again, these could all be the same type or they could be different crystals.

When gridding a property, you can make the grid as large as you wish, so you could energize just your house, or you could include any land around the property. As with grids around a room, grids around a property could include a crystal at the corner of each boundary or at each of the compass points. You would also include a crystal in the center to focus the energy. Putting crystals at ground-floor level is sufficient to protect or energize the whole property. As I said before, it is the intention that is important, but if you would like to connect your crystals to affirm the grid, be sure to include your focus stone. You can program the focus stone with your intention to add more energy to the grid. Ensure that any programming is carried out in a positive manner—for example, "to energize this house with positive loving energy" or "to protect the area inside this grid from any energy detrimental to the health of the occupants."

When choosing crystals for your room or property grid, you may choose crystals according to their metaphysical properties. For example, crystals like rose quartz are good for creating a loving atmosphere, whereas kyanite would be good for deflecting any negative intentions aimed at the occupants of a house back to the person who sent them.

Another reason for gridding a house would be if you have energy lines (natural or created by humans) running through the house. Using a plan, a rough drawing, or a map of the property or land in question (this does not have to be to scale, a hand-drawn representation is fine), ask your pendulum whether there are any energy lines running through the property. Run the finger from your free hand around the outside of

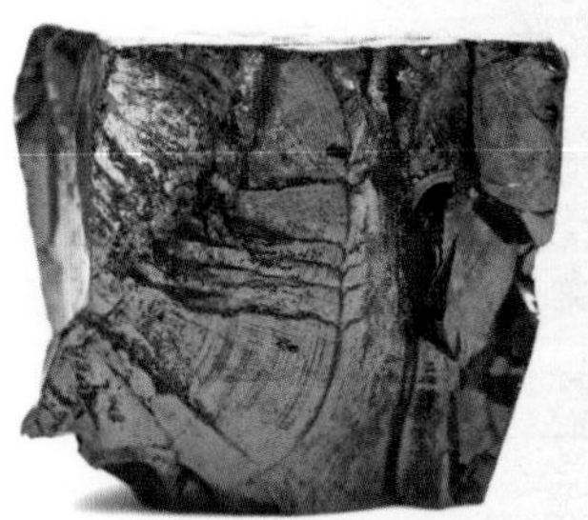

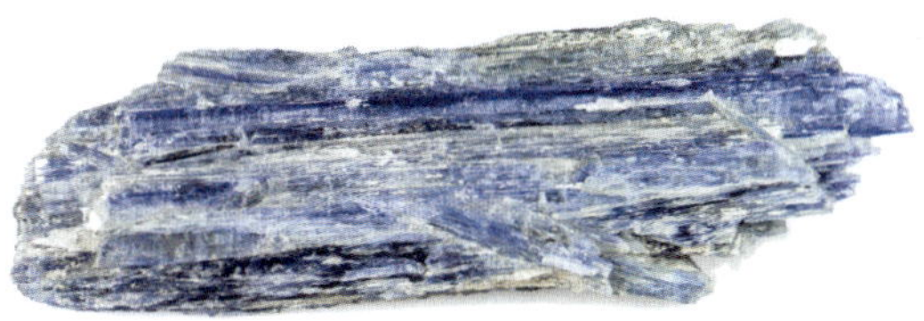

your building plan and you will see your pendulum swing at any points that represent locations where lines enter or exit the property. You could also walk through the rooms with dowsing rods or a pendulum. Normally, natural energy lines, such as ley lines, Hartmann lines, or Curry lines, do not affect our health, but if you have a line that goes across your bed or other place in which you sleep, it could affect the quality of your sleep. This is because when we sleep, everything relaxes and slows down. If we are lying in the path of strong energy during this time, it diminishes the restful and restorative nature of our sleep. The same is true if there are electric pylons or other types of EMFs (electromagnetic fields) like TV masts outside your property.

You can place crystals where the lines enter and exit the property to block the effects of energy lines. I discovered that there was a natural line that entered my house and traveled across my son's bed, then moved over my bed, all the way from bottom to top. I placed a large smoky quartz cluster under my son's bed by the wall and another large smoky quartz cluster under my bed by the wall. I used my pendulum to find the precise location that would be most effective. I also placed a small selenite piece on each side of the smoky quartz, which helped to clear any unwanted energy from the crystal.

For EMFs, you may need to place crystals all along the entry wall. These could be placed outside the house, or they could be buried in a line across the garden. Use your pendulum to find the right location.

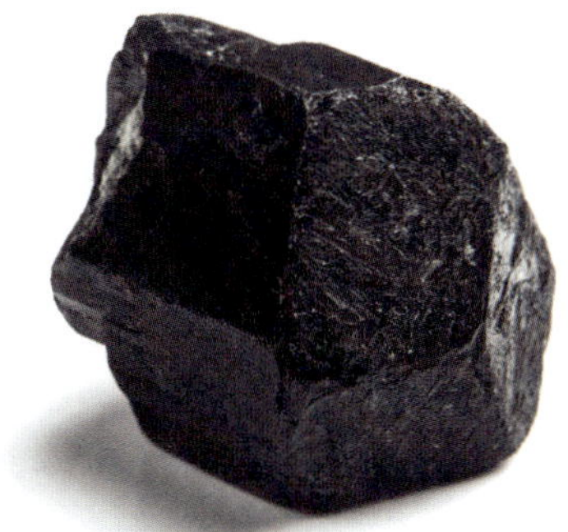

Crystals like black tourmaline, lodestone, magnetite, and shungite are excellent for protecting you or your family from detrimental energy sources. Incidentally, shungite is pronounced "shunkite."

Manifestation Grids

Grids dedicated to helping you achieve a desire are based on sacred geometry. Everything in the universe forms from the same shapes. If you overlap two identical circles so that their centers touch each other's perimeters, the overlapping portion is called the *vesica piscis.*

Repeating this pattern with seven circles (six circles linking through a central circle) gives us the Seed of Life.

If this pattern is repeated with nineteen circles, it forms the Flower of Life.

There is also the Fruit of Life, which is formed by surrounding a circle with six non-overlapping circles, then placing a circle at the edge of each of those circles so that you have thirteen in total.

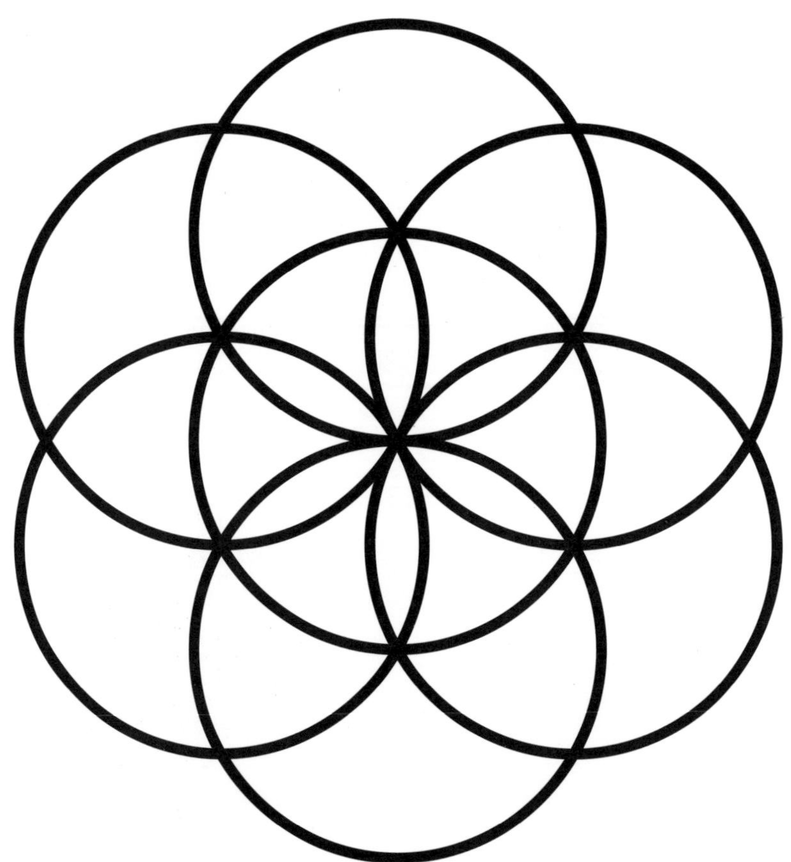

Seed of Life

If you join the center of each circle in the Fruit of Life to all the other circles, you will end up with Metatron's Cube. From the Flower of Life there is the Kabbalah Tree of Life, and there are also hexagons, triangles, and so on.

On an interesting note, when you look at these patterns in 3D, you can create all of the shapes of the crystal systems as well as the merkaba shape. There are also the platonic solids, which are 3D shapes with all of the faces and sides the same size and length. The platonic solids are cube, tetrahedron, dodecahedron, octahedron, and icosahedron. For the purpose of grids, however, we work with 2D shapes.

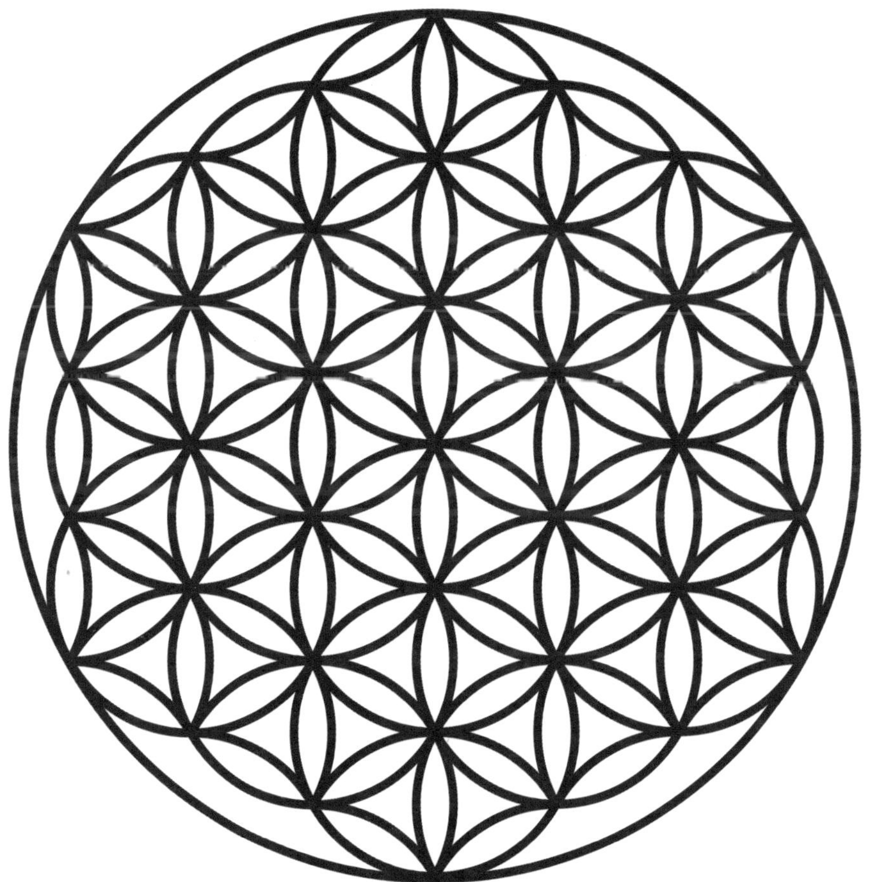

Flower of Life

Which Grid Shape to Use

You do not need to have a picture of the shape to place the crystals on—simply visualize the particular pattern you have chosen. You could write an affirmation on a piece of folded paper to place under your focus stone, or you could add pictures from magazines that show what you are working to manifest, such as a new house, or a smiling couple to represent a happy relationship.

A circle may be used when you wish to focus on a project. You may create as many circles of crystals as you like around the focus stone. This kind of grid is useful when you want to enhance something like a school project or some other kind of "homework."

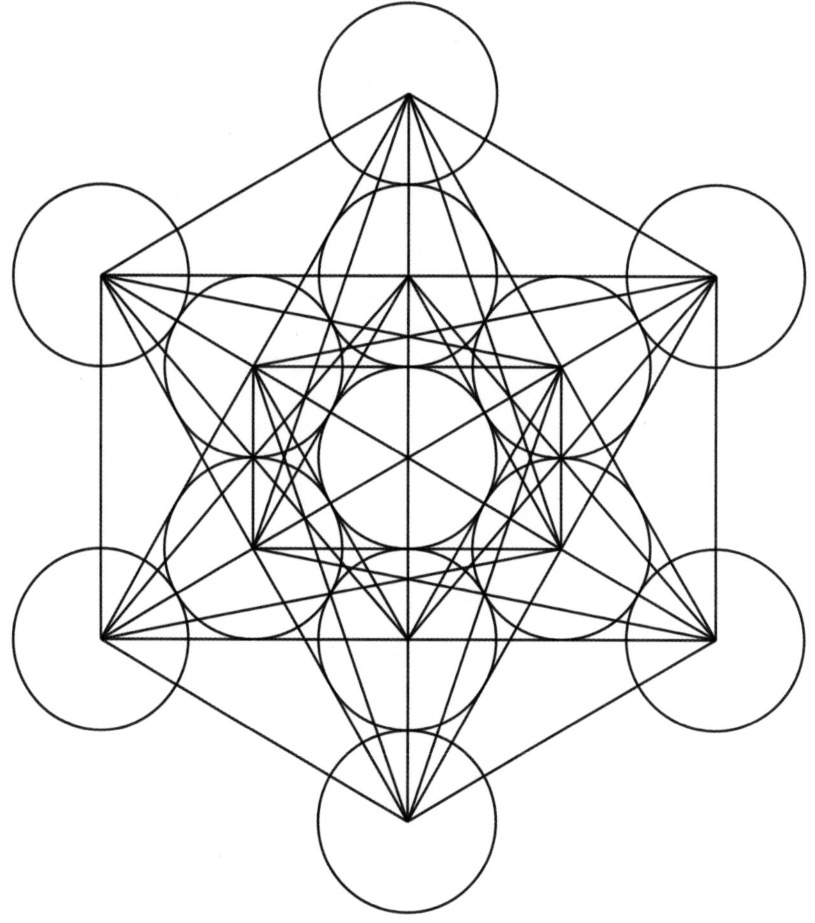

Metatron's Cube

The *vesica piscis* is a shape sometimes used to represent female genitalia. As such, this shape of grid would be good for a creative project that you want to move from being a dream to reality, perhaps by starting your own business. You could use the *vesica piscis* shape as the two overlapping circles if you wanted to bring the right kind of energy to group work or a partnership.

The Seed of Life might be used in a situation where you want to research an idea before putting it into action. This could be something like coursework or a report in which you want to make sure you have included all you want to say before submitting it.

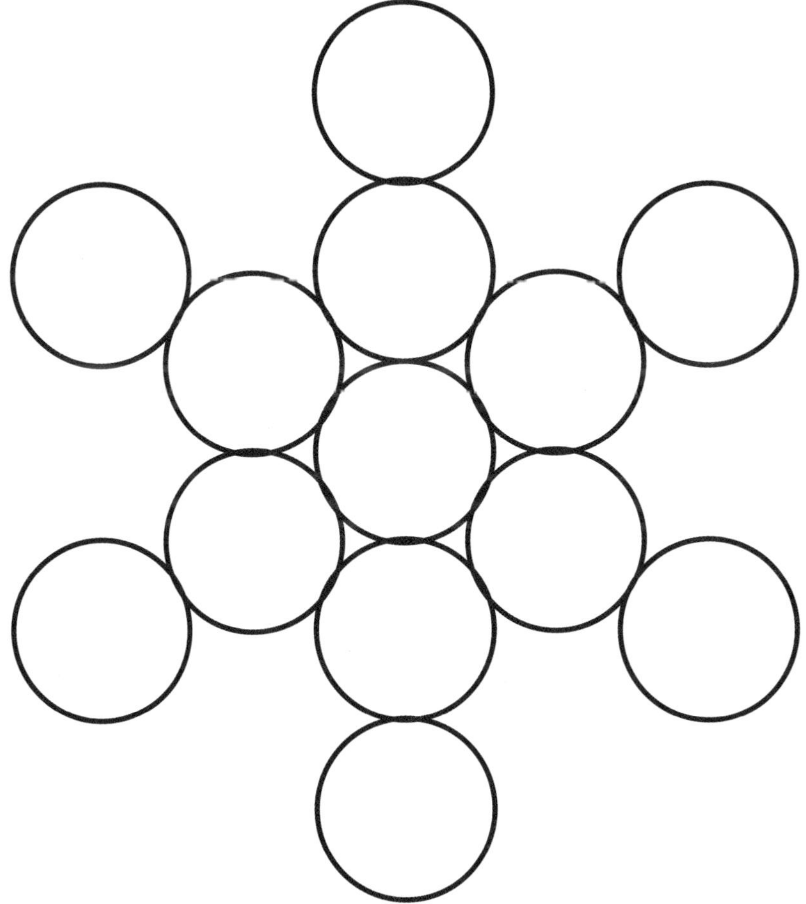

Fruit of Life

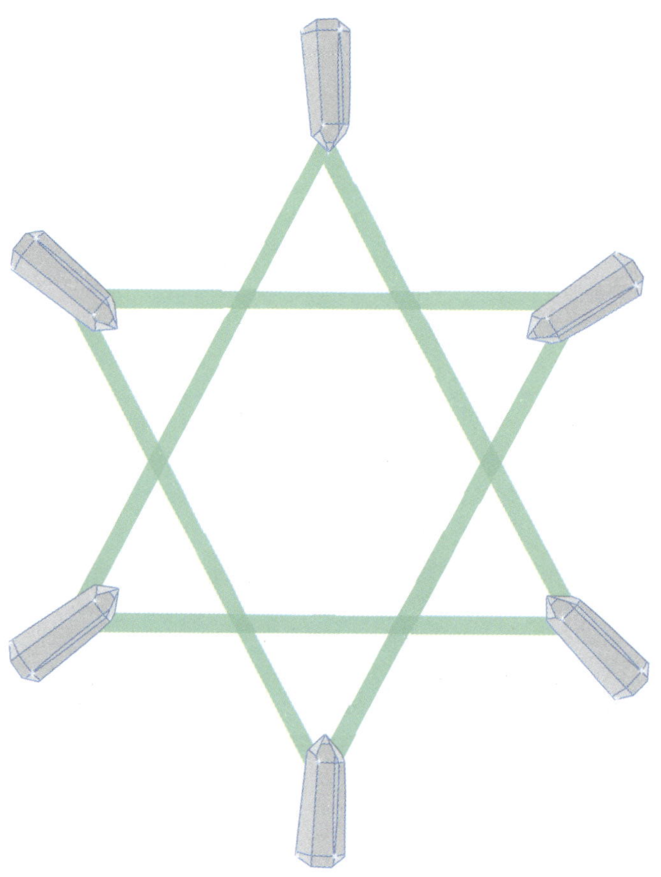

Seal of Solomon

The Flower of Life is a good shape for enhancing what you already have, so it encourages growth and abundance but also balance and calmness by letting things happen at the right time. This grid has a variety of uses, from manifesting a new house to attracting new relationships, improving finances, and soothing tensions in stressful situations.

As mentioned, the Seed of Life lies within Metatron's Cube. Metatron is an archangel who can be called upon to assist you with your spiritual journey, so this grid can be useful for helping you to look within and to develop your spiritual self but also for integrating spiritual studies into your life.

The Seal of Solomon shape can also be used. As with the merkaba, the downward-pointing triangle represents female energy, and the upward pointing triangle represents male energy. This shape is also seen as the symbol of the heart chakra. This would be a good shape for bringing balance into your life or to your emotions. If you are using crystal points in this grid, the direction would depend on whether your focus stone is programmed to release something from your life or to bring something into your life. For example, if you are overwhelmed with the number of tasks you are trying to cope with at the moment, facing the points outward could help you to release or delegate any jobs on which you do not need to spend your time. If you are grieving, facing the points inward would bring in healing energy.

Any shape you create can also be surrounded with a protective circle of crystals to guard against outside influences.

Forming the Grid

Feel free to use whichever crystals you like, or choose a combination based on the properties of different crystals presented in the book that is specific for your need or intention. To set up a grid, pick your grid shape, and add the crystals onto the grid. Remember to keep your intention in mind while you do it.

All manifestation grids have a focus stone. This is the central crystal that represents your wish or desire. As with gridding a property, you may like to program your focus crystal with the reason for your grid—for example, to attract abundance or to help heal heartbreak. Then you build up your pattern based on which sacred geometry shape you have chosen. This is usually done by placing the crystals at intersections where lines meet. In the case of a circle or *vesica piscis*, you would position crystals evenly around the circumference.

Depending on the kind of grid you have set up, you may like to include crystals that are good at moving energy directionally. These could include points that will move energy in one direction, such as quartz, citrine, and amethyst; or crystals that move energy in both directions, such as striated crystals, including tourmalines or selenite; or double terminated crystals with a point at both ends, which are usually quartz varieties like Herkimer diamonds.

There is some debate on whether the crystals should point inward to the focus stone or outward to bring focused energy out. I suggest that you use your intuition or pendulum to ascertain which direction would be appropriate for your personal grid.

Single-Stone Grids

For grids that are very simple—for example, a focus stone and four stones surrounding it—you may want to use exactly the same crystal for each position. Of course, you can use the same crystal for grids with many stones if you wish, but I like to bring in different energies to bigger grids, to add another aspect to my intention.

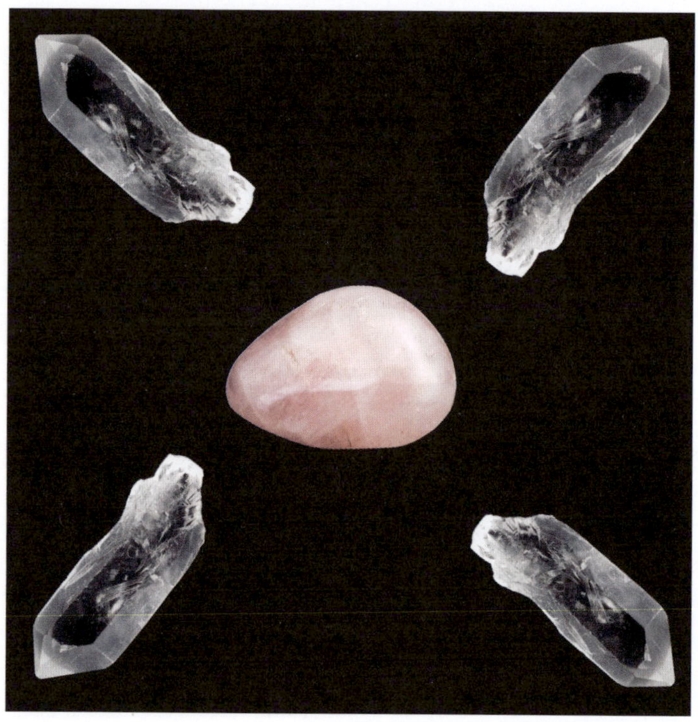

Multiple-Stone Layouts

If you are using different crystals, you can balance the energy of the grid by having an even number of each crystal and making the layout symmetrical. There is also a train of thought that recommends using stones from the same crystal "system." (See chapter one, "About Crystals.")

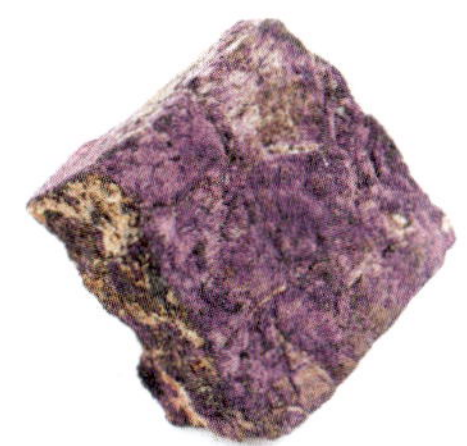

Orthorhombic crystals could be used if there is a situation that you find stressful and you decide to disperse some of the tension—for example, if you are being bullied or if you have problems with neighbors. The orthorhombic system is good for releasing tension and anxiety and for bringing relaxation and focus.

Crystals with this system include topaz, zoisite, shattuckite, chrysocolla, chiastolite, peridot, and purpurite.

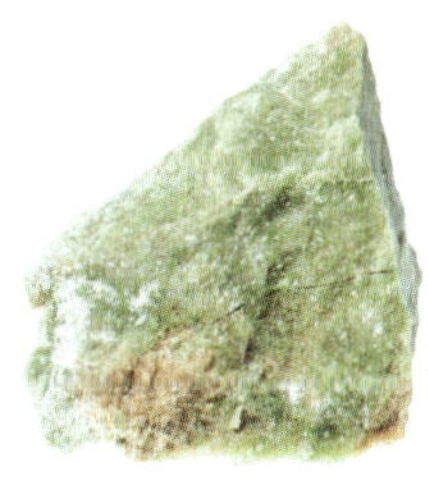

Tetragonal crystals may help in your grid if something in your life is causing you pain and you need to let go and move on. This could be a broken relationship or grieving for a loved one who has passed away. These crystals can be good for attracting people if you are feeling isolated or you want to reconnect with certain people. The tetragonal system is good for releasing and clearing old emotions and negative patterns of thinking, bringing clarity and balance. This would be good for anyone who has insulated or closed themselves off from others, as it would help them to connect and adopt a more positive attitude.

Crystals with this system include apophyllite, zircon, chalcopyrite, idocrase, scapolite, and tugtupite.

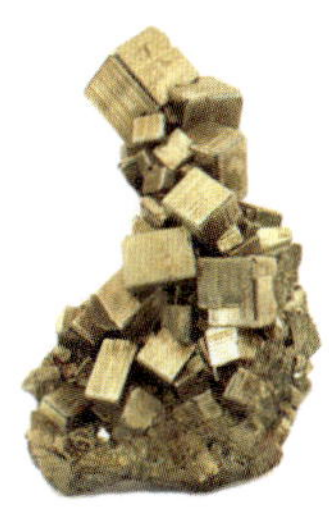

Cubic crystals have an energy structure that represents steady progress, so these could be used in grids aimed at building on what you already have, such as perfecting existing skills or working toward gaining new ones. The cubic system is good for structural and physical repair, such as helping to repair broken bones and healing wounds.

Crystals with this system include fluorite, garnet, spinel, iron pyrite, halite, lapis lazuli, sodalite, and diamond.

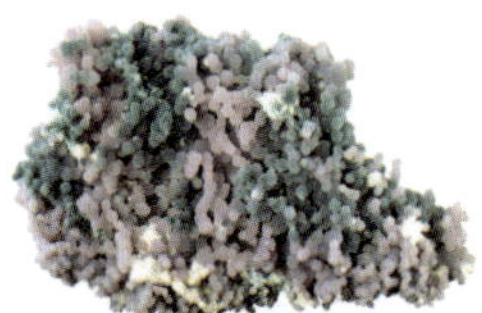

Trigonal crystals may be used on a grid where the intention is to boost your confidence or help you work through anxiety issues. The trigonal system has an energy that is balancing and calming. This helps the person to be in the present moment and to focus on making decisions. Trigonal crystals are also good for protection from other energies. This could be good for people who are finding it hard to make choices due to lack of confidence or due to being ungrounded.

Crystals with this system include some quartz varieties, chalcedony, aventurine, tourmaline, carnelian, jasper, agate, and chrysoprase.

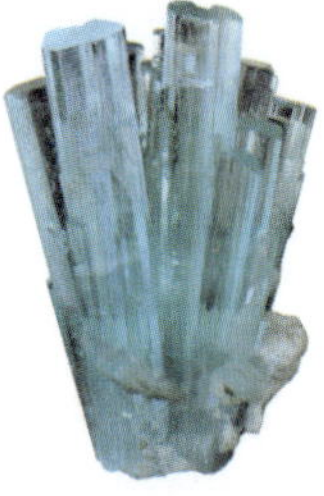

Hexagonal crystals can be used in grids where you want to work toward a goal or where your desire is to manifest something that will help you to grow as a person, such as a new job or relationship. The hexagonal system can bring clarity and focus by clearing mental turmoil. It is also good for integrating spirituality and self-development. This could help a person to meditate as well as help with transformation and growth.

Crystals with this system include some quartz varieties, rhodochrosite, calcite, emerald, sapphire, apatite, aquamarine, and hematite.

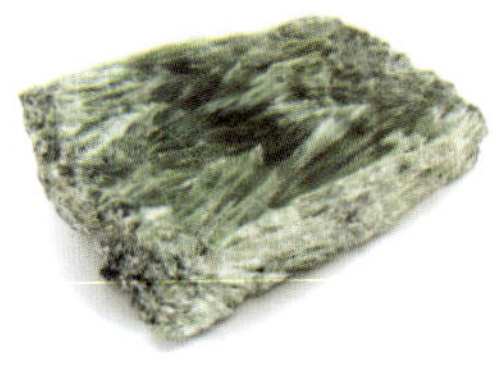

Monoclinic crystals may be helpful if your grid is set up to assist you with evaluating some part of your life—for example, if you want to enhance your intuition. The monoclinic system is good for clearing stagnant energy and stimulating clarity and purpose. This would be helpful for people who feel stuck in a rut, or for those who are finding it hard to let go of the past and move on.

Crystals with this system include kunzite, jade, malachite, seraphinite, chrysotile, howlite, selenite, azurite, charoite, zeolite, lepidolite, and serpentine.

Some Notes

It is important that your grid is set up with the intention that it be for the highest good of everyone involved. This is even more important if your desire directly involves other people in some way, such as forming new relationships or rekindling old ones.

If you are setting up a healing grid for someone else, make sure you have their permission. If it is not possible to obtain permission (if the person is in hospital, for example), have the intention that if this person does not wish to receive the healing energy, then it would go to someone else who is happy to receive it.

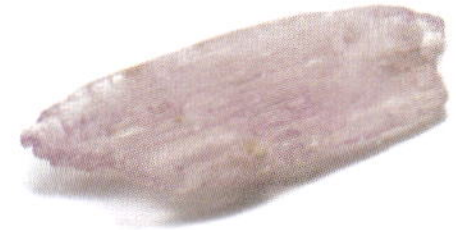

Triclinic crystals can assist you with working to deflect other people's opinions and comments that could have affected you on a subconscious level. They are also good for grids aimed at changing beliefs that stop you from achieving success, such as "I can't . . ." or "I'll never be able to . . . ." The triclinic system balances by calming and moving energies on different levels. This would be good for people who find change difficult due to self-limiting beliefs.

Crystals with this system include sunstone, labradorite, turquoise, amazonite, kyanite, clevelandite, and ulexite.

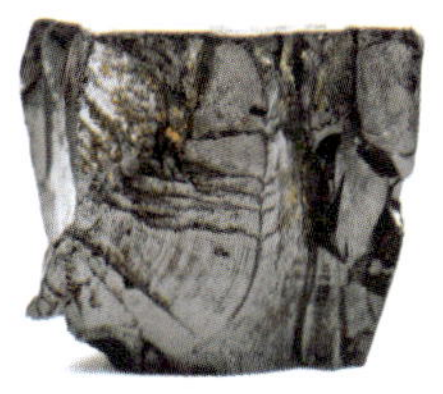

Amorphous crystals can be used with grids, although they can shift energy quickly, so you may want to consider whether quickly clearing energy is appropriate at this time. These are crystals with no internal structure, such as obsidian (which is molten glass), amber (tree resin), and moldavite (meteorites), among others. Amorphous crystals shift energy.

Other crystals with this system include jet, opal, limonite, girasol, tektite, and shungite.

❋ ❋ ❋

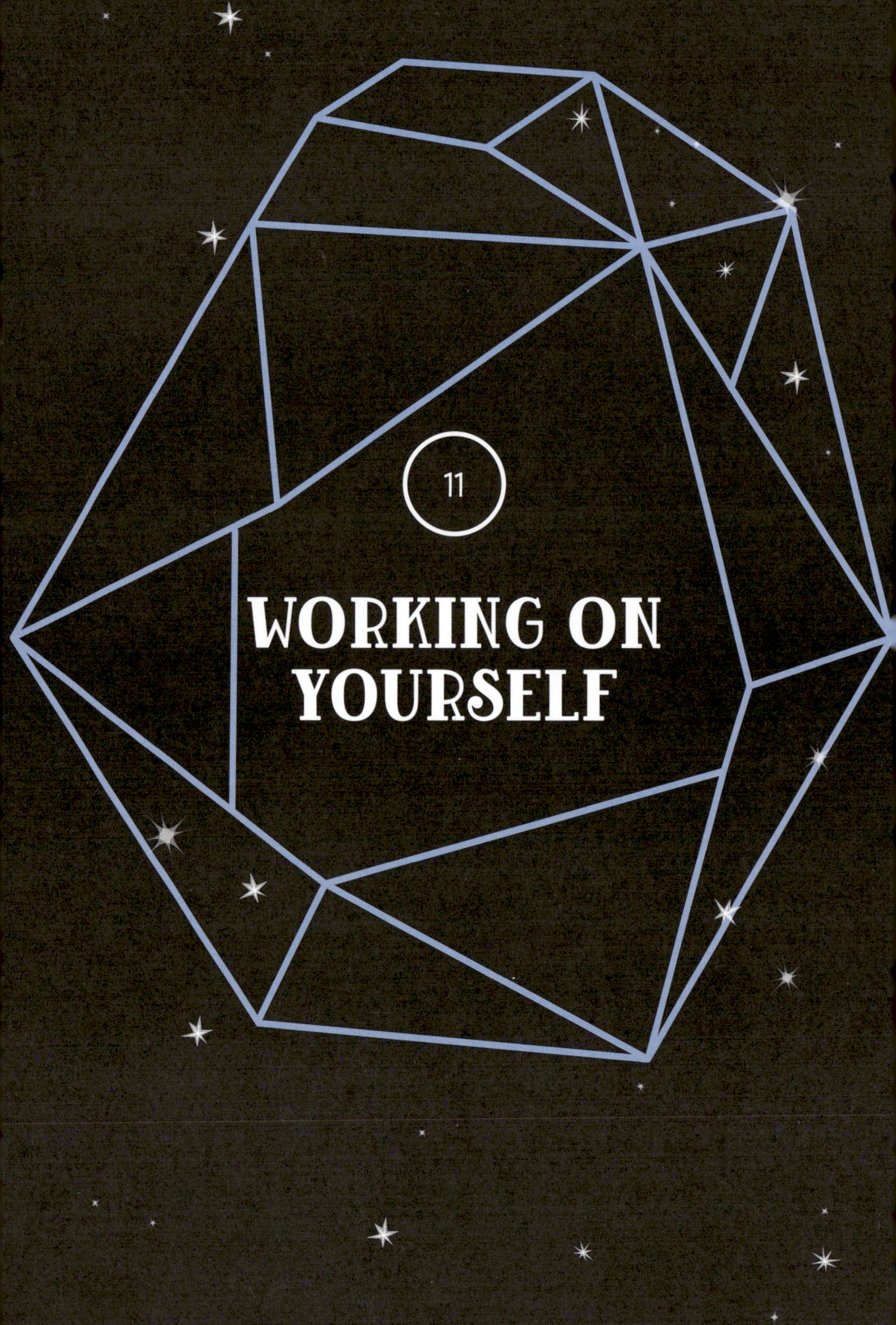

11

WORKING ON YOURSELF

As mentioned in the first chapter, crystals can help us to shift everyday stress and bring calmness and balance. Crystals can also help us to face any issues that we have and work through them: for example, anxiety, fear, anger or lack of self-confidence and self-love.

Working on yourself is a bit like cleaning an old bare room. To start with, you may like to sweep the walls and floorboards to get rid of the cobwebs and dust, just like gradually letting go of everyday worry and stress. Then, after a while, you may like to wash the walls and floorboards to get some of the dirt out, which could be likened to reflecting on the issues that are causing you stress. You may notice that the floorboards need sanding to get some stains off—this would be the point you start taking action to address the source of your stress.

As you begin to work with crystals, they clear the easy stuff first, such as the issues that you are quite happy and willing to let go of. Eventually, you will find that you are going a bit deeper. You may find that after doing a different layout, or even after spending longer than you normally do in a layout you're familiar with, memories of past events may surface or you could even have more-vivid dreams than usual. This is because after you've cleared issues on the surface, you can start working at a deeper level and slowly shift the old patterns and ways of thinking that could be holding you back.

Balancing and Calming

When I start to feel under pressure from all that is going on in my life, one of my favorite layouts for releasing a bit of tension and stress is a *balancing and calming layout.* You will need:

- one single terminated quartz,
- one single terminated smoky quartz, and
- one rose quartz tumblestone.

Lie down and place the smoky quartz below your feet, pointing away from your body, to ground you. The quartz goes above your head, pointing upward and away from your body, to connect you to universal energy, God, gods, goddesses, and so on, and the rose quartz goes at your heart. Just lying with these crystals for a few minutes helps me to feel a lot calmer.

Self-Development

Self-development can be as slow and steady as you want, and go as deep as you wish. Although this book is aimed at helping you to work by yourself, do seek help from others if there are issues that you are struggling to cope with. I use my crystals all the time to aid me with whatever issues I'm dealing with, but there have been times that I've felt the need to try other therapies, such as Reiki, acupuncture, breathing techniques, and essences, to name a few. Sometimes we reach a point where we know we have to let go, but we don't know how: this is where someone else can step in and help us to shift everything along. To go back to my room analogy: if you know there's a potential problem under the floorboards, sometimes it's better to call in someone to help you, rather than to try to muddle through fixing the problem yourself.

Effects of Working with Crystals

While using crystal layouts on yourself, try to be relaxed and calm. Some people have told me that while I'm working on them they experience warm, fuzzy energy where the crystals are placed or see bright colors behind their closed eyes. But sometimes, if there's an energy blockage, or some energy is being cleared concerning an issue that you are currently focusing on, you may have a different experience. It is perfectly normal to observe fleeting symptoms, such as ears popping, leg or knee pain, or limbs jerking. You may also experience a feeling in one of your chakras, such as headache, blocked throat, or heart palpitations. It is worth sticking with the layout until the feeling subsides, because it is usually an indication of energy building up at a blocked area, and it should shift after a few deep breaths in through your nose and sighed out through your mouth. If you feel bothered or worried, remove the crystals and place a red or black crystal between your feet to ground yourself. After doing a layout on yourself, make sure you are fully grounded before continuing with your day.

The same may happen if you are wearing a new piece of jewelry or carrying a newly purchased crystal around with you. I once took a new tumblestone to work with me and throughout the morning, I began to feel light-headed and spaced out. It took me a couple of hours to figure out that the way I was

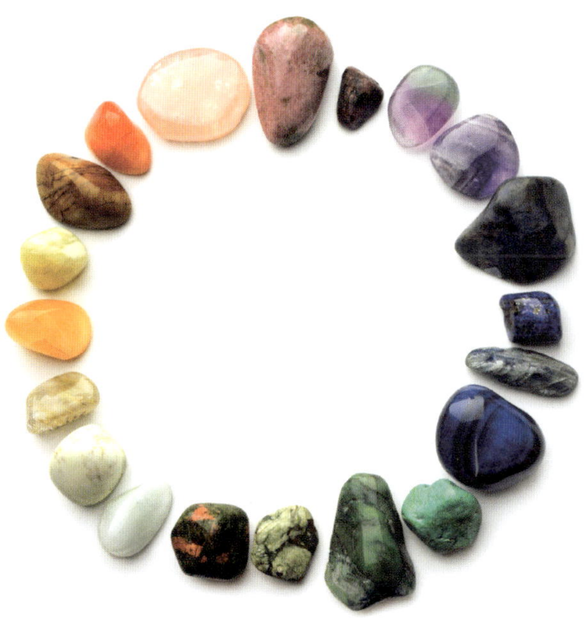

feeling was due to the crystal; once I had removed it from my person and done a grounding visualization, I felt a lot better!

I advise carrying or wearing only a small number of different crystals at a time, to avoid being overwhelmed with too many energies at once. When it comes to crystals, more is *not* better. In the same way that you would not listen to several pieces of music at once, you will be able to focus (either consciously or subconsciously) more on what you are experiencing if there are fewer energies to interact with.

After you have been working with crystals, it could take up to three days for your energy to settle, especially if you have been using a layout that you haven't experienced before or you have done more than one layout on yourself. Always make sure you drink plenty of water over the three days—this will help you to assimilate any changes.

Sometimes, although you are feeling great right after doing a layout, you may soon grow quite tired, and this can lead you to feel off-color for a few days. This is nothing to worry about, because just as every person experiences conventional medicine in a different way, so we all have different responses to crystal layouts. You may find that you need to go to the bathroom more frequently for a day or so. Just be aware of how you feel, and if the symptoms last for more than a few days or if you are worried, then seek medical advice.

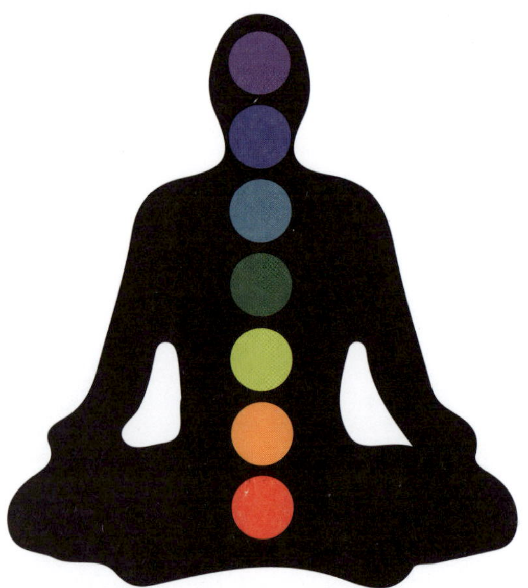

Working on Your Chakras

This is a very simple combination of working with crystals and meditations for opening and closing your chakras. You need to open them before you start, and you should close them once you have finished your work in order to prevent yourself from feeling spaced out or being upset by vivid dreams.

Opening Your Chakras

There are many methods of opening and closing chakras, but this is the one my friend Roberta Vernon uses:

- Gather light from the universe and bring the light down to your crown chakra.
- See the crown chakra as a purple lotus (water lily), and imagine it opening and allowing the light to enter through it.
- Let the light come down as far as the forehead chakra, at which point a large blue eye opens up.
- Allow the light to come down as far as the throat, at which point a pale blue cornflower opens up.
- Let the light come down to the heart chakra, where some green leaves open up.

- Allow the light to come down to the solar plexus chakra, and see a large yellow daisy or dahlia open up.
- See the light moving down to the sacral chakra, where a large orange marigold opens up.
- Now let the light travel down to the base chakra, where a big red poppy opens up.
- Then allow the light to filter down through the legs and to fill the whole body and the surrounding aura.

Closing Your Chakras

Once you have finished your crystal chakra healing or meditation session, you need to close your chakras. It is actually more important to close the chakras than to open them, because they open of their own volition as soon as you do any kind of psychic or spiritual work. Chakras that have been left open can lead to bad dreams, feelings of psychic invasion, and other uncomfortable sensations.

- Start by imagining the light that has reached down into the earth being turned off, and turn off the light in your legs until you reach the base chakra.
- Turn off the light up to the base chakra and carefully close the red poppy.
- Next, turn off the light up to the sacral chakra and close the marigold.
- Take the light up to the solar plexus chakra and close the yellow daisy, while turning the light off.
- Now move up to the heart chakra, turning off the light as you go and closing the leaves.
- Move to the throat chakra, where you close the blue cornflower and turn the light off.
- Now bring the light up to the third eye and close it firmly, shutting off the brow chakra.
- Push the light out from the crown chakra and close the purple lotus flower.
- Finally, send the light off into the universe, where it can give healing to those who need it.

A Reminder of the Chakra Colors

As a reminder, the colors of the chakras are listed below. They are the same as the colors of the rainbow.

Base or Root Chakra Red: Garnet or red jasper

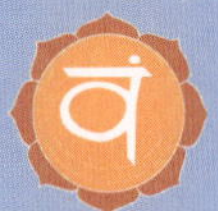

Sacral Chakra Orange: Carnelian or sunstone

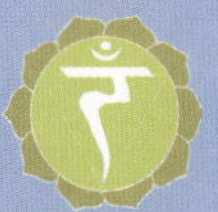

Solar Plexus Chakra Yellow: Citrine, topaz, or amber

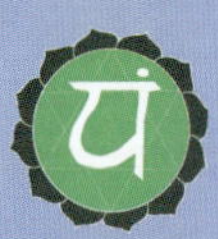

Heart Chakra Green: Emerald or agate

Throat Chakra Light blue or greenish blue: Turquoise or blue lace agate

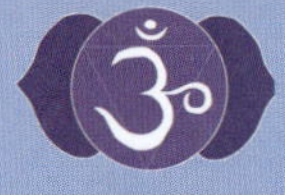

Brow Chakra Dark blue: Sodalite, lapis lazuli, or sapphire

Crown Chakra Purple: Amethyst, tanzanite, or clear quartz

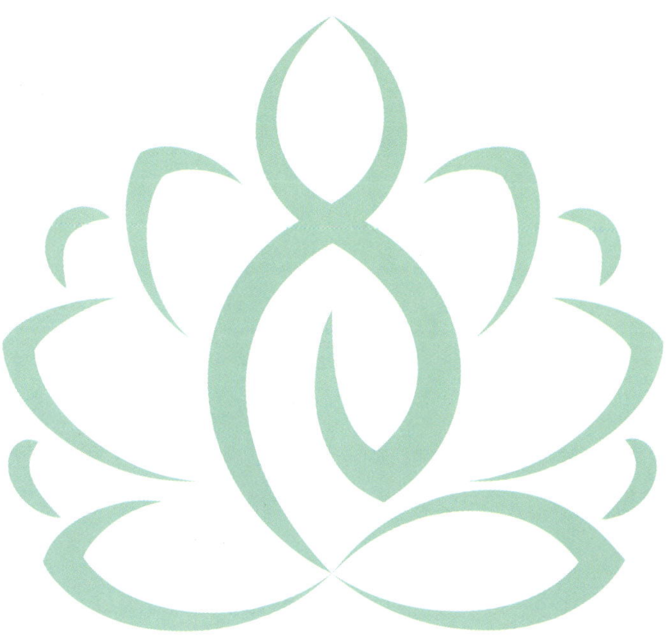

Combining crystals and the chakras for self-healing is simple and safe. Do this in a quiet place where you won't be disturbed. You can burn incense, light candles, or have music playing quietly in the background. Make yourself comfortable, close your eyes for a few minutes, and breathe regularly. Then begin to concentrate gently on the chakra associated with the problem you wish to heal. Hold an appropriate crystal against the chakra that you want to heal, and meditate upon the chakra and the crystal. Once you have finished the meditation, close your chakras.

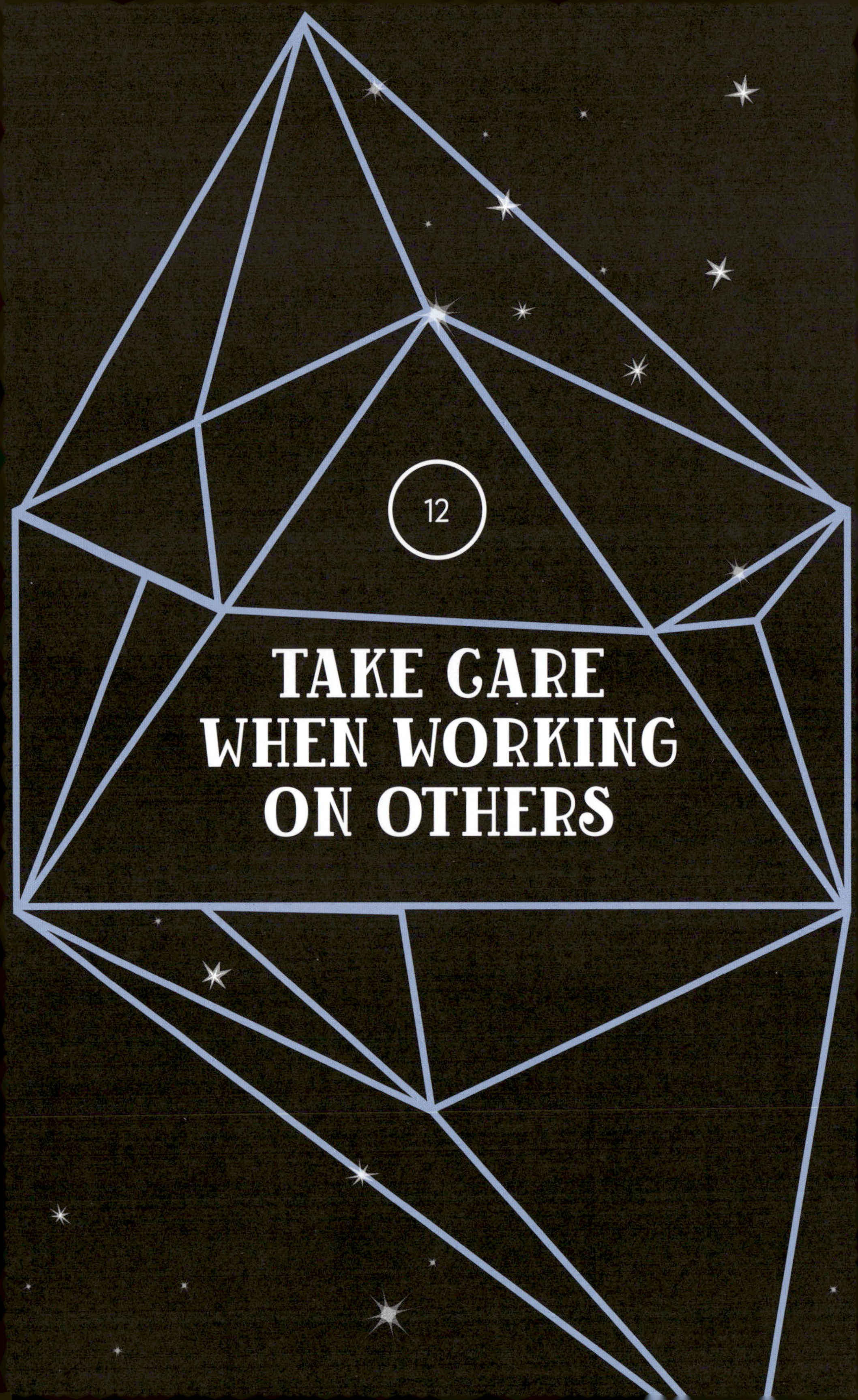

12

TAKE CARE WHEN WORKING ON OTHERS

When working on other people, you need to be more careful than when using the crystals on yourself. This is because you connect to the person you are working with, and it is very easy either for you to pick up energy from them or for the person to pick up energy from you. In simple terms, this could mean that anything you clear away from them could be absorbed by you.

I suggest that you always follow these steps before carrying out any crystal therapy or healing on another person.

- Always tap yourself in before beginning.
- Ask your pendulum if it is safe and appropriate for you to work on this person.
- Ask your pendulum if either of you needs protection crystals. A crystal can be placed under the client's pillow if he or she needs one and in your pocket if you need one.
- Have the intention in your mind to do only what is safe and appropriate at this time before selecting layouts and crystals.

Make sure that you intend to carry out only what is safe and appropriate at this time. For instance, you may set the intention "to clear away anything associated with X illness," but this may not be the right thing for you to do. We all want those who are sick to get better, but the illness itself may not be the issue that the person needs to work through at this time.

If the person you are working on begins to feel unwell or starts to cry, quietly remove all the crystals and place grounding stones between his feet. This is simply a response to the shifting energy. Making sure you remain calm and grounded, and that you ground your client's energy, will help him to settle.

Some Important Tips

It is very important that you make sure the person you are working on is grounded at the end of the session. Either place a black or red crystal between their feet or get them to do a grounding technique as described earlier in this book.

After working on someone, I like to run my hands through the client's aura, from the head to the feet, because this helps me reaffirm his or her boundaries and my own. I usually do this three times, and then run my hands through my own aura. I start at my head and move my hands down to my feet about an inch away from my body, making sure that I do all sides of my body. You could also spray some gem essence down the client's body to clear the aura. Be sure to shield your client's eyes when doing this.

Always make sure that the person experiencing the therapy, whether this is you or someone else, drinks plenty of water in the three days following the session to help the energies settle.

Three- or Five-Line Clearing

- Ask your pendulum if it is safe and appropriate to work on a particular person at this time. If the answer is "no," do not proceed!
- Ask if either of you need a protection crystal. If the answer is "yes," then use your pendulum to choose the specific crystal and place it accordingly.
- Ask your pendulum if you should start above the head or below the feet.
- Start your pendulum swinging forward and backward (neutral swing), and move up or down the center line of the body. At some point the pendulum will start to swing in a circle instead of neutral swing, which means it is clearing some energy. Stay in that place until your pendulum

stops circling and returns to neutral swing, and then you can continue to move up or down the center line. Carry on until you have passed over the whole length of the body and a bit beyond.

- Return to where you started, which will be at the head or the feet, and proceed again, but this time, slightly away from the person's body and in line with one of the shoulders. It doesn't matter which side you do first.
- Once you have done this line, continue with a third line, level with the other shoulder.
- If you wish, you can extend the line on each side, going out the same distance as you did for the shoulders, but be sure to complete both shoulder lines before moving farther out.

Group Work

If you have a group of people who are interested in learning about crystals and want to know how to experience the energy of the crystals, you could try this exercise:

- You will need twelve amethyst points.
- Make sure everyone is centered and grounded before you begin.
- Elect one person to carry out the exercise. This person should dowse to see if he needs a protection stone.
- In the meantime, everyone else writes their name on a piece of paper and hands it to the leader. Each of them should then find somewhere to sit or lie down for a few minutes.
- The leader then puts the names in a pile and surrounds them with a circle of twelve amethyst points facing inward. The amethyst net will raise the energy in the enclosed area.

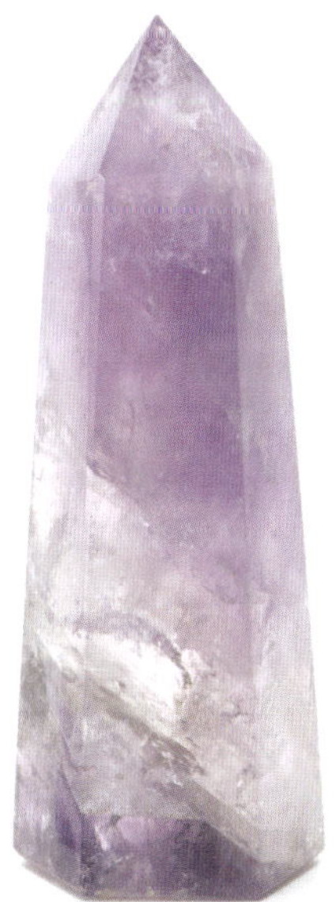

- Next, a crystal is placed on top of the pile of names for a couple of minutes. Then that crystal is removed and replaced by a different one for another couple of minutes. To make the energy quite different, I suggest using a purple stone with a higher frequency, then a red or black crystal, which has the lowest frequency. Using the red or black crystal after the purple one would start to ground the group.
- Remove the crystal from the center of the amethyst net, and then dismantle the net while everyone slowly sits up and makes sure they are well grounded.

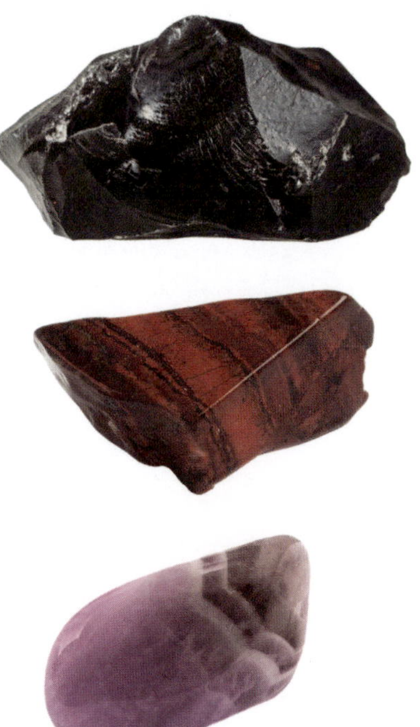

Have a discussion to see whether people felt a difference when lying between the crystals. Remember that it's fine for some of the group to feel nothing out of the ordinary, as it sometimes takes practice to develop one's sensitivity.

Working on One Person

You can place the amethyst net around a person, and this can be good to use if the person is feeling a bit down. Simply place one point above the head pointing down and one point at the feet pointing up, and then spread the rest of the points evenly around the body, all facing inward. Dowse to see how long the person needs to remain in the net.

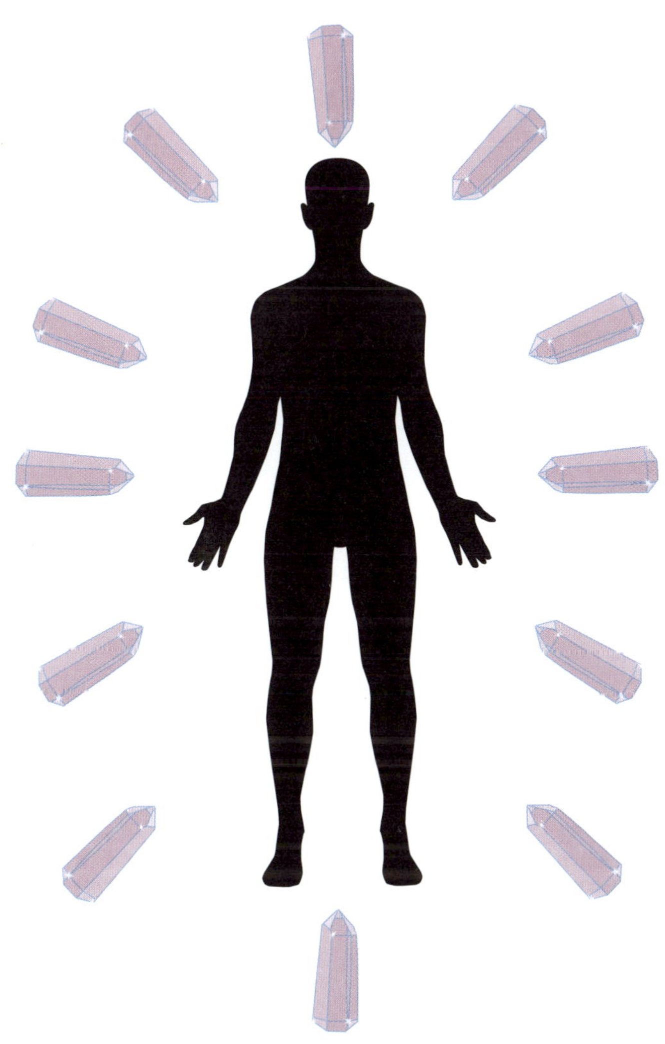

✵ ✵ ✵

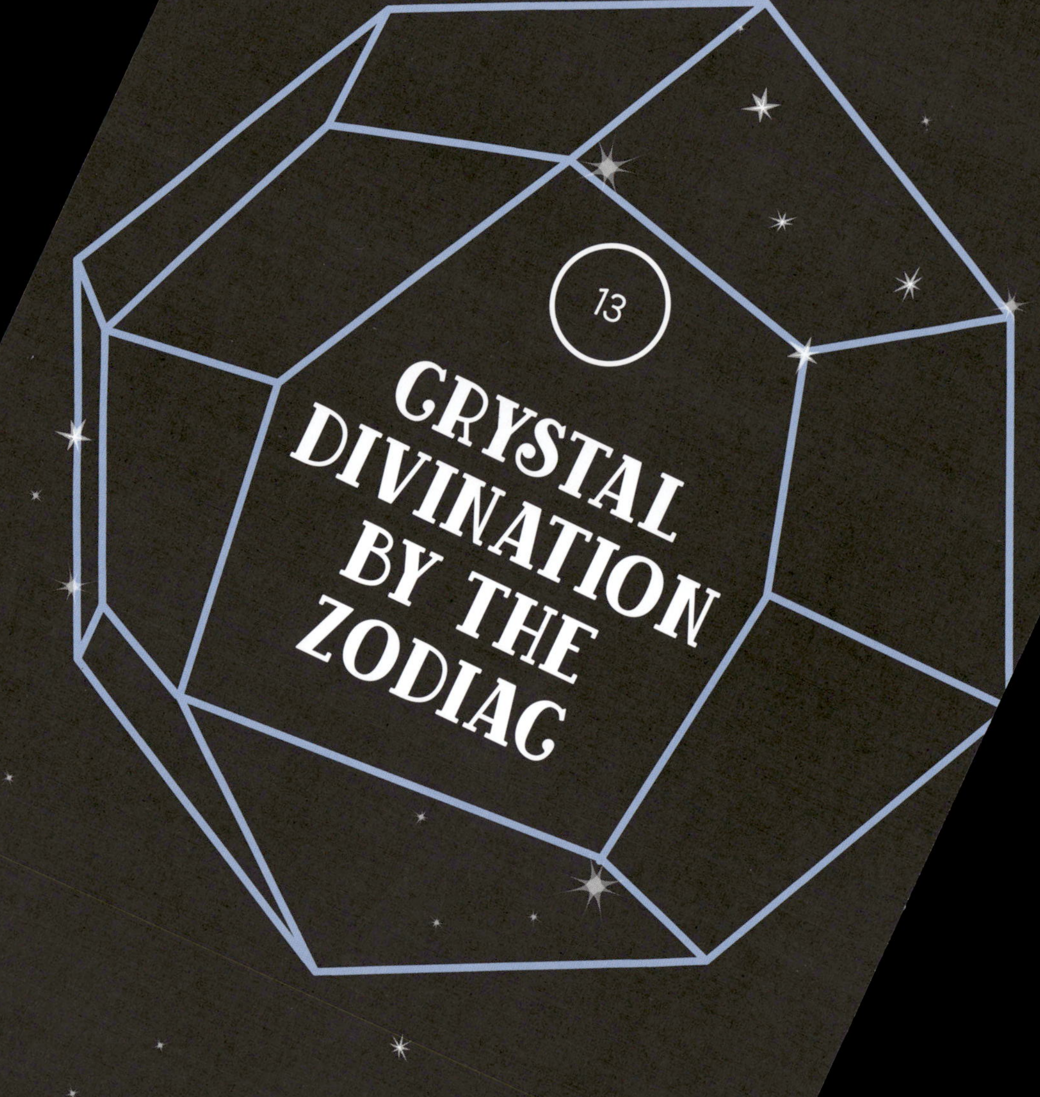

13 CRYSTAL DIVINATION BY THE ZODIAC

Crystals can be used for divination purposes. *Divination* is the art of foreseeing what energies will be around a person in the future, helping to give us an idea of what issues or events may arise. There are different methods of crystal divination, and the way I work is by using a circular printout of an astrological wheel. If I am working on myself, I keep the "intention" in my head that the chart represents the energies that will be around me this week. The center of the circle represents what will happen today or tomorrow, and the area that is closer to the edge of the circle represents a time that is later in the week. Any crystals that fall outside the circle relate to energies that will be around me in the following weeks.

Each crystal has a different type of energy and characteristic, and the astrological sign in which a crystal falls can give an indication of any issues or important events that may be coming up. For me, knowing what kind of energy is going to be around me enables me to feel prepared, and it assists me in remaining calm when events threaten to stress me out. By meditating with a crystal, you will get an idea of the energy or situation that the crystal represents.

The astrological signs on the divination board represent the characteristics of each star sign, or the issues that relate to a particular sign.

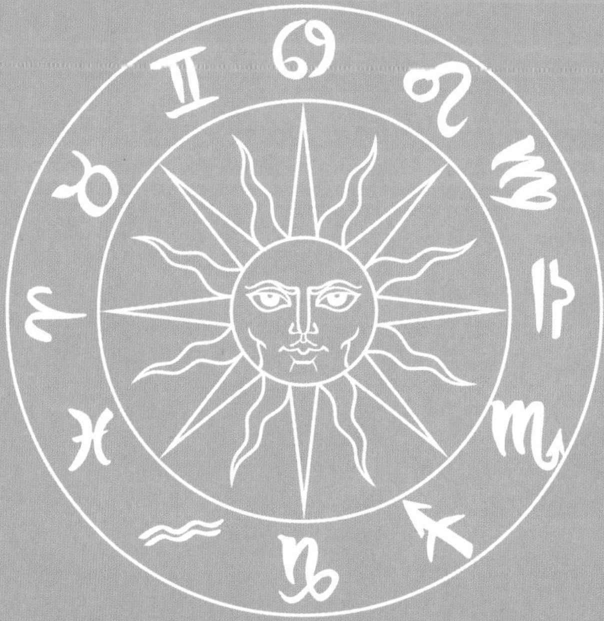

Aries

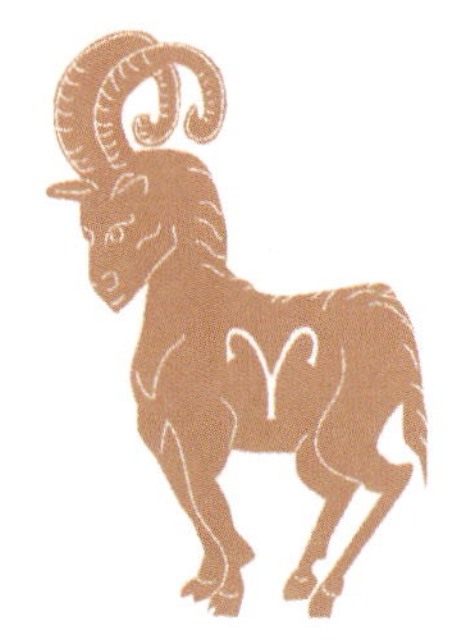

Key words: *appearances, individuality*
Arians are good at promoting themselves and pushing forward with projects. A crystal in this sign may be telling you what you need to show to the world or what you need to keep in check. It is an assertive sign, so it can suggest that you need to stand up for yourself, but it could warn against being too aggressive.

Taurus

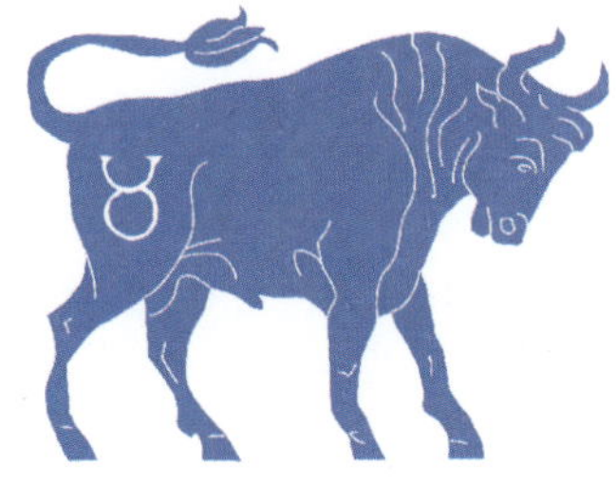

Key words: *money, finance, possessions, values*
Taureans love owning things and spending money on the finer things in life, so crystals that fall here could be telling you about your financial situation, such as a windfall or spending too much, but also highlighting issues that are important to you. This sign loves good food and luxury, so it may denote a pleasant treat or a warning against being too self-indulgent.

Gemini

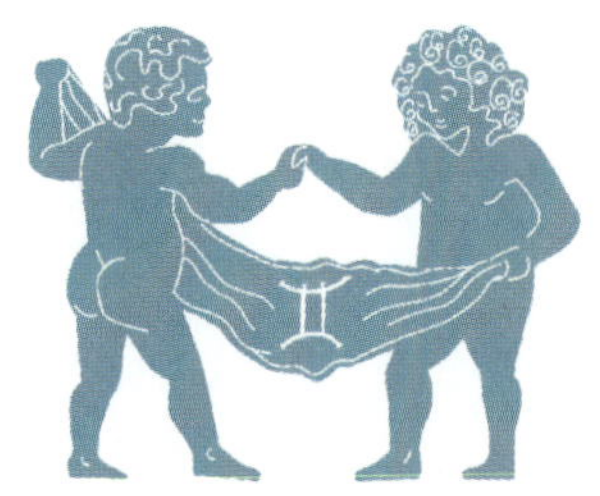

Key words: *communication, siblings, neighbors, gossip, travel*
Geminis are great talkers and are usually very active people. Crystals in this sign often hint at news and other information that will come to light, or the crystals may be saying that you need to speak up. There could also be travel on the horizon or issues with people close to you. You may have to speak up or, on the other hand, guard your tongue.

Cancer

***Key words:** home, roots, family, stability, protection*

Cancerians are very family orientated and will work hard to make their home life secure. Crystals that fall here could either be suggesting ways for you to strengthen your ties with family or possibly be hinting at issues regarding them that you will need to work through. This sign can relate to property and premises or even a small business of your own, so pay attention to any suggestions.

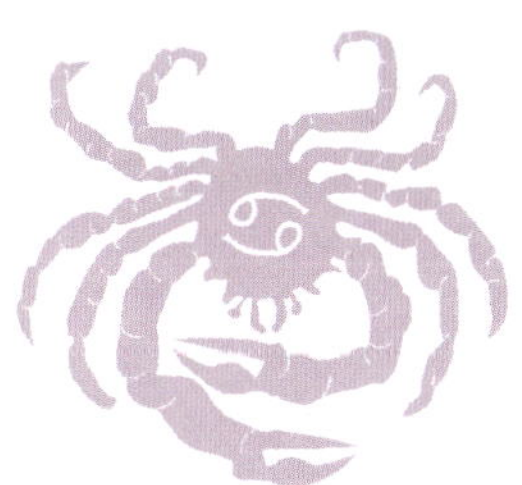

Leo

***Key words:** creativity, romance, leisure, children, gambling*

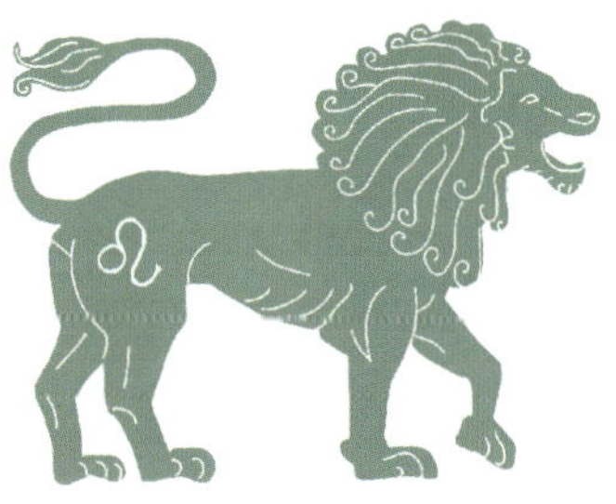

Leos enjoy the limelight and taking part in many activities. They often like to be in control of a situation or group. A crystal here may suggest upcoming opportunities in your leisure time, or it may offer you creative ideas. It may also pertain to children or the birth of an idea, or warn of any risky situations. Leo also rules children, so the youngsters in your family may soon be in need of attention.

Virgo

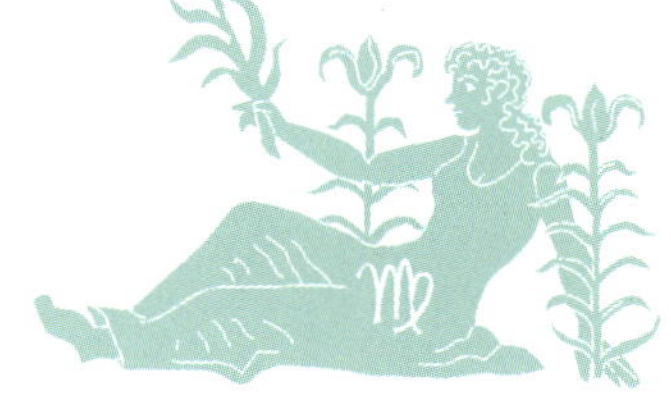

***Key words:** work, healing, service, health issues, crisis points, pets, routines*

Virgos are often called perfectionists because they take great care when doing jobs, which is why this sign covers work and routines. Health issues and crisis points are also included as this star sign does very well with organizing and sorting out these situations. Crystals falling in this sign highlight a situation or issue that will require attention to detail.

Libra

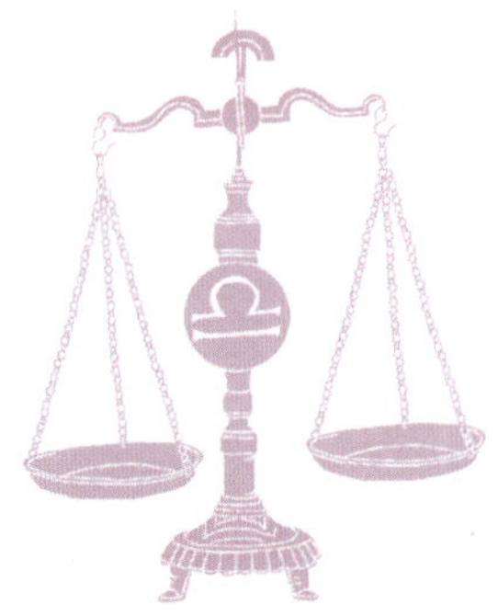

Key words: *relationships, partnerships*
Librans like balance, hence the symbol for this star sign is a pair of scales. Crystals that fall here usually indicate ways of keeping a balance with relationships with friends, family, and partnerships, and this can include business partnerships. You may need tact and diplomacy when tackling an upcoming problem.

Scorpio

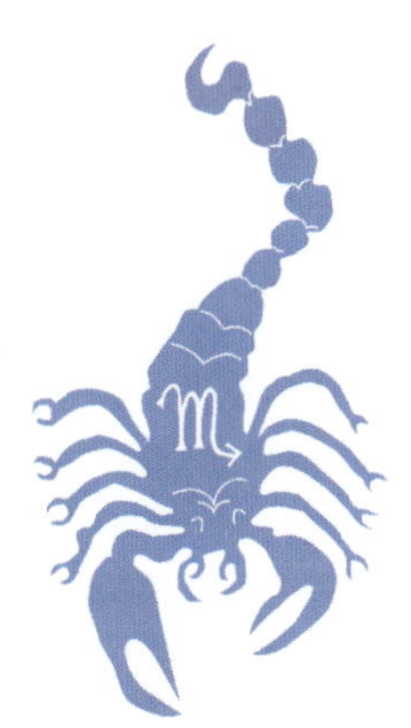

Key words: *other people's money, endings, beginnings, deep emotions*
Scorpios have a lot of passion, and they are also sharp-eyed when it comes to spotting details. Crystals here can signify beginnings and endings, as well as something that triggers deep emotions. This sign relates to important financial dealings that involve others, such as mortgages and loans, so you might need to look into these.

Sagittarius

Key words: *education, travel, religion, philosophy, expansion*
Sagittarians are broad-minded and often enjoy traveling and learning. Crystals in this sign could hint at future travel plans or suggest ways in which to expand your knowledge. This sign always wants to look beyond the obvious, so it could be encouraging you to look into psychic or spiritual matters, or warning you not to become obsessed with them.

Capricorn

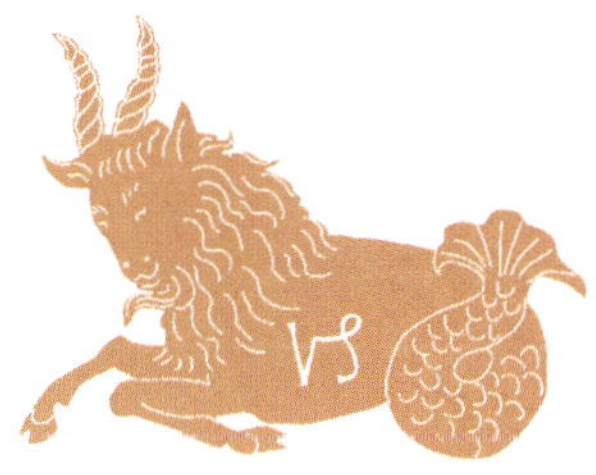

***Key words:** career, ambition, status, reputation, planning*

Capricorns are generally hardworking and sensible, so they like to plan ahead and work steadily toward their goals. Any crystals that appear in this sign refer to an area of your life that requires hard work, like a career or planning for the future. This sign can represent authority figures who might be helpful to you, or who might become troublesome to you, so keep an eye out for either of these.

Aquarius

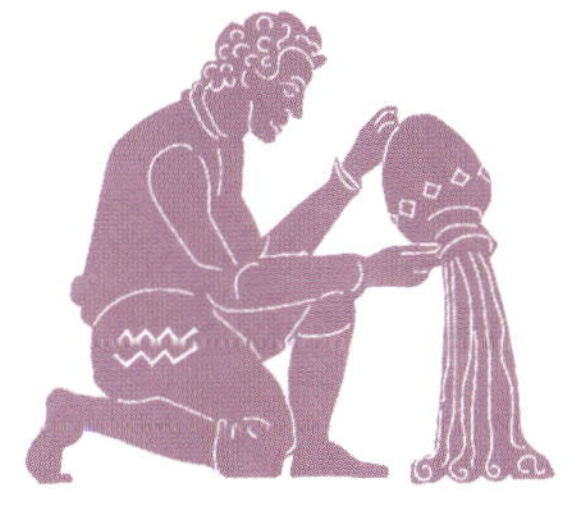

***Key words:** friends, social life, group issues, ideals*

Aquarians tend to have many acquaintances, and they flow easily in group situations. Crystals here mostly refer to group energies, such as meeting with friends, committees, local politics, clubs and societies, social events, and other group activities. This is a sign of unconventionality and originality, so you might come up with some terrific ideas, but you might also become somewhat unrealistic.

Pisces

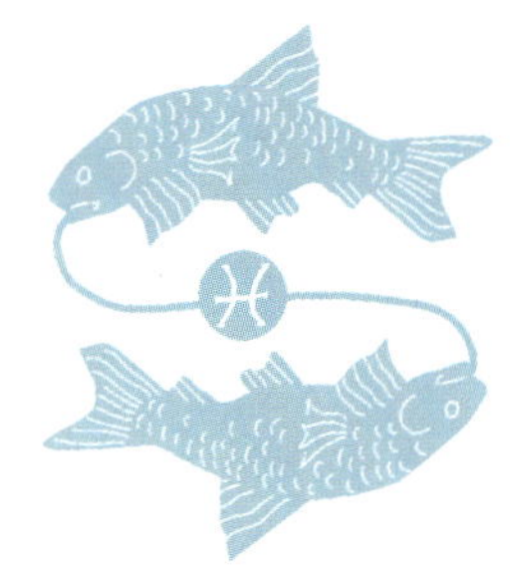

***Key words:** introspection, silence, self-sabotage, secrets, unconscious thoughts*

Pisceans are intuitive and have very creative ideas and dreams, but they often overthink, which can lead to finding problems that don't exist. Crystals that fall here could be either pointing out where you are blocking your own progress or suggesting areas of your life that may need a bit of analyzing or those that would benefit by meditating upon them.

Crystal Meanings

These are a few of the crystals I use and the meanings they carry within them.

Crystal		Possible Meanings
Smoky quartz	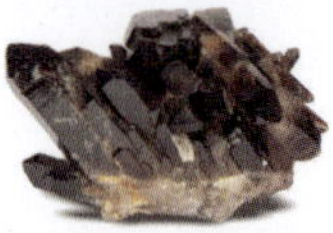	Endings, beginnings, things that aren't clear yet
Clear quartz	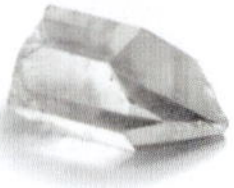	Clarity, honesty, being transparent
Labradorite	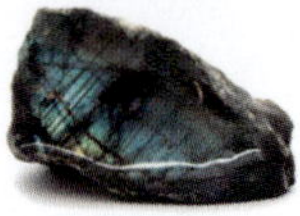	Surprise, unexpected events or ideas
Aventurine	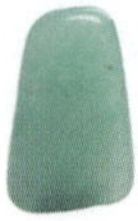	Opportunity, chance, freedom
Citrine	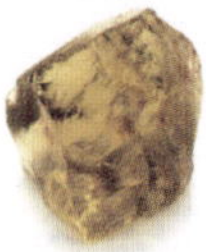	Happiness, uplift
Calligraphy stone	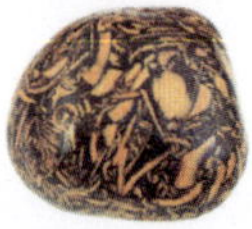	Documents, written communications

Crystal		Possible Meanings
Obsidian		Hidden, deep feelings; sudden change
Tiger's eye		Sociable, friendly interactions
Selenite		Fluctuating feelings, uncertainty
Fluorite		Coordinating (projects or people)
Rose quartz		Love, gentle appreciation
Rhodonite		Confidence or insecurity
Rutilated quartz		Being busy, tying up loose ends

Crystal		Possible Meanings
Amber	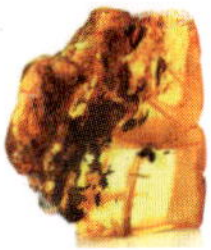	Enlivening, stimulating, electric
Amethyst	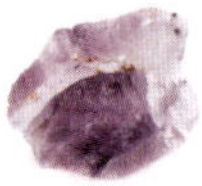	Self-control, calming, considerate
Carnelian	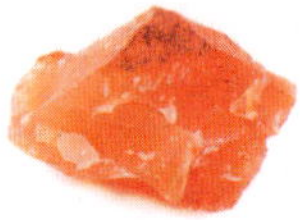	Healing, creative, sympathetic
Sodalite	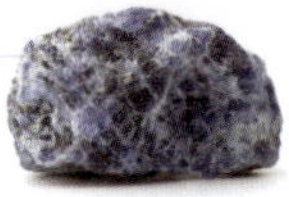	Mediator, communicator, nonjudgmental
Milky quartz	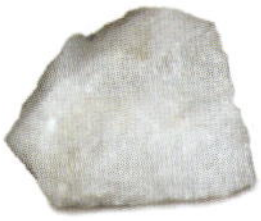	Unclear, insubstantial, vague
Turquoise	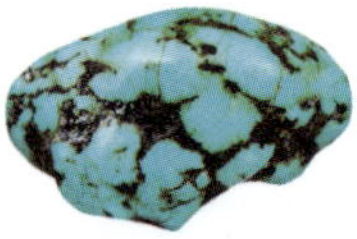	Immune, protective
Moldavite	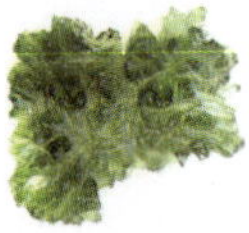	Expansive, pushing boundaries

Casting the Crystals

I keep my crystals in a bag and select them blindly. You can choose your crystals by intuition if you like to do it that way, but I prefer to do it without looking so that I'm not influenced by my favorites or led to avoid the stones that I'm reluctant to work with. I pick one crystal to give an overall idea of the energy that I will experience for the upcoming week and then select twelve other crystals (one for each sign of the zodiac). I hold all the crystals in my hands above the center of the astrological wheel and ask the question in my mind, "What energies will be with me this week?" I then open my hands to release all the crystals so that they will fall into the appropriate zodiac sign. Don't drop them from a height—you will end up with crystals rolling everywhere! Dropping them one to two inches above your chart is fine. Also, you may not want to do this with very soft crystals, because they could shatter.

At this point I look for patterns, such as a grouping or a line of crystals. This would suggest they are connected to the same event or issue. I suggest writing down which crystals fall in which sign and also note the date and perhaps the day of the week when you experience this energy. Note down any ideas that come into your head about possible meanings. You can then review your week as you go along.

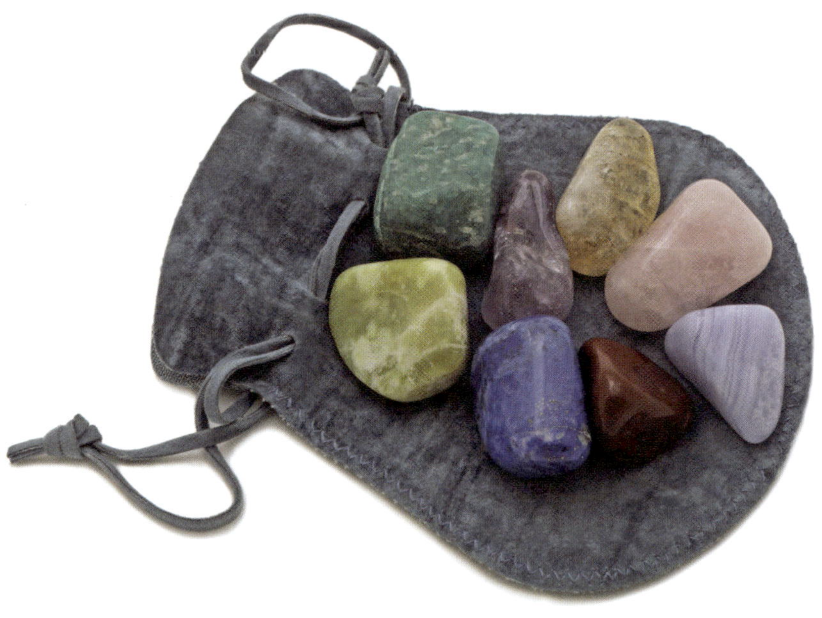

Until you get used to possible meanings for each crystal, it may be easier to look at each day in retrospect and analyze what happened and how the crystal's placement applies. Make sure that you are grounded before you begin divining, as this can help you trust your intuition more easily.

The Magic Square

This is an idea taken from feng shui and it is called the Magic Square. It is an ancient Chinese system that shows how the energies work in your home or in your place of work.

Each line of numbers in the Magic Square adds up to fifteen, whether counted horizontally, vertically, or diagonally, which does indeed make it a magic device!

The number fifteen also relates to the fifteen-day divisions of the Chinese year that helped the ancient sages to work out the best times for planting, growing crops, building houses, and so on. All of this adds to the mystical nature of the Magic Square numerology system. Note that the Magic Square always points toward the south.

		South		
Southeast	4	9	2	Southwest
East	3	5	7	West
Northeast	8	1	6	Northwest
		North		

First draw the Magic Square design and then draw a rough sketch of your property, making sure that the property plan fits neatly over the Magic Square.

If any of the numbered squares fall outside the plan of the house, the way to solve these problems is to place small mirrors on the walls facing into the missing or shortened areas. This is a feng shui method of protection.

The Magic Square Energies

Each area relates to a desire, aspiration, or need, so reinforcing any area of your life and your home that is giving you trouble can help to improve your circumstances. Do take only one area at a time, though, because trying to enhance multiple areas simultaneously will cause confusion, and you might end up with headaches as a result of the overexcited energies flying around.

The nine numbered areas are:	
1	Planning, career, profession
2	Education, knowledge
3	Children, creativity
4	Communication, mentors, friends
5	Health, life force
6	Wealth, prosperity
7	Family, well-being, celebrations
8	Marriage, love, romantic happiness
9	Reputation, status, fame

1. Improve career prospects by placing red jasper here.

2. To improve your mind, seek wisdom, pass exams, and make achievements, place a blue lace agate here.

3. To start a family or get a creative venture off the ground, reinforce this area with tiger's eye.

4. Improve communication skills and make new friends by placing turquoise crystals here.

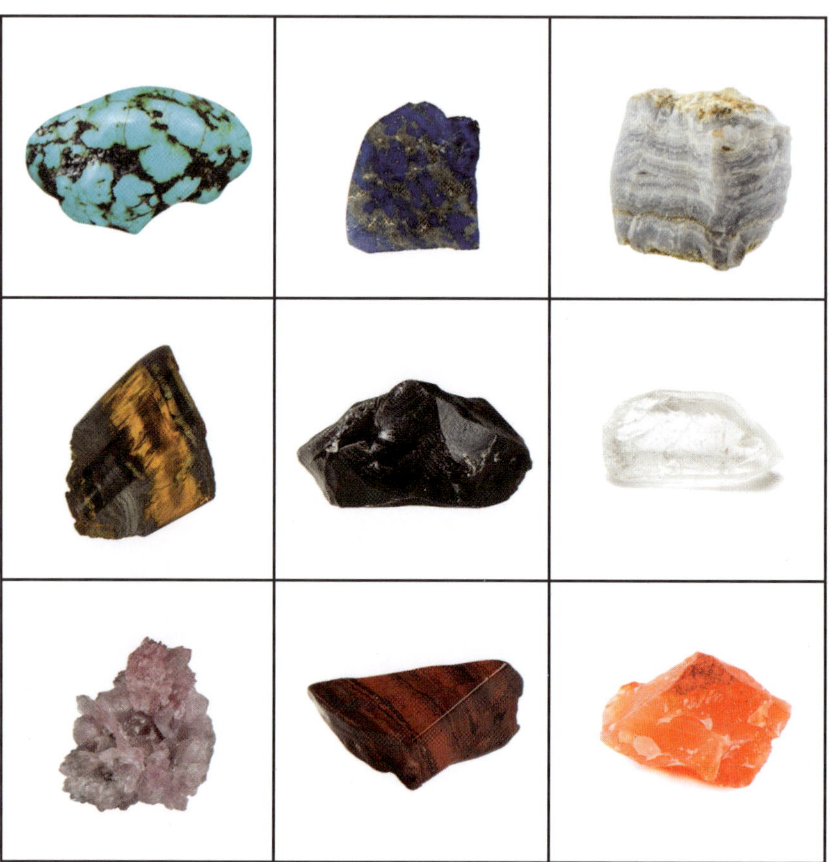

5. A piece of obsidian or black onyx will help to protect you from harm, while citrine could boost your health.

6. For more abundance, place a carnelian here.

7. A piece of clear crystal in this area will be beneficial to family relationships.

8. If you are hoping to find a wonderful, loving partner, a piece of jade or some rose quartz here may help.

9. Improve your reputation with a blue stone, such as sodalite, lapis lazuli, or turquoise.

Divination with the Magic Square

Draw the Magic Square design on a large sheet of paper and hold a small selection of cleansed and charged crystals in your hands. Drop the stones onto the Magic Square (not too high a drop—the stones would scatter too far or possibly break up). Where the stones land will show you the areas of your life that are due to become important in the near future and how these areas may be influenced. For instance, an energetic crystal would enliven the area, whereas a softer one would have a calming effect.

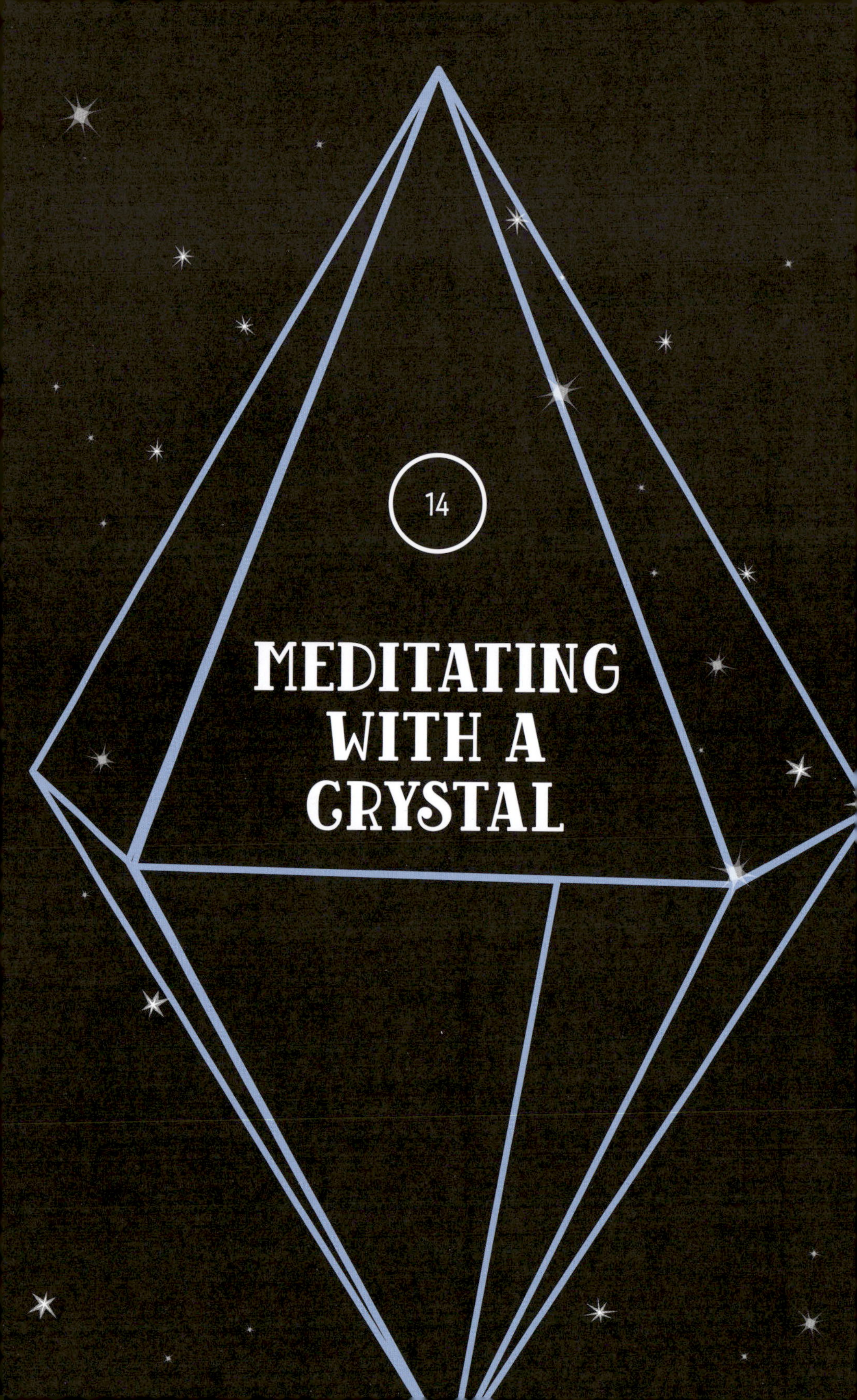

14

MEDITATING WITH A CRYSTAL

Meditating with your crystals is a lovely way to work with a crystal's energy. If you would like to connect with a new crystal or one from your existing collection, this can be as simple as sitting with the crystal in your hands and focusing on how the crystal feels, both physically and energetically.

Crystals can also be used during a meditation to quiet the mind or to make sure you are grounded if you find yourself drifting away. If you are new to meditation, you can choose a crystal to help you remain focused. I find black crystals good for meditation, because they help me to ground and stay focused.

A Busy Mind

If your mind is so cluttered with day-to-day problems that you find it hard to meditate, try holding a piece of sodalite in your hand while doing some yoga-breathing. For this, you need to breathe in through your nose on a slow count of four, hold your breath for another count of four, and then let the breath out slowly, making a concerted effort to relax your shoulders as you breathe out. Now do the same two more times.

Incidentally, if you suffer from palpitations, particularly when you are trying to get to sleep, this yoga-breathing method will often stop them or, at the very least, will slow them down so that you can relax and fall asleep.

As it happens, sodalite is an excellent healing stone, so if you are in any kind of pain or suffering from any ailment, a bit of yoga-breathing with a sodalite crystal in your hand will often help you to feel better.

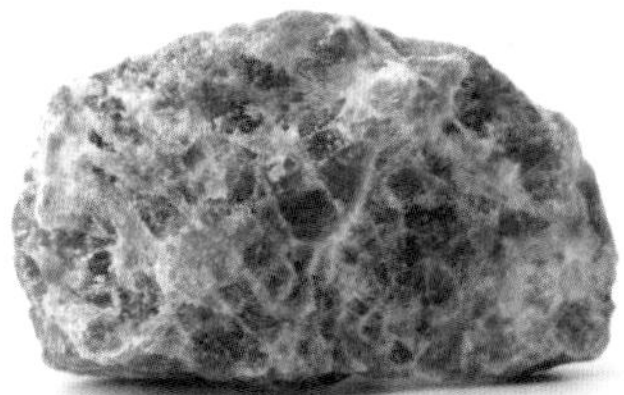

A Meditation to Enable You to Meet the Spirit of the Crystals

In this meditation, your intention is to experience the energy of the crystal, as if it were a being that you could converse with. As always, make sure your chosen crystal is cleansed and dedicated before you begin.

- You are standing at the entrance to a cave. Take a moment to examine the entrance, make sure you are grounded, and then enter the cave.
- Keep walking until you see a door. On this door is a replica of the crystal you are holding. Put your hand on this crystal and announce your intention to meet the spirit of the crystal.
- Repeat twice more so that you have set your intention three times.
- Open the door and enter.
- Keep walking until you meet the being who represents the spirit of the crystal.
- Now you may ask any question you wish—it may just be "What do I need to know today?" or you may wish to ask the spirit about the best way to work with this particular crystal.
- When you have finished, thank the spirit of the crystal and retrace your steps to the entrance of the cave.
- Take a moment to bring yourself fully back into your body before opening your eyes.

It doesn't matter if you can't see any pictures in your mind when you meditate—just have the intention in your head and you will find words or feelings coming to you. Similarly, if you cannot hear what the spirit of the crystal is trying to say, or if nothing comes to you, just relax and enjoy being in the company of your crystal. Sometimes you may need to try again another time with the same crystal in order to receive a message, and even then, you may not receive the message as words but, instead, as pictures or emotions.

At a workshop I was running, there were two people who did not visualize pictures during the meditation. One person just felt the energy of the crystal and felt a presence standing behind her. The other person saw lots of bright, swirling colors. I suggested that they might like to create their own meditation to attune themselves to their crystal and to use their unique way of perceiving the energy. If you are meditating as part of a group and comparing your experiences, please do not feel that, because you did not see or feel anything, you are not "as good" as everyone else; we are all different and experience energy in different ways. There is no "wrong" way to meditate—the aim is simply to switch off from everyday life, and this can take a lot of practice.

I strongly encourage you to write about what you experienced, because even though you may not understand all that happened at the time, the symbolism may occur to you later in the day or even at a later date.

Always make sure that you are fully grounded after meditating; if you aren't, you may feel too relaxed or spaced out and you may not be able to focus on your day properly.

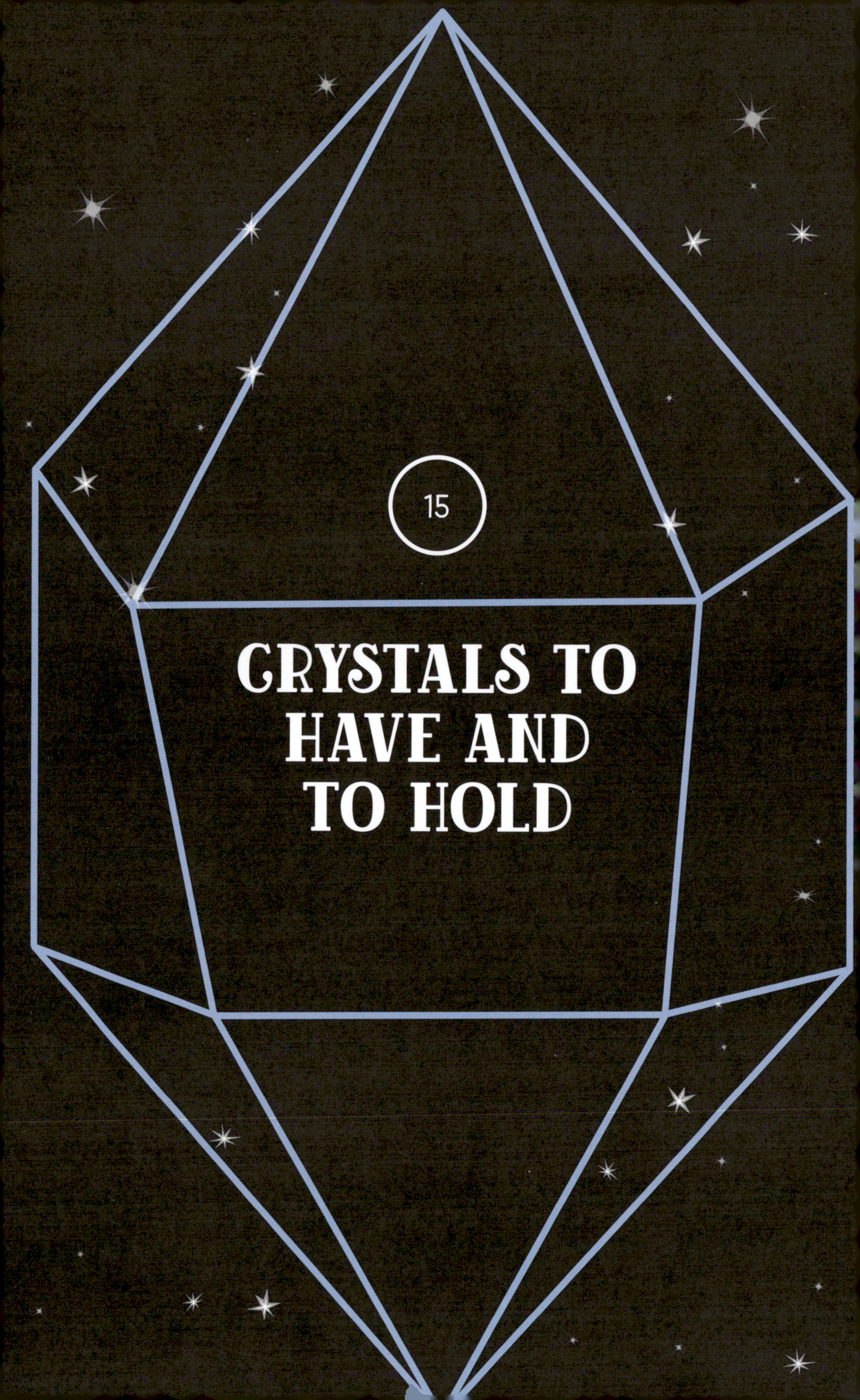

15

CRYSTALS TO HAVE AND TO HOLD

Your first step for picking crystals is to decide what those who work as healers call *intention*, which simply means deciding what you want to happen, or in this case what you need from a crystal. It is important to be extremely clear and specific about your aim, and the next step is to find a crystal possessing the appropriate attributes for your intention.

Never forget the importance of cleansing and charging your crystal, partly to rid it of previous influences and partly to give it the energy it needs. When using a crystal in this way, it is important to cleanse and re-charge it regularly, in order to obtain the maximum benefit. Carry the crystal in a pocket for the next few days, or until you achieve the benefit that you need from it.

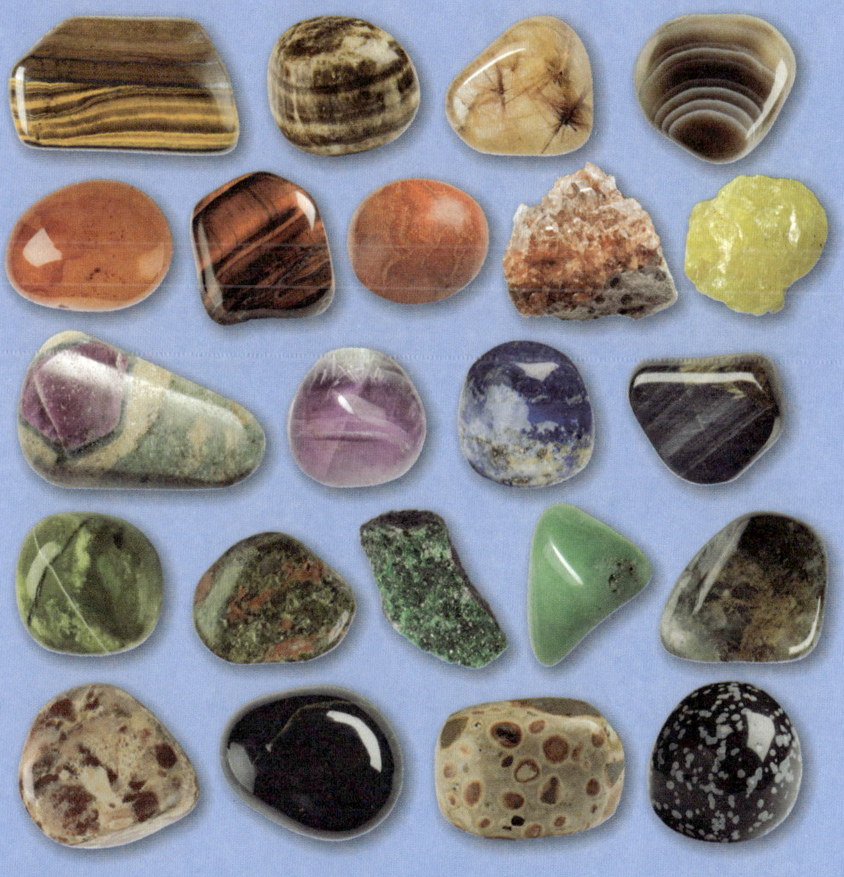

Crystal Usage

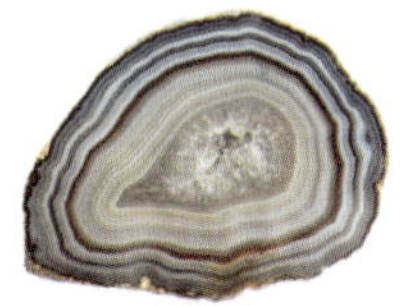

Agate, Banded

This crystal will ground and focus you, and it will remove fear.

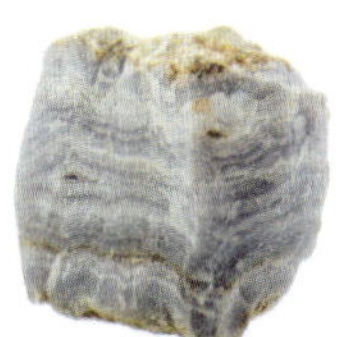

Agate, Blue Lace

When one door closes and another opens, this crystals it will help you cope. It will help you to express yourself pleasantly and clearly.

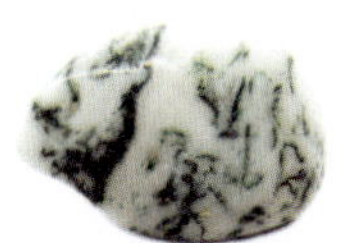

Agate, Moss

This stone help develop intuition, and it can bring peace of mind and spirit.

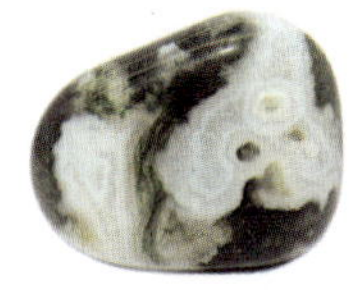

Agate, Tree

If your ego is getting the better of you, wear a little tree agate to help you gain equilibrium. This crystal helps relieve stress, makes for clear thinking, and can aid meditation. Tree agate is said to increase plant growth, so it might be worth putting a piece of it near your favorite potted plant.

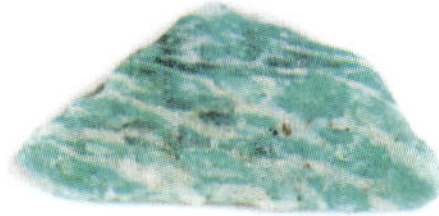

Amazonite

Amazonite helps to increase self-esteem and heal the emotions while soothing jagged nerves. It is also good for areas where there is electricity or computers or if you live near pylons or phone masts, as it helps clear geopathic stress. And it is useful when you are faced with new projects, especially those that need some money to help in getting them off the ground. This is a helpful stone when abundance and prosperity are needed.

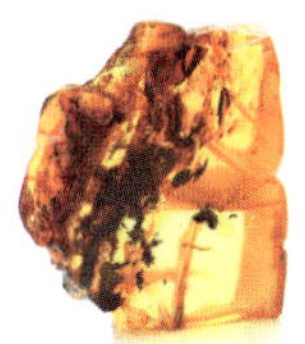

Amber

This lovely, warm stone is not a crystal because it is a very ancient tree resin. It gives energy when you need it, can ease depression, and can lift your spirits if you are unhappy. It also can help cleanse the aura or protect the home. My friend Sasha wears amber if she is ill with colds or chest infections. Interestingly, amber was widely used in medieval times by women when they went into labor!

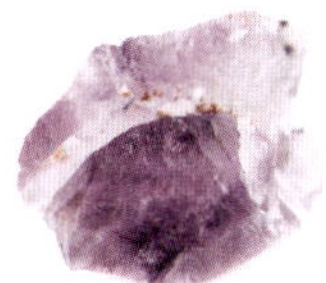

Amethyst

This is a good stone to put in an area where there is electricity or computers or if you live near pylons or phone masts, as it helps clear geopathic stress. This crystal aids intuition, is a great healer on both the practical and spiritual levels and can even be used when cleansing the aura. Holding a bit of amethyst is said to help you recover from a hangover! This crystal helps you to think straight, but it also helps those who wish to become more spiritual. It helps soothe and calm, and even deal with addictions.

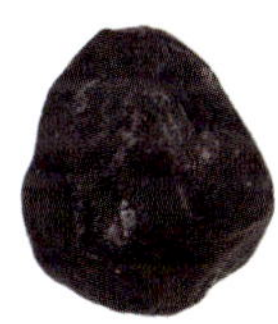

Apache Tears

This crystal is a form of obsidian. It is considered a great stone for bringing a positive view of life and bringing good luck.

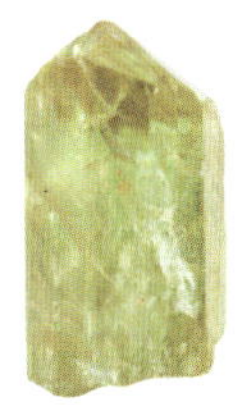

Apatite

Apatite will get you up and running and help you communicate clearly. It is also useful if you want to make new friends and contacts.

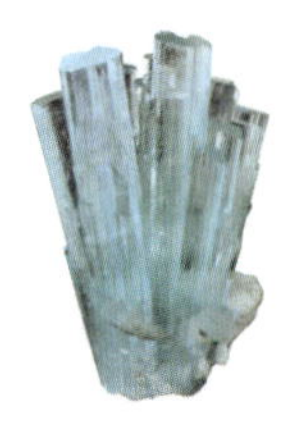

Aquamarine

This beautiful semi-precious jewel helps you get through rough times and helps you become more compassionate.

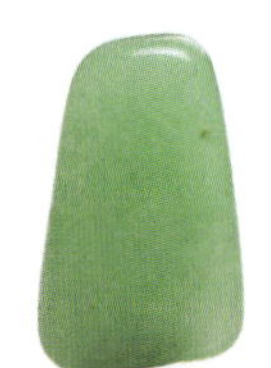

Green Aventurine

This crystal brings good fortune and increases creativity but also helps you get over emotional hurt. It is also useful for bringing prosperity and abundance.

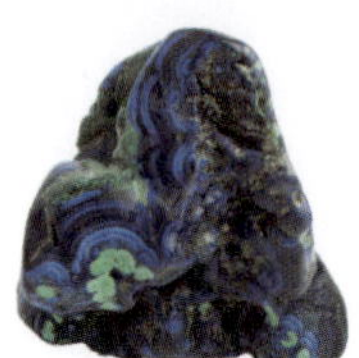

Azurite

Azurite helps you see clearly and drop silly or harmful ideas.

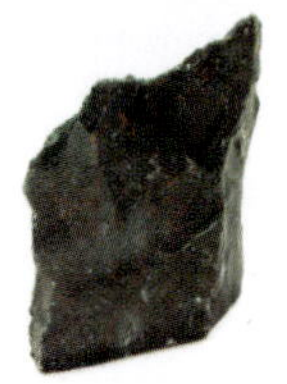

Bloodstone

This calming stone will clear your mind of fear, confusion, and obsession. It helps you to let go of the past and old hurts. It can be useful when you need perseverance.

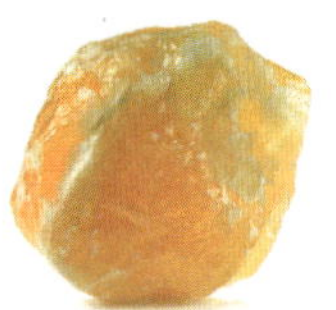

Calcite

This brings psychic protection and energy.

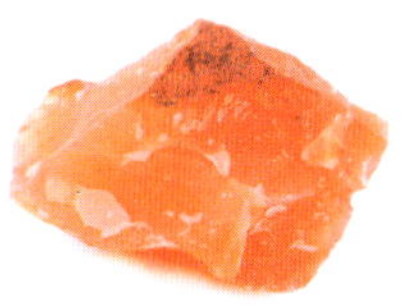

Carnelian

This crystal has many uses. It helps you make and keep money, and be successful in business ventures. Carnelian promotes friendship and improves your love life and sexuality. It helps you feel less envious of others and prevents them from being jealous of you. It inspires courage, brings clear thinking, and helps you make decisions. Carnelian is even said to aid fertility and creativity.

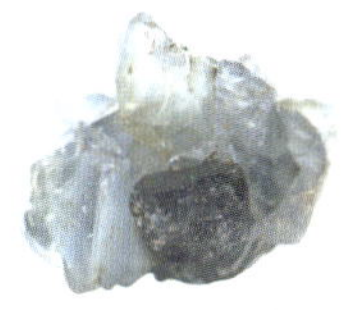

Celestite

This crystal is an aid to communicating and bringing peace.

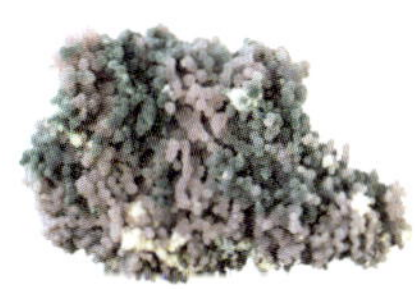

Chalcedony

Chalcedony helps you feel better and makes you a little happier.

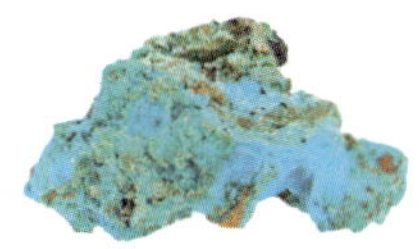

Chrysocolla

This is a good stone for emotional matters, and it brings confidence. It can ease tension and anxiety. This crystal also banishes bitterness, resentment, and anger against those who are unkind to you.

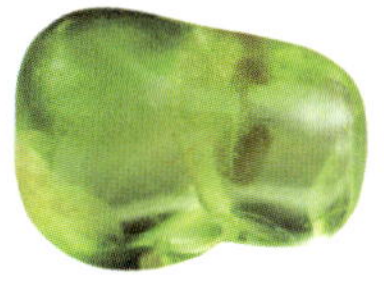

Chrysolite

Chrysolite can help you to come to terms with the past.

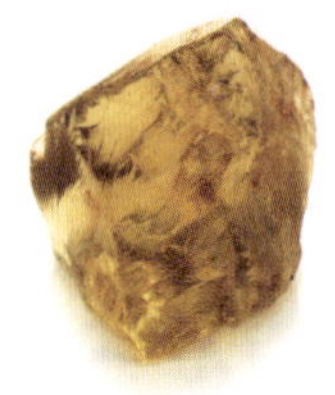

Citrine

This crystal can help you make money when you need it, and it can be useful in tricky negotiations or in business generally. If you are struggling to get something off the ground, wearing a piece of citrine can help. Citrine also gives confidence and power when you need it. It can bring inspiration, and it is said to help dispel fatigue.

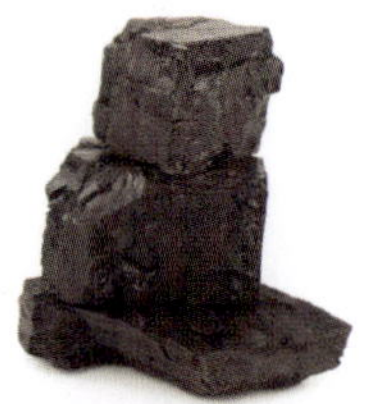

Coal

Coal is an organic substance, not a crystal, but it is said to bring courage when it is needed. It also has protective qualities, so it can be useful to keep a little in your bag when traveling.

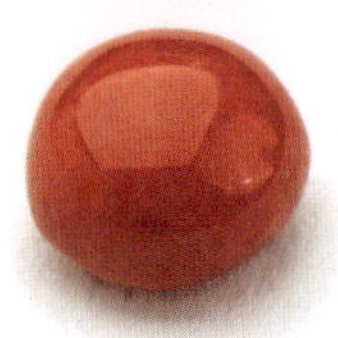

Coral

An organic substance from the sea, this beautiful stone brings love and friendship.

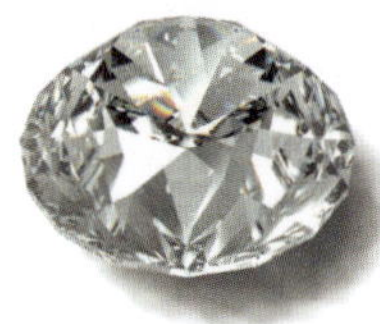

Diamond

This stone relates to the upper chakras, so it is said to help you connect to the universe and to the spiritual world. It also helps you clarify your thoughts.

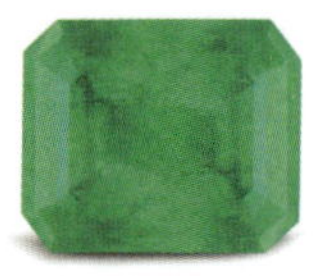

Emerald

This stone links with the heart chakra, so it relates to unconditional love, but it also heals mental and physical problems.

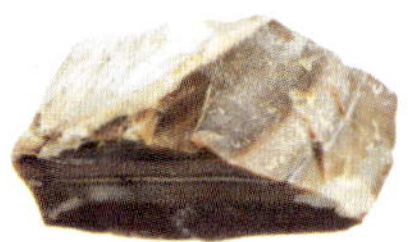

Flint

You will find this very common stone on beaches and riversides all over the world. It represents toughness, so keep a bit of flint in your bag or your car when involved in difficult work situations. It also offers grounding and practicality, so use it whenever you feel that you need common sense or bringing back down to earth after doing spiritual work.

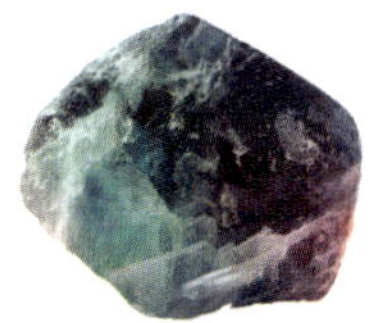

Fluorite

Fluorite combats fear, worry, and anxiety, and it helps your mind to be more logical and sensible. This is said to be an aid to psychic powers, especially that of clairaudience, which is the ability to hear the words of a spiritual guide or those who have passed over.

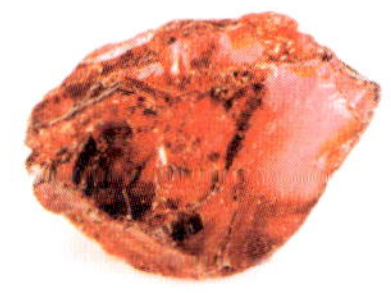

Garnet

This precious gem is also called a *carbuncle* when cut as a cabochon rather than with facets. It helps when you are downhearted, and it helps you to be patient and to finish what you start.

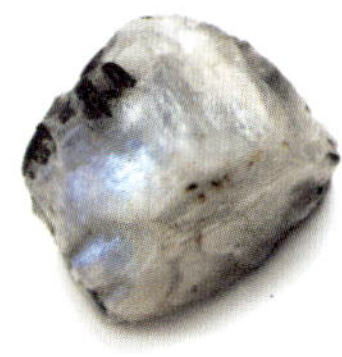

Halite

Halite is helpful when you need to declutter your home or your life. It also helps release unwanted emotional ties.

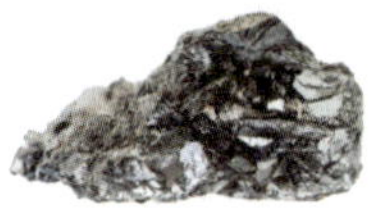

Hematite

This slightly magnetic rock can be used for healing in the same way that magnet therapy can. You can even put it under your pet's bed if the animal is unwell. It is said to aid psychic development and promote self-esteem where it is needed. This can help you to clear away unwanted karmic ties and events from the past.

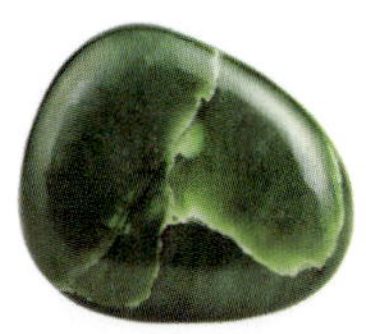

Jade

This stone brings peace to the home, and it is useful for healing the mind and the spirit. It is said to bring luck, long life, and friendship.

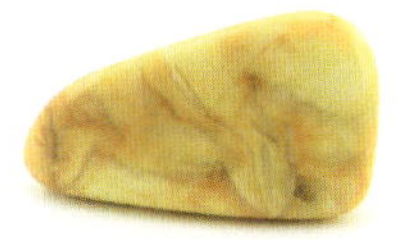

Jasper

This is a good grounding stone. Put it near your feet if you feel spacey or stressed out. It brings peace and helps you get through hard times.

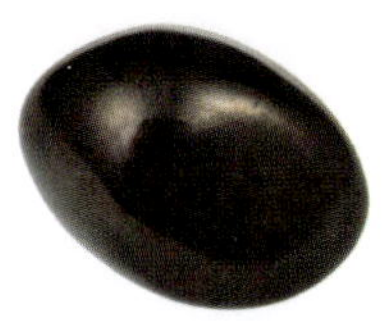

Jet

This is a protective stone that tradition says helps to keep evil spirits at bay. Today it is used to give courage when you are going through tough times.

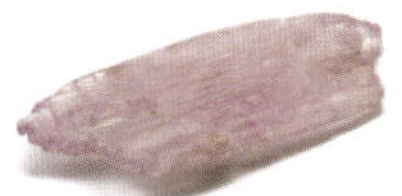

Kunzite

Kunzite helps to relieve emotional stress and settle the emotions. It might be useful to those who are looking for love.

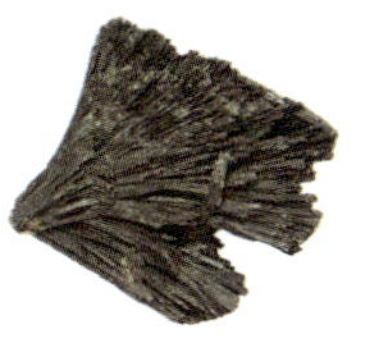

Black Kyanite

This is a useful stone to hold when doing a chakra-clearing meditation as it's very good at cutting away what you no longer need.

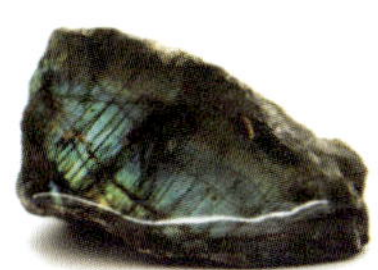

Labradorite

It is said that labradorite helps develop psychic powers. It also enables you to erect psychic boundaries when you need them, and it can help at times of change.

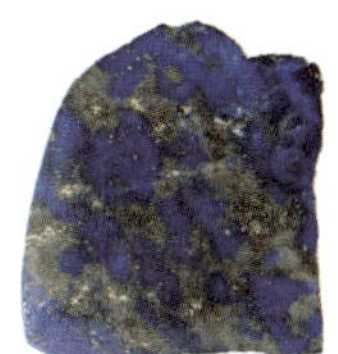

Lapis Lazuli

This beautiful crystal is said to help develop the sixth sense. It stimulates the intuition and psychic gifts. It is also said to be inspirational and at the same time healing. It is a great aid to clear communication. This stone can help clear past karma, and it can help you find the truth in a situation.

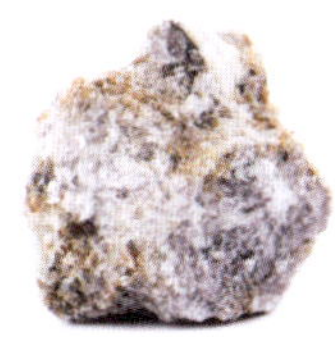

Lepidolite

This can help rid you of negativity and anxiety.

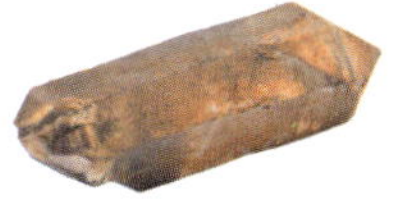

Lithium Quartz

A calming stone, lithium quartz can help you become less stressed.

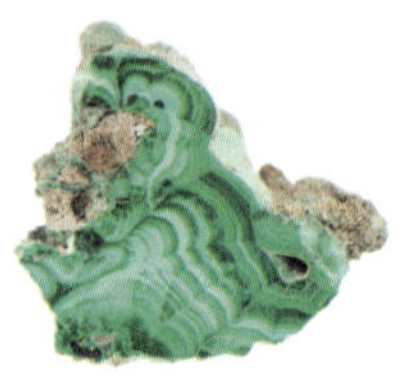

Malachite

This healing stone helps with mental and psychic problems. It can help you recover from anger and unhappiness and helps to mend a broken heart.

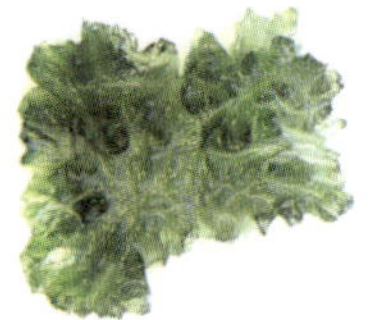

Moldavite

Moldovite is good at times of change and new beginnings.

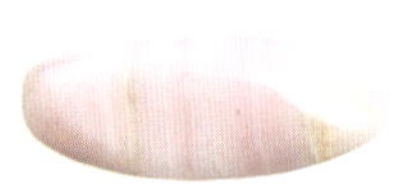

Mangano Calcite

This stone helps with heartache.

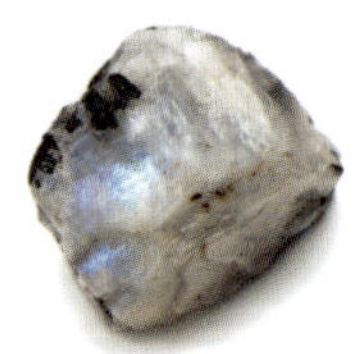

Moonstone

Moonstone is said to aid fertility. It is also said to bring harmony and emotional balance in difficult situations.

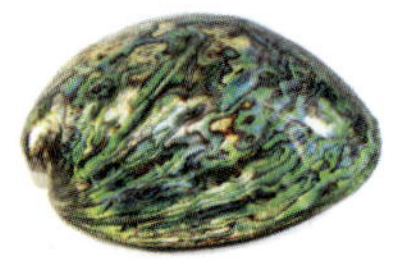

Mother-of-Pearl

This isn't a crystal—it's a shell—but it is said to be useful in matters of love.

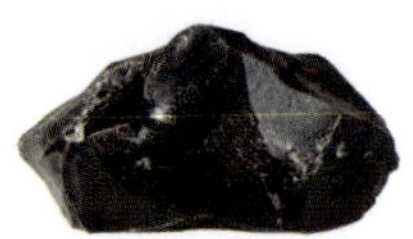

Obsidian

This is a very useful stone as it gives protection in difficult circumstances and can even help you face down bullies. It is also useful if you want to develop your psychic gifts.

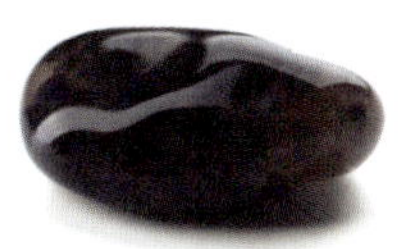

Onyx

Like obsidian, onyx gives protection in awkward circumstances and creates a protective psychic shield around the wearer. It helps you to recover from grief and bereavement. This is also a useful stone to wear if you are away from home, as it has protective qualities. It is said to bring happiness in love and marriage.

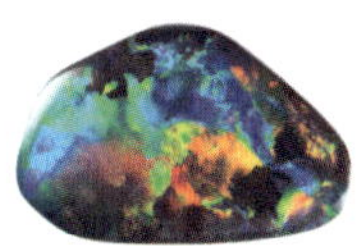

Opal

This stone helps you see the other person's point of view, and it can balance emotions that are overwrought.

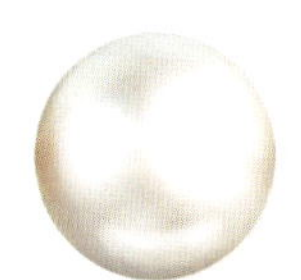

Pearl

The pearl isn't a crystal—it's an organic substance from the inside of an oyster—but it is a lovely piece of jewelry that talks of love. It is said to bring self-esteem and self-confidence.

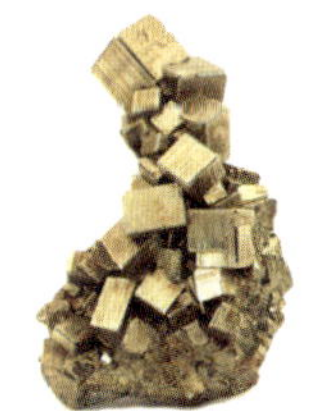

Iron Pyrite

Iron pyrite is said to allow you to tap into and understand new ideas. It can also bring success in business.

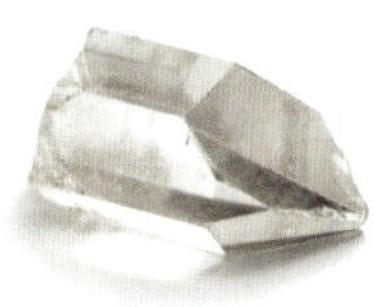

Quartz, Clear

Clear quartz can be used in place of any other crystal, especially for meditation and crystal grids. It is said to boost the immune system and it is a good aid to meditation and channeling. It is often used as a magic wand, yet is also calming and peaceful.

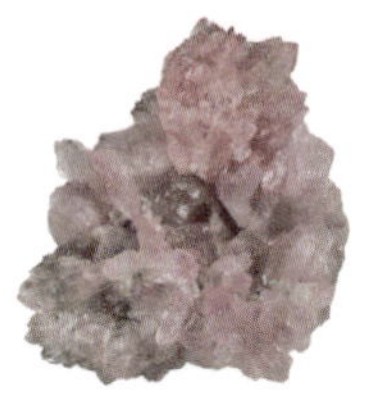

Quartz, Rose

Everyone loves this beautiful stone that is so involved with the idea of love and happy relationships. It attracts love, brings comfort, and relieves grief, while bringing friendship and harmony. Rose quartz can be soothing, but also energizing, in matters of love.

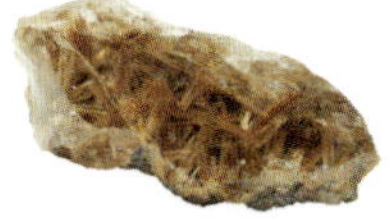

Quartz, Rutilated

Rutilated quartz brings self-confidence and helps clear the chakras or other blockages.

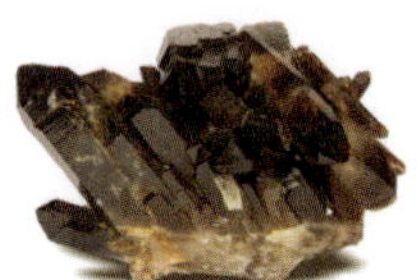

Quartz, Smoky

This stone has many uses, including healing, de-stressing, and ridding oneself of negative emotions. It can protect you and your home from geopathic stress, so it is a good one to keep near your computer or other electrical equipment. It is said to help if you want to become telepathic. And it helps when you need courage, especially when recovering from trauma and loss.

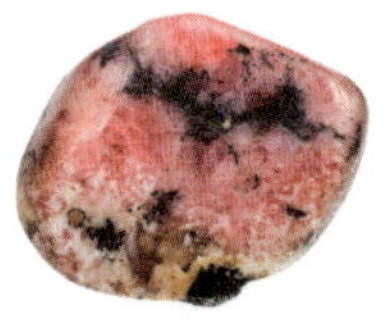

Rhodonite

Rhodonite encourages the growth of confidence.

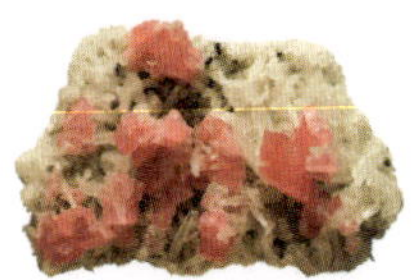

Rhodochrosite

Rhodochrosite helps mend a broken heart, and it helps you to listen to good advice.

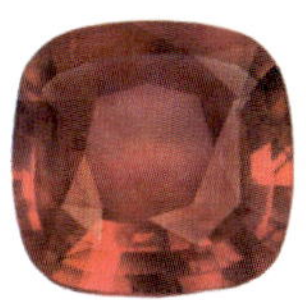

Ruby

Ruby is a powerful gem that helps you to survive financially. It is also associated with passion.

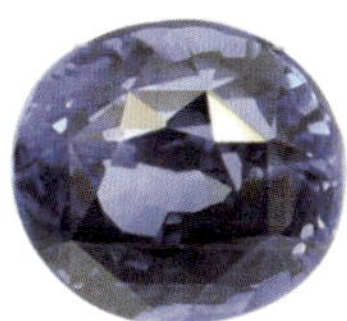

Sapphire

This gem helps you think straight and enhances intuition. It is said to bring luck.

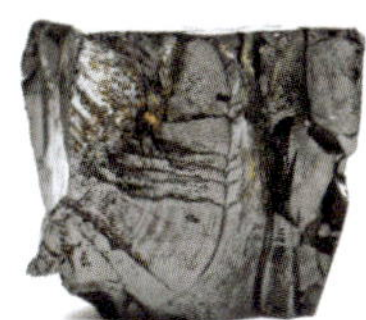

Shungite

This stone comes from Russia and is really rather special. It is great for combating geopathic stress, which can be electricity from computers, electrical power lines, phone masts, or just too many electronic gadgets in the home or in your surroundings. I keep one on the desk with my computer, and it does save me from getting headachy after too much time spent at work. It is also a stone of protection, so if you feel like you're under attack or if you have to deal with difficult people, keep a piece of this in your pocket. If you need help with changeable circumstances so that you can make a fresh start, this is the crystal for you.

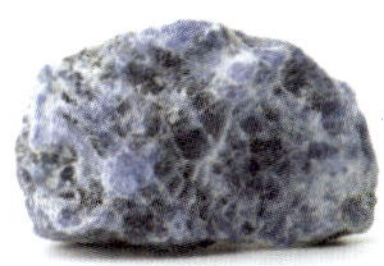

Sodalite

This great healing stone is also useful for healing on an emotional and mental level. It aids thinking processes and promotes sleep, as it helps you to become less stressed out.

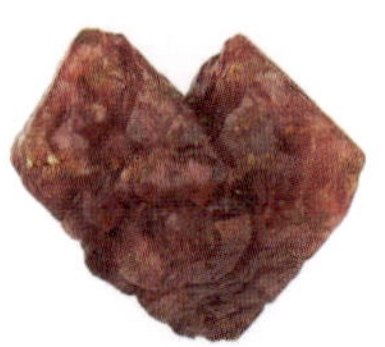

Spinel

If someone attacks you on an emotional level, wear or carry this stone to protect you from feeling hurt.

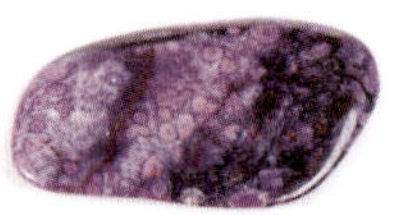

Sugilite

This is a calming stone that also helps you to obtain spiritual insight. It is helpful when you need to respect and love yourself.

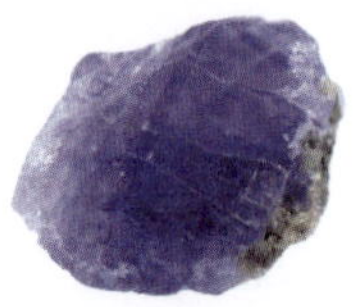

Tanzanite

This beautiful gem helps you to move on in times of change. It also helps to heal heartbreak.

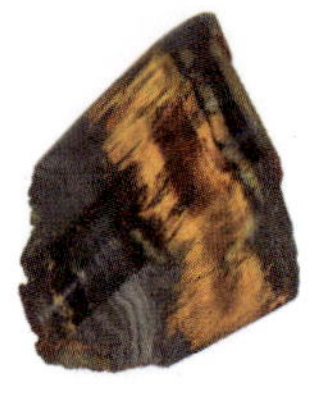

Tiger's Eye

This lovely stone is protective, but it also helps when you need inner strength and confidence, patience, and persistence. It is said to be useful for those who are looking into past lives or investigating metaphysical subjects. Tiger's eye is said to promote creativity.

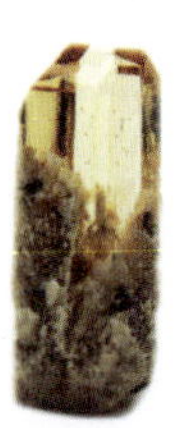

Topaz

The beautiful topaz encourages psychic development and clairvoyance. It can be useful for creative people and those who work in some field of art. It is said to help you pass messages by telepathy.

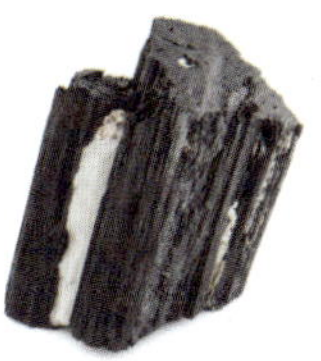

Tourmaline, Black

This protective stone is useful around the house in times of troubles, as it repels all negative energies and protects you from destructive forces. It is a useful stone to keep by you when bullies are around.

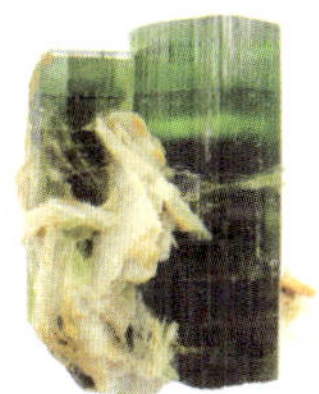

Tourmaline, Green

If you are short of money, green tourmaline may help you to earn or obtain what you need; it is also useful when you are involved in a creative venture.

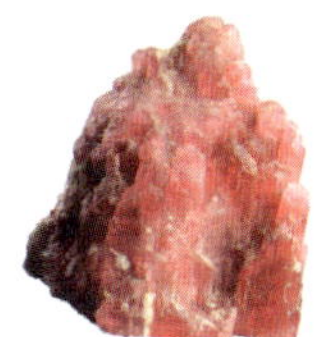

Tourmaline, Pink

This stone is associated with femininity, and it is said to help the sexual organs. It helps macho men to see things from a woman's point of view.

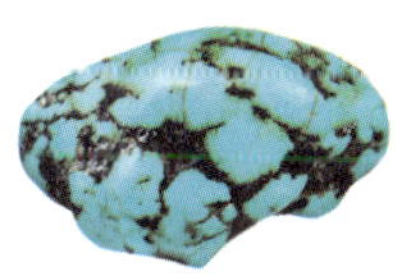

Turquoise

This calming and healing stone is great to wear when you are stressed out or overemotional. It is said to bring luck, love, and money, so it is a wonderful all-around stone.

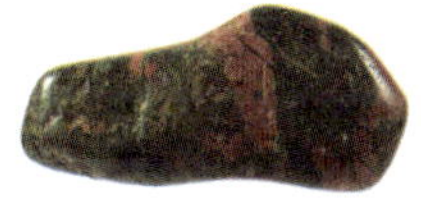

Unakite

If you are in emotional or spiritual pain, unakite will help. It will also help you to see your real needs and inner or higher consciousness.

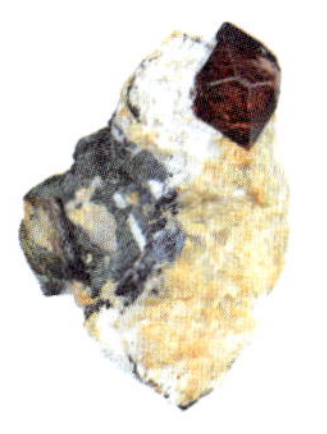

Zircon

Zircon helps you to develop your psychic powers, and it encourages creativity and original thinking. (It is the red crystal in the rock shown here.)

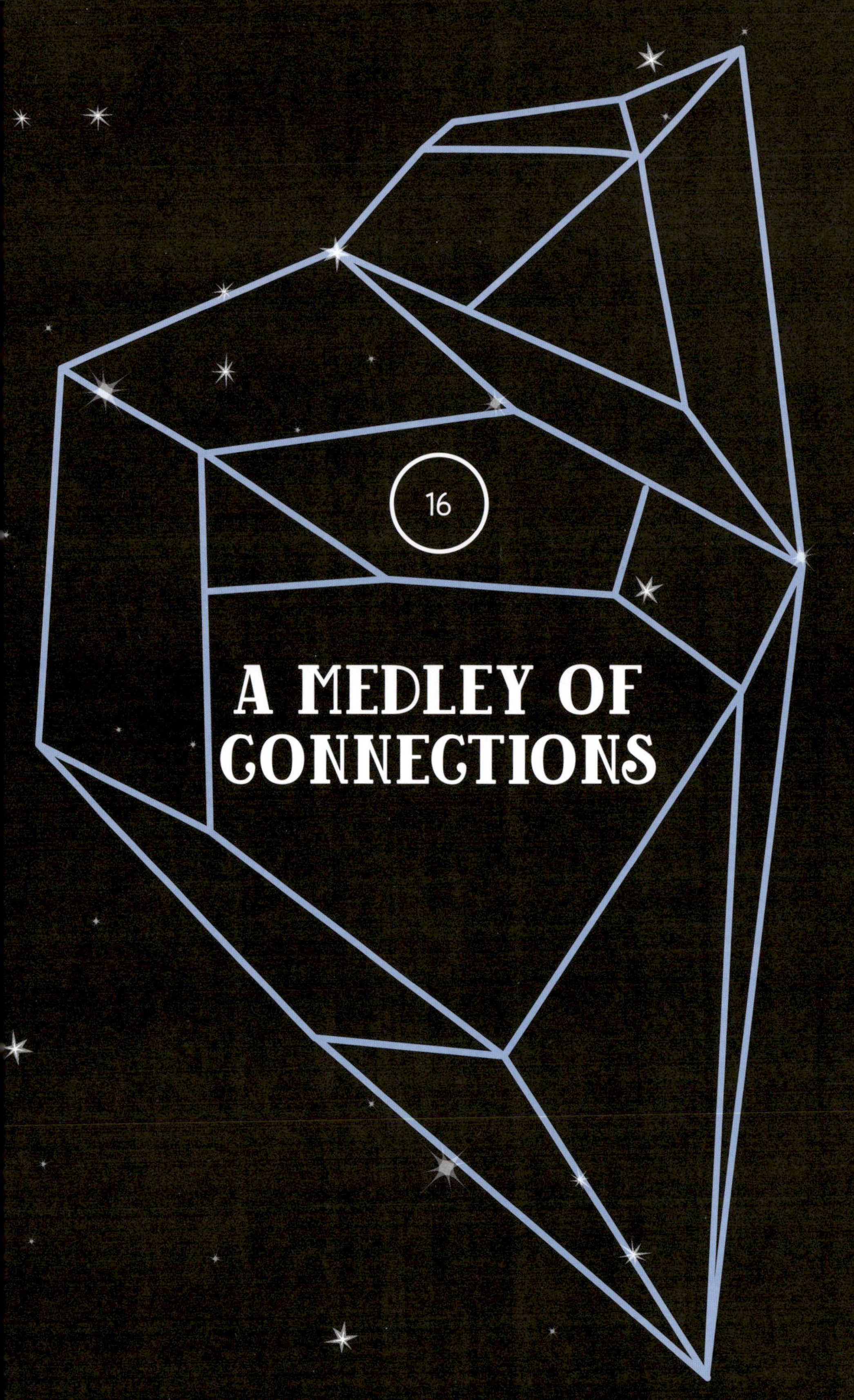

16

A MEDLEY OF CONNECTIONS

This light-hearted chapter shows links between divination systems, planets, colors, and crystals.

The Astrological Alignments for the Chakras

Before the invention of telescopes, the ancient world knew of the Sun, Moon, Mercury, Venus, Jupiter, and Saturn. These are linked to the chakras and crystals in the following way:

The Base, or Root, Chakra

Linked with Scorpio and Mars,so try jasper, garnet, or ruby.

The Sacral Chakra

Associated with Cancer and the Moon, so select carnelian or amber. Also select pyrites, pearl, and mother-of-pearl.

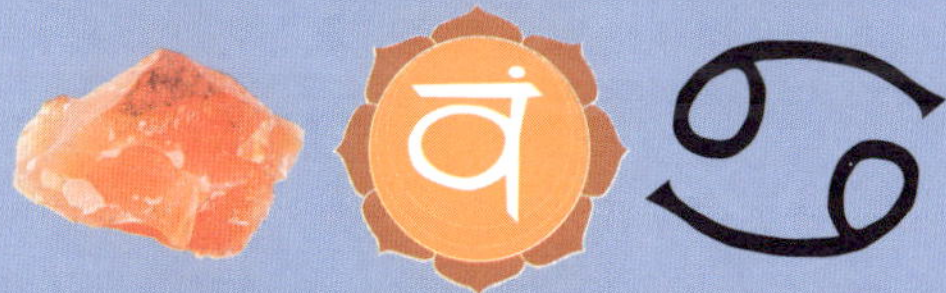

The Solar Plexus Chakra

Connected to Leo and the Sun, so use tiger's eye or citrine.

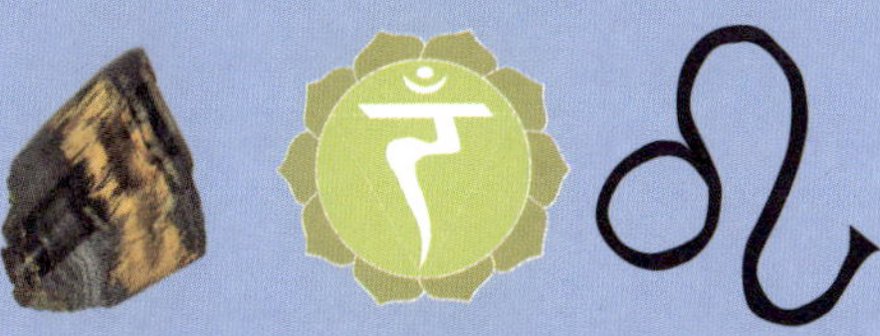

The Heart Chakra

Linked with Libra and Venus, so choose rose quartz, emerald, or jade.

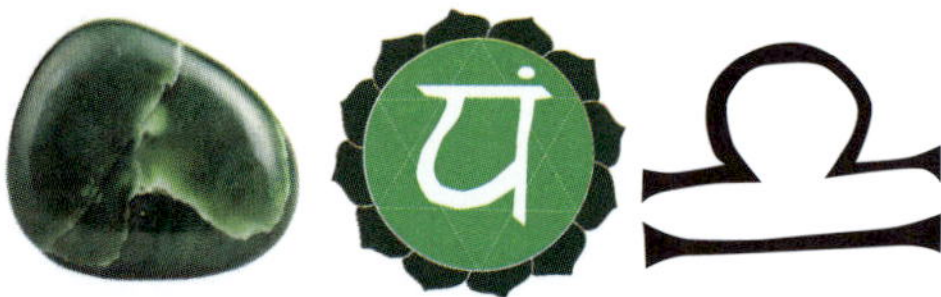

The Throat Chakra

Linked with Virgo and Mercury, so opt for aquamarine, turquoise, or blue lace agate. Oddly enough, Mercury can also link with tiger's eye or citrine.

The Brow, or Third Eye, Chakra

Associated with Pisces and Jupiter, so use lapis lazuli or sodalite. Also, blue-green agate would do, along with aquamarine and turquoise.

The Crown Chakra

Connected to Capricorn and Saturn, so try amethyst, moonstone, or clear quartz, but you could also choose Saturnine crystals, such as obsidian, flint, or black tourmaline.

Birthstones

There are many traditions and lists for birthstones. Here is one that you might find useful.

January: Garnet	February: Amethyst	March: Aquamarine
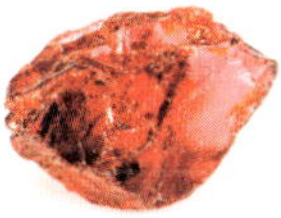	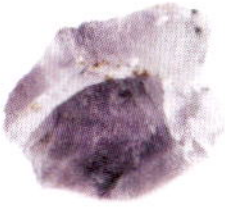	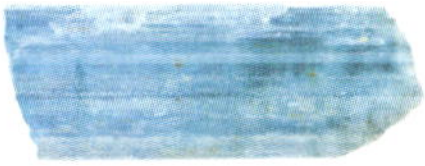
April: Diamond	May: Emerald	June: Citrine
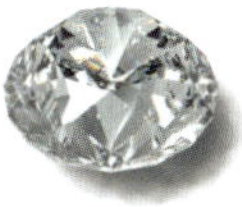	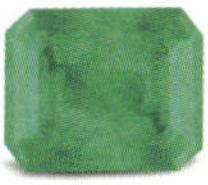	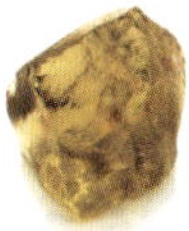
July: Pearl	August: Onyx	September: Rose quartz
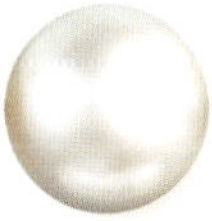	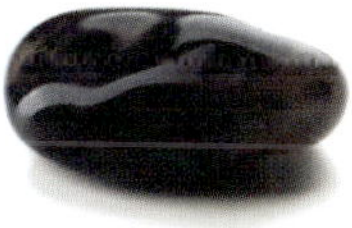	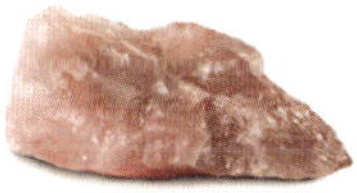
October: Carnelian	November: Obsidian	December: Tiger's eye
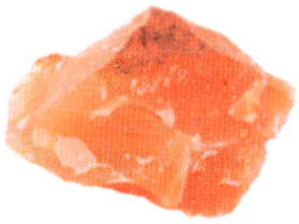	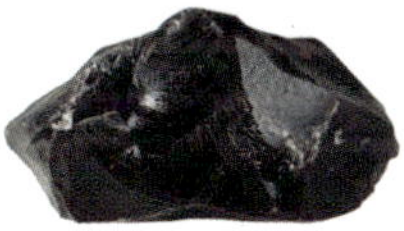	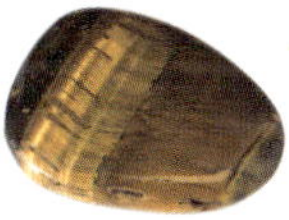

The Zodiac Colors

These are the colors for the zodiac, so it is only a matter of selecting crystals from your collection to fit the signs. Remember that clear quartz will do for any that you don't have.

Sign	Colors
♈ Aries	Red
♉ Taurus	Pink or green
♊ Gemini	Yellow, or black and white variegated
♋ Cancer	Pearly white or silver
♌ Leo	Gold or orange
♍ Virgo	Mulberry or soft beige
♎ Libra	Green or pink
♏ Scorpio	Dark red or purple
♐ Sagittarius	Royal blue
♑ Capricorn	Gray, brown, or black
♒ Aquarius	Glowing blue/green colors or aquamarine
♓ Pisces	Sea green or blue

Chinese Astrology

The Chinese take directions very seriously, and each is linked to a color, so selecting a crystal for the direction is an easy thing to do. If, for instance, you are traveling northward for some important purpose, you could take a crystal with you for protection or for luck. The center is always important in Chinese mythology, as it refers to the emperor's palace, the seat of ancient power, and China itself.

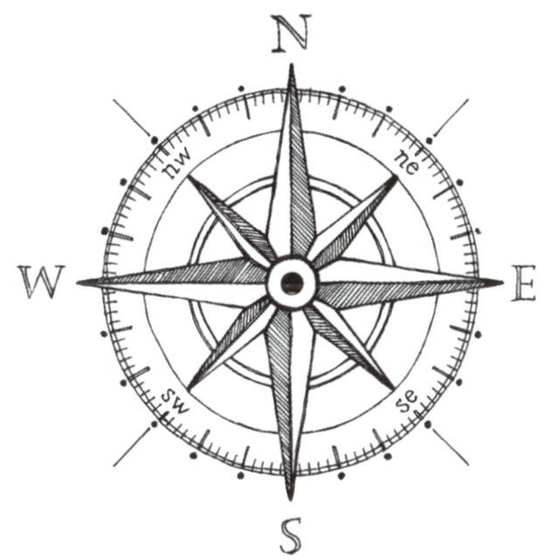

North
Symbol: The turtle
Color: Blue or black
Crystal: Onyx

West	Center	East
Symbol: The tiger	Symbol: The emperor	Symbol: The dragon
Color: White	Color: Yellow	Color: Green
Crystal: Pearl	Crystal: Yellow diamond	Crystal: Emerald

South
Symbol: The phoenix
Color: Red
Crystal: Ruby

Numerology

You might like to wear a crystal that connects to your Life Path Number. This is found by adding together the digits in your date of birth.

Example: October 21, 1992
Add up the digits: 10 + 21 + 1992
Or: 1 + 0 + 2 + 1 + 1 + 9 + 9 + 2 = 25
Now add the 2 and the 5 to make a single-digit number: 2 + 5 = 7
Therefore, the person's Life Path Number is 7.

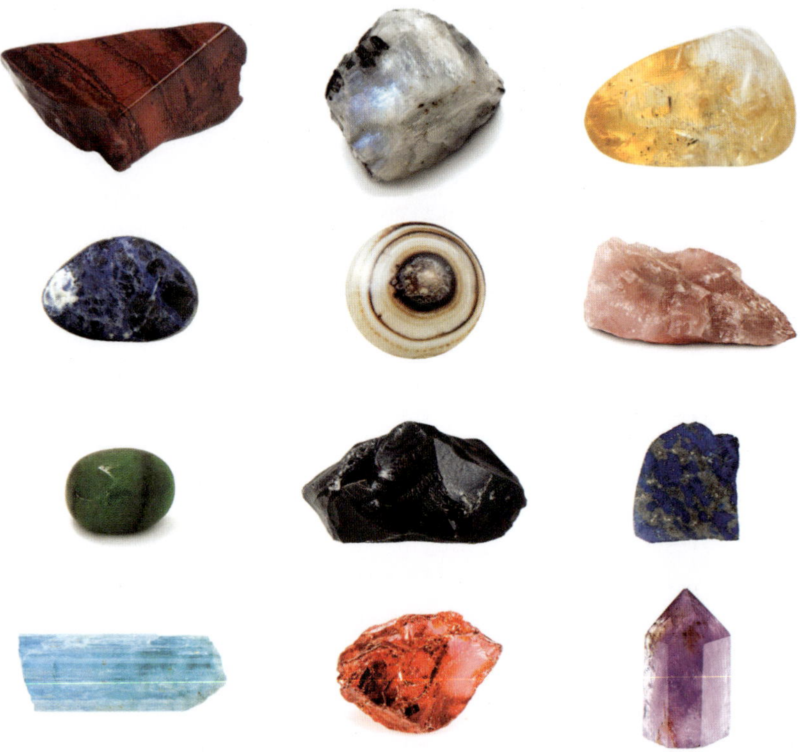

Number, Color, and Crystal Correspondences

Any crystals of a color that matches the number will do, so the ones I've listed here are just my own suggestions.

One
Planet: Mars
Color: Red
Crystal: Jasper

Two
Planet: Moon
Color: White
Crystal: Moonstone

Three
Planet: Sun
Color: Yellow
Crystal: Citrine

Four
Planet: Earth
Color: Blue
Crystal: Sodalite

Five
Planet: Mercury
Color: Brown
Crystal: Agate

Six
Planet: Venus
Color: Pink
Crystal: Rose quartz

Seven
Planet: Neptune
Color: Sea green
Crystal: Green agate

Eight
Planet: Saturn
Color: Black
Crystal: Obsidian

Nine
Planet: Jupiter
Color: Blue
Crystal: Lapis lazuli

Eleven
Planet: Uranus
Color: Blue/green
Crystal: Aquamarine

Twenty-Two
Planet: Pluto
Color: Dark red
Crystal: Garnet

Thirty-Three
Planet: Chiron
Color: Purple
Crystal: Amethyst

❋ ❋ ❋

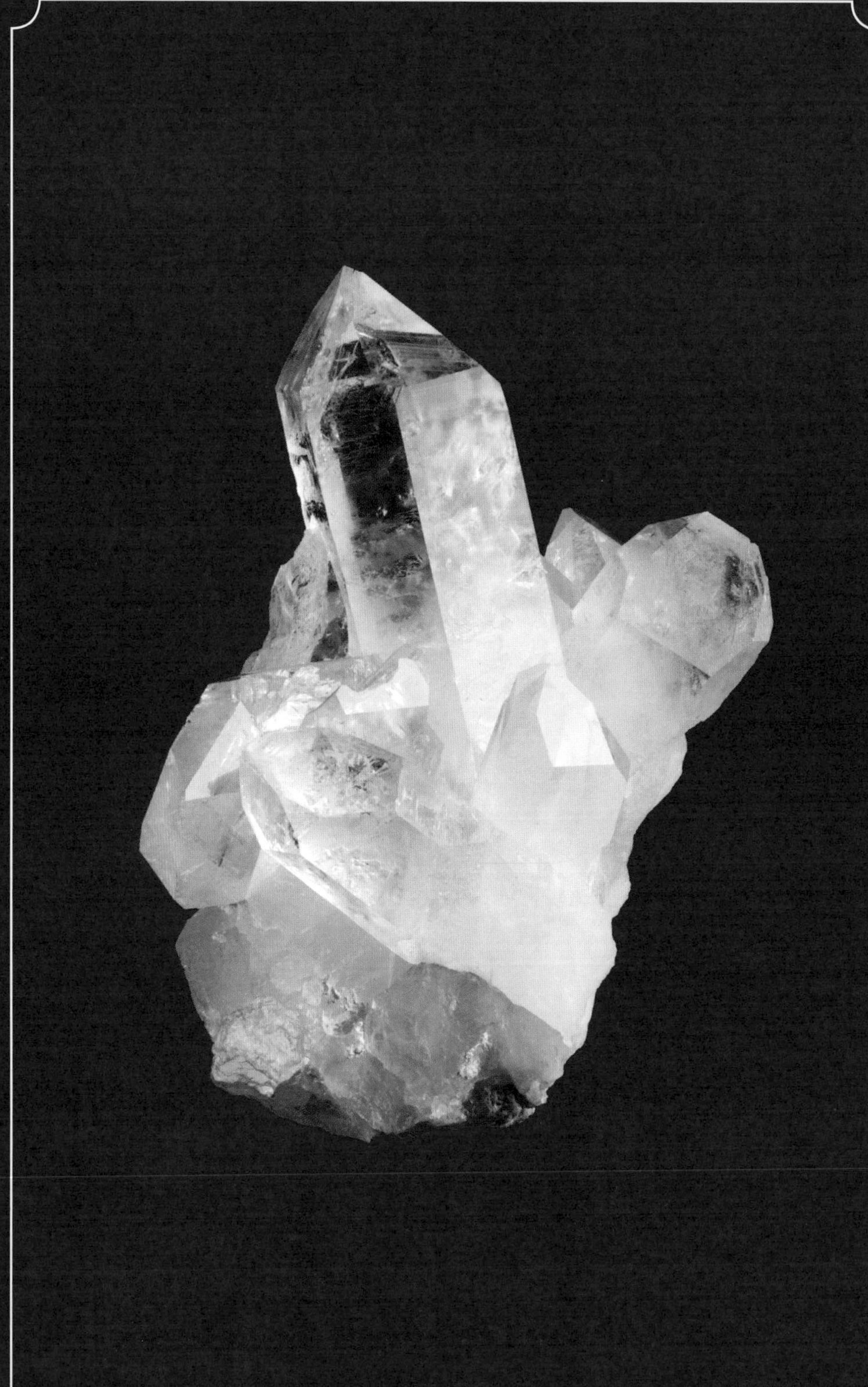

CONCLUSION

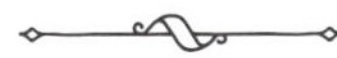

Crystals are beautiful, fascinating, and full of positive energy, and we all love them, whether for healing and other kinds of help, or just for their physical qualities. So, I hope you find my book enjoyable and useful in your quest for life, love, spirituality, and joy. With all my very best wishes to you and your loved ones,

Bernice Cockram

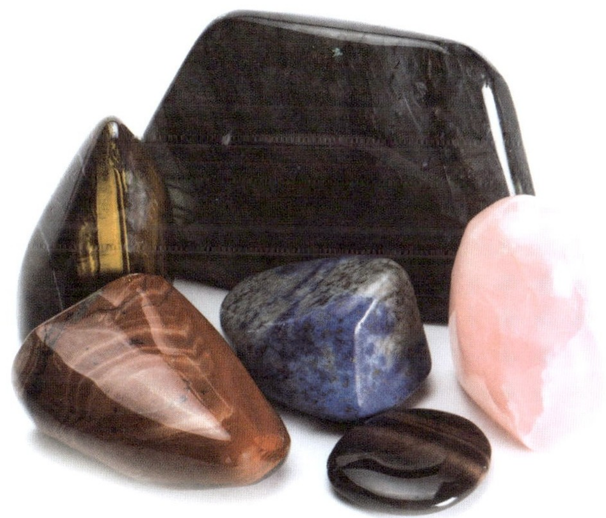

ABOUT THE AUTHOR

Bernice grew up on a farm in rural Devon, UK. Even though she now lives in a city, she spends a lot of time in the countryside, visiting Dartmoor and walking around local woods. There are also many beaches in the area that she likes to visit.

She worked for many years as a secretary, before giving up work to raise her son. Just a few years later, her life started moving in a different direction when she discovered crystal healing and self-development.

Nowadays, Bernice likes to keep herself busy. As well as being a crystal therapist and having two part-time jobs, she enjoys volunteering at the Devon Family History Society, researching her family tree, and helping other people research their own ancestors. Her hobbies include learning to play the harp, walking, cycling, learning British Sign Language, and, of course, collecting crystals—a hobby she shares with her teenage son.

INDEX

IMAGE CREDITS

Right (rt), Left (l), Top (t), Bottom (b), Center (c), Row (r),

Cover: crystals © Vasilius/Shutterstock.com; grid © Lina003/Shutterstock.com; stars © intueri/Shutterstock.com; frame © painterr/Shutterstock.com; background texture © Andrius_Saz/Shutterstock.com.

All interior Illustrations by Terry Marks, except:
crescent moons and stars on 1, 3 © Lion's mane/Shutterstock.com; mandalas on 1, 3 © Bildagentur Zoonar GmbH/Shutterstock.com; quarter moons and stars on 1, 3 © intueri/Shutterstock.com; 11 © Olga Batseva/Shutterstock.com; 13 © Brett Hondow/Shutterstock.com; body on 14, 81, 109 © Martial Red/Shutterstock.com; 15 (b) ©Kaia-Liisa/Shutterstock.com; 15 (t) © Green angel/Shutterstock.com; 17, 43 (r2), 132 (r5) © Bjoern Wylezich/Shutterstock.com; 19 © Iryna_Khomenko/Shutterstock.com; 21 © MaryValery/Shutterstock.com; 22 (b) © SHIK_SHIK/Shutterstock.com; 23 (b), 51 (r4), 76, 117 (r3), 122 (r2c) © Tamara Kulikova/Shutterstock.com; 24, 34, 84 (b), 95 (r2), 137 (r5), 141 (r3), 25 (t), 43 (r4) © bjphotographs/Shutterstock.com; 25 (b) © aninata/Shutterstock.com; 30, 31, 35, 40 (r2), 40 (r3), 42 (r3), 43 (r3), 46 (r1), 47 (r4), 49 (r3), 50 (r2), 51 (r1), 68 (b), 69 (b), 71 (bl), 74 (c), 74 (b), 77 (c), 92 (rose quartz), 93 (r2), 108 (t), 116 (r6), 117 (r1), 117 (r6), 118 (r6), 122 (r1l), 122 (r2c), 131 (r4), 133 (r4), 133 (r5), 135 (r2), 136 (r2), 136 (r1), 136 (r4), 138 (r6), 138 (r3), 140 (r4), 143 (r4), 146 (r2), 146 (r1), 147 (r4c), 147 (r1rt), 150 (r3c), 150 (r1rt), 150 (r2c), 150 (r4l) © vvoe/Shutterstock.com; 32 © Peryn 22/Shutterstock.com; 33 (b) © Alex DeG/Shutterstock.com; 33 © Rachel Hoyt/Shutterstock.com; 39 © Anna Soelberg/Shutterstock.com; 40 (r1) © ArtOfPhotos/Shutterstock.com; 40 (r4), 46 (r4), 52 (r3), 85 (b), 92 (clear quartz), 94 (r3), 95 (r1), 116 (r3), 122 (r1rt), 130 (r2), 131 (r3), 132 (r4), 136 (r5), 137 (r1), 137 (r2) © Roy Palmer/Shutterstock.com; 41 (r1), 77 (t), 116 (r1), 140 (r3) © Pancrazio De Vita/Shutterstock.com; 41 (r2) © carlosvelayos/Shutterstock.com; 41 (r3), 44 (r3), 52 (r2), 118 (r7), 138 (r2) © Jiri Vaclavek/Shutterstock.com; 42 (r1), 68 (c), 108 (c), 122 (r3c), 132 (r3), 145 (r1), 150 (r1l) © aregfly/Shutterstock.com; 44 (r3), 70 (c), 116 (r5), 116 (r2), 134 (r1), 134 (r2), 135 (r5), 138 (r4), 139 (r5), 147 (r2rt), 150 (r1c) © J. Palys/Shutterstock.com; 44 (r4), 117 (r2), 122 (r2l), 142 (r3), 145 (r2) © olpo/Shutterstock.com; 42 (r2) © Pisut Phaetrangsee/Shutterstock.com; 42 (r4) © Henri Koskinen/Shutterstock.com; 44 (r1), 118 (r1), 131 (r1) © ntv/Shutterstock.com; 44 (r2), 134 (r4), 136 (r3) © Alexandar Iotzov/Shutterstock.com; 45 (r2), 135 (r1), 147 (r2c) © Sergio33/Shutterstock.com; 45 (r4), 138 (r1) © Epitavi/Shutterstock.com; 46 (r2), 133 (r2) © yul38885/Shutterstock.com; 46 (r3), 85 (t) © wiiz/Shutterstock.com; 47 (r1), 73 (c), 118 (r4), 125, 141 (r4) © optimarc/Shutterstock.com; 47 (r2) © Bramthestocker/

Shutterstock.com; 47 (r3), 73 (b), 122 (r1c), 137 (r3), 146 (r3), 150 (r3rt), © Ademoeller/ Shutterstock.com; 48 (r2), 53 (r1), 53 (r2), 142 (r3) © PNSJ88/Shutterstock.com; 48 (r3) © Linnas/Shutterstock.com; 49 (r2), 49 (r4), 50 (r1), 50 (r4) © Albert Russ/ Shutterstock.com; 49 (r4), 140 (r5) © MarcelClemens/Shutterstock.com; 51 (r2) © Yellow Cat/Shutterstock.com; 51 (r4), 118 (r5) © Aleksandr Pobedimskiy/Shutterstock.com; 52 (r1), 108 (b), 117 (r4), 135 (r3) © La corneja artesana/Shutterstock.com; 53 (r3) © Nika Lerman/Shutterstock.com; 53 (r4) ©Kagai19927/Shutterstock.com; 61 © Elchin Jafarli/Shutterstock.com; 67 © JuliRose/Shutterstock.com; 69 (c), 118 (r2), 118 (r3), 122 (r3rt), 130 (r5), 131 (r2), 133 (r1), 137 (r4), 142 (r2), 145 (r2), 146 (r4), 147 (r4l), 147 (r1c), 41 (r4), 43 (r1), 48 (r1), 48 (r4) © Coldmoon Photoproject/ Shutterstock.com; 71 (c), 116 (r4), 132 (r2), 45 (r1) © Anastasia Bulanova/Shutterstock.com; 71 (br), 72 (br), 94 (r1), 94 (r2), 117 (r5), 122 (r3l), 132 (r1), 133 (r3), 140 (r1), 143 (r6), 45 (r3), 77 (b) © Ozef/Shutterstock.com; 84 (t) © Cagla Acikgoz/Shutterstock.com; 86, 152 © Peter Hermes Furian/Shutterstock.com; 87, 27 © Svesla Tasla/ Shutterstock.com; 88 © SkillUp/Shutterstock.com; 89 © Lina003/Shutterstock.com; 93 (r1) © Moha El-Jaw/Shutterstock.com; 93 (r3), 130 (r1), 139 (r4) © Dafinchi/ Shutterstock.com; 99 © Miiisha/Shutterstock.com; 100 © NBeauty/Shutterstock.com; 103 ©redstone/Shutterstock.com; 107 © mykeyruna/Shutterstock.com; 111 © Fribus Mara/Shutterstock.com; 117 (r7), 140 (r2) © Suponev Vladimir/Shutterstock.com; 119 © Nikki Zalewski/Shutterstock.com; 126 © Zdenek Sasek/Shutterstock.com; 129 © Triff/Shutterstock.com; 130 (r3) © Stellar Gems/Shutterstock.com; 130 (r4), 142 (r5), 50 (bc) © Nastya22/Shutterstock.com; 134 (r4) © Alexander Hoffmann/Shutterstock.com; 134 (r5), 147 (r2l) © ikonacolor/Shutterstock.com; 135 (r4), 147 (r1l), 150 (r4c) © lmfoto/Shutterstock.com; 138 (r5) © Shelly Still/Shutterstock.com; 139 (r1), 147 (r3c) © Africa Studio/Shutterstock.com; 139 (r2) © Bildagentur Zoonar GmbH/ Shutterstock.com; 139 (r3), 147 (r4l) © Toscanini/Shutterstock.com; 141 (r1), 141 (r2) © NickKnight/Shutterstock.com; 142 (r1) © Yut chanthaburi/Shutterstock.com; 143 (r1) © TonelloPhotography/Shutterstock.com; 143 (r2) © Gozzoli/Shutterstock.com; 143 (r5) © Mali lucky/Shutterstock.com; 147 (r3rt), 150 (r2rt) © Richardson Peterson/Shutterstock.com; 147 (r4rt) © Oliver Mohr/Shutterstock.com; 149 © LoveDesignShop/Shutterstock.com; 150 (r2l) © Martina Osmy/Shutterstock.com; 150 (r3l) © Doru Cristache/Shutterstock.com; 150 (r4rt) © DaleS/Shutterstock.com; 152 © Peter Hermes Furian/Shutterstock.com; 153 © Vereschagin/Shutterstock.com